EXPECT A MIRACLE

EXPECT

BOOKS BY DAN WAKEFIELD

New York in the Fifties
*The Story of Your Life: Writing a
    Spiritual Autobiography*
Returning: A Spiritual Journey
*All Her Children: The Making of
    a Soap Opera*
Supernation at Peace and War
*Between the Lines: A Reporter's
    Personal Journey*
The Addict: An Anthology
Revolt in the South
*Island in the City: The World of
    Spanish Harlem*

NOVELS

Selling Out
Under the Apple Tree
Home Free
Starting Over
Going All the Way

A MIRACLE

The miraculous things

that happen

to ordinary people

DAN WAKEFIELD

Thorsons
An Imprint of HarperCollinsPublishers

Grateful acknowledgement is made for permission to reprint
the lyrics of 'Colorado (The Blizzard)', words and music by Judy Collins.
Copyright © Rocky Mountain National Park Music.
Reprinted by permission of Judy Collins.

Thorsons
An Imprint of HarperCollins*Publishers*
77–85 Fulham Palace Road,
Hammersmith, London W6 8JB

First published by HarperCollins*Publishers*, New York, USA 1995
This edition published by Thorsons 1996
1 3 5 7 9 10 8 6 4 2

© Dan Wakefield 1995

Dan Wakefield asserts the moral right to
be identified as the author of this work

A catalogue record for this book
is available from the British Library

ISBN 0 7225 3331 4

Printed and bound in Great Britain by
Caledonian International Book Manufacturing Ltd, Glasgow, G64

To Sara Davidson,
my colleague, friend, and ally,
who is not afraid to believe in miracles
and to create them,

and

to the memory of Ollah Toph,
"Aunt Ollie," poet and seer,
who showed me in my youth there is more
to the world than we can know
with our five senses.

*We never acknowledge miracles—we're stingy,
we don't share our miracles, and they die on us.
How blessed we are, but there's no acknowledgment
of it, we never mention it. If we don't speak of it,
we diminish the possibility of miracles.*

Father Gerald O'Rourke

*All is a miracle. The stupendous order of nature,
the revolution of a hundred millions of worlds around
a million of suns, the activity of light, the life of all
animals, all are grand and perpetual miracles.*

Voltaire

Contents

Introduction
  Accepting Miracles   1

1 *Miracles Then and Now*   7
2 *In Search of Miracles*   36
3 *Miracles of Healing*   65
4 *Miracles of Recovery*   94
5 *Miracles of Love*   118
6 *Miracles of Creation*   143
7 *Miracles of Encounter*   164
8 *Miracles of Presence*   191
9 *Everyday Miracles*   221

Afterword
  The Miracle of the Miracle Book   249
Acknowledgments   255
About the Author   259

EXPECT A MIRACLE

ACCEPTING MIRACLES

Sirens wailed and red lights flashed in the dark of four o'clock in the morning. I crawled from a car that a friend had just driven head-on into a cement retaining wall on an S-curve in south Chicago. Barry had a skull fracture and was still unconscious as I listened to the doctors calling to him while they worked through the night to try to save his life. As the passenger beside him in a car that was moving forty miles an hour when it hit, I "should have been killed," according to one of the policemen who first arrived on the scene. Yet all I had suffered at first glance was a broken thumb. "Your son is lucky," the attending doctor told my parents with a jolly laugh when they arrived from Indianapolis the next day. "He can go home this afternoon."

When I complained that my back hurt so badly it felt like it was on fire, the doctor shrugged it off with the diagnosis that my discomfort must be from "sleeping in a strange bed." When taken to emergency the night before, I had said my shoulder hurt, so they had taken an X ray of it; but nothing appeared to be wrong. Now my worried parents insisted on a further examination, and after a full set of X rays was taken, two doctors and a nurse came running toward my bed with sandbags and pulleys, shouting, "Don't move!"

I was put into traction, where I would remain immobilized for the next three months. The X rays revealed a broken and dislocated fifth cervical vertebra. Had I jerked my head strongly to the left or right, I could have been killed or paralyzed from the waist down. That I was going to emerge unscathed, after walking around at the scene of the crash, walking in to emergency, getting into bed, tossing and turning in sleep, waking and sitting up, and moving around for more than twelve hours without restraint or caution was "a miracle," the doctors said.

Oh yeah? "Miracles" weren't part of my vocabulary as an Ivy League intellectual, a freshly minted collegiate atheist, with a head full of Sartre's nothingness and Hemingway's anti-prayer "Our *nada,* who art in *nada.*" Miracles were part of the unenlightened understanding of my middle-class, middle-western parents, part of the world I'd left to go East to college and now scorned. I called it "lucky" and attached the same term to the full recovery of my friend who was driving the car, after he lay unconscious for sixteen days. I managed to turn our good fortune around to a negative interpretation more appropriate for my sophisticated image as a college wise guy: "If we really were lucky, we wouldn't have been in an accident at all!"

That's what I said aloud, anyway, to challenge my parents and entertain my pals who came to visit me in the hospital. Still, in the privacy of my own mind, as I lay in traction for the next three months, missing the fall semester of my senior year at Columbia, I thought often of Ollah Toph, my mother's remarkable cousin who was known in the family as Aunt Ollie, loved by some, and feared by others because of her psychic powers.

I loved her, and as a teenager I loved to go to her small house, which reminded me of a pioneer's log cabin, hidden among trees way out on the north side of town. There was something special about the place, other-worldly and yet welcoming, just like Aunt Ollie herself. This beautiful, snowy-haired lady of great dignity and reverence was in her eighties then, and she not only read and wrote poetry on spiritual themes that was published in the local papers, she played the organ that sat in her living room and sometimes, if the moment seemed right, took my hand, squeezed her eyes shut, and told me things she saw, invisible to others.

Spirits appeared beside a person that only she could see, and glimpses of past and future. Ollah Toph was a serious, devout member of the Spiritualist church, and in one of her scrapbooks I saw a yellowed clipping from the *New York Times* that reported her attendance as an American delegate to a world Spiritualist conference in London that was also attended by Arthur Conan Doyle, among other believers. You could not request her to exercise her psychic powers in any way; that would have been an insult, like asking that she "tell your fortune." It was not a game or a trick. The experience was serious, solemn—indeed, sacred.

One evening when I was fourteen years old she took my hand and closed her eyes and told me I would go far away to college but that my education would be unexpectedly interrupted just before I finished. I would be near death, she said, but I would recover and complete my education—just as it all happened. She also told me that night that after college I would go on a voyage across the oceans to a distant land, but farther than Europe, a prediction I vividly recalled as I stood on the deck of a Zim Lines ship on my way to Israel a year after graduation. Was her foretelling only luck or chance? Was my survival of such a dangerous injury the same kind of luck or chance?

I had to dismiss the "miracle" talk, which didn't jibe with my brash new skepticism. After all, I reasoned, no force had snatched me out of the way, no voice (that I heard) had told me to keep myself still—I was just in a nasty accident and had the luck to get out alive and fully functional. Cursing my "bad luck" became even more intense when I was put in a body cast that went from my waist up over my head with a hole cut out for the front of my face. My forehead and most of my cheeks and chin were covered by the plaster. The most terrifying part of this was not primarily the confinement (though that was frightening enough, especially when the hot plaster was wrapped tightly over me the first time), but even more the fact that I wouldn't be able to wash my face for three months. My parents worriedly warned me that our family doctor confirmed what I already feared: The acne that tormented and depressed me through high school and college (so deeply troubling it led to thoughts of suicide) would inevitably grow worse with my skin encased in plaster, without soap or water or even air to reach it for this extended length of time. I had nightmares of how awful I would look when the cast was removed, and I braced myself, fearing the worst.

Knowing my anxiety, my parents came to be with me when the cast was removed, and when the plaster was cut away from my face, they gasped. My God, was it even worse than they expected? There were tears in their eyes. The doctor handed me a mirror. I looked to see my face, uncovered. It was clear. For the first time since the acne erupted with a vengeance during my freshman year in high school, seven years before, it was gone. It would never really bother me again. In some unforeseen way, some way not explainable by physical, medical knowledge, coming as the result of a circumstance anticipated to make matters worse, the scourge that darkened my adolescence and early youth was suddenly removed.

The word *miracle* flashed in my mind. I didn't speak it out loud, though, even then. It was 1953. My heroes were Hemingway and Fitzgerald (who declared "all wars fought, all Gods dead" when his own generation came of age in the twenties), and I didn't want to be square. But miracles were still familiar to me, part of my heritage.

I grew up with miracle stories from the Bible—Moses parting the Red Sea, Jesus healing the crippled and restoring sight to the blind. These stories stirred a deep response in me, a kind of recognition. I later "learned" or was taught or told—in college and the Freudian psychoanalysis that followed—that such feelings were only wishful thinking, for kids and the unenlightened or for needy neurotics looking for false reassurance, people who weren't psychically strong enough to know and accept the fact that they were alone in the universe. I blotted out my own impulses of belief with alcohol and drugs until I crashed at age forty-eight and turned to a different path, following inner pulls toward prayer, spiritual community, and physical discipline.

Fourteen years later my life still has its full share of jarring ups and downs, changes of fortune, defeats and discouragements, unexpected and sometimes seemingly insurmountable challenges, along with great fulfillments, satisfactions, and pleasures. Sometimes in the down times my old collegiate cynicism surfaces again, taunting me with questions of what it all means, anyway. Look how I've just made a stupid mistake, a damaging decision, and I can't even blame it on drugs or alcohol because I don't use them anymore!

Then I realize that until my life began to turn in a healthier direction in 1980, I would have told you with complete conviction I was simply the kind of person who couldn't get along without booze. Except for two agonizing weeks of sobriety imposed by trying to recover from alcoholic sickness (drying out so I could start again) for twenty-three years I had not got through a day without drinking. Before I stopped, my regular consumption was about half a gallon of wine a day. It was part of my life;

essential, like fuel, to my functioning—to living at all. I would have sworn that for better or worse I simply couldn't live without it. Certainly such a history of dependence would have set the odds against me.

Maybe, in my wildest dreams, I could imagine that if I discovered some amazing discipline that gave me complete control over my mind and body, like becoming a Kung Fu master (though I couldn't really imagine that, either), I might be able to become so strong I could live a life without alcohol—a life of continual stress from resisting the need and temptation, of course. If you had told me the day would come when I would not drink anymore simply because I no longer had the desire to drink—that the deep, ingrained compulsion to drink was "lifted" from me, was no longer part of who I was—I would have dismissed the idea as insane. Or a miracle.

It happened. Today I am not afraid to use the word. It is, in my own life, in my own terms, a miracle.

Today I am more aware of and attuned to miracles not only from my own experience but also from the privilege of coming into contact with people all over the country and the world who are seekers, who have opened up to the possibility of miracles in their lives. After writing my book *Returning: A Spiritual Journey*, which chronicled my own turn toward health and spirit, I began leading workshops in spiritual autobiography at churches, adult education centers, spiritual retreats, and conferences around the country. I hear true stories of people moving from darkness to light, or seeking the light, and experiencing or discovering what they consider miracles in their own lives and others'.

Of course I don't believe or suggest that anyone can order miracles on demand or that the best or even good people are "rewarded" with them. I am painfully aware that, in the words of Rabbi Harold Kushner's book, bad things do happen to good people. All the time. Rabbi Kushner himself prayed for the healing and the life of his son, who was born with a terrible disease that not only doomed him to an early death but condemned him to the suffering of growing physically old while still alive and young, a torturous nightmare that was real. There are no people more devout or generous of spirit than Harold Kushner and his wife, Suzette, and yet no miracle, medical or spiritual or any other kind, saved their son or spared them the agony of watching him live and die in pain.

Yet out of the pain came *When Bad Things Happen to Good People*, a book that brought emotional and spiritual healing, comfort, and relief to millions of people all over the world. That was its own kind of miracle—not the one Rabbi Kushner desired with all his heart, but the one he received anyway. You can't request a miracle or determine what kind you get if you do get one. It's a mystery.

My own experience and observation of the past decade leads me to believe, however, that we can prepare ourselves for the possibility of miracles in our lives. We can create an atmosphere in which miracles—at least in the categories of transformation and healing—are more likely to occur. I know that we can become awakened to the miracles of daily existence that we have become blinded to, cut off from, too numbed to perceive. I lead an exercise in "looking close" at something in nature, as a kind of meditation, by selecting a natural object—a flower, a leaf, a piece of fruit—and looking at it intensely for twenty minutes, discovering what is really there, noting it, drawing it, and then writing about what we've discovered. This simple exercise can lead to a personal experience of miracles as defined by Willa Cather in her novel *Death Comes for the Archbishop*, a definition whose fulfillment is available to all: "Miracles . . . seem to me to rest not so much upon faces or voices or healing power coming suddenly near to us from afar off, but upon our perceptions being made finer, so that for a moment our eyes can see and our ears can hear what is there about us always."

Chapter 1

MIRACLES
THEN AND NOW

W e are living in a new "Age of Miracles."
When I was a college student at Columbia in the 1950s, I never thought I would live to see such a time, or in fact that such a time would come again. Miracles were part of the dark, dead past, part of childhood—my own and that of the human race. Freud and science had replaced God and spirit as the way of finding answers to the mysteries of life.

In a literature course at Columbia in 1953, the legendary professor Mark Van Doren, a Pulitzer Prize–winning poet and mentor of students from the Trappist monk Thomas Merton to Beat writers Jack Kerouac and Allen Ginsberg, said that in most great literature until the modern era the source of power and change was God, or the Gods, from the Bible and the Greek epics and plays to Dante's *Divine Comedy*. Van Doren cited a newly published story called "A Change of Air" by one of the students in our class, Ivan Gold, in which a formerly promiscuous young woman in a tough neighborhood on Manhattan's Lower East Side goes off to a mental hospital and returns "a different person," one who no longer wants random, meaningless sex. The off-stage power that transforms her, Van Doren pointed out, was psychiatry, not God, which reflected our society's new understanding of the way the world works. It wasn't a "miracle" but the application of new "scientific" principles.

There were to be no more miracles, because everything that happened could be "explained" by one or another branch of science, from psychology to physics. The atom was unlocked, and so was the unconscious;

we believed ourselves to be masters of our own fate, even "Masters of the Universe," as Tom Wolfe later described the wheeler-dealers of Wall Street who thought of themselves with the grandiose title of the children's comic book and TV heroes.

As a boy in Indianapolis in the 1940s I had thrilled to a Baptist Bible study class when the minister and his wife told us miracle stories they dramatized with homemade artifacts, such as a brown paper bag made to look like a rock placed over a fountain to reenact Moses striking water from a stone. A decade later, fresh out of Columbia, I thrilled to a hard-drinking, chain-smoking Sarah Lawrence graduate who said she had gone to an ethical culture Sunday school, where miracles were explained by scientific reason. I asked her to give me an example, and she said, "Parting the waters of the Red Sea." What's the explanation? I asked. The girl tilted her chin up, exhaled a thin stream of smoke, and said with throaty authority, "Low tide."

In the turbulent sixties, *Time* magazine ran a cover story announcing that "God Is Dead," and Harvey Cox's *The Secular City*, which told how religion might still remain relevant, became the surprise theological best-seller of the decade.

A quarter of a century later Professor Cox, a popular and distin-guished teacher at Harvard Divinity School, was putting the finishing touches on *Fire from Heaven,* his new book about the phenomenon of the miracle-conscious Pentecostal movement, the fastest-growing Christian denomination in the world.

Discussing the shift from the death of God to the current acceptance of miracles, Cox told me at his home in Cambridge, Massachusetts, "The modern world was not satisfied when meaning and mystery was taken away—the churches have been unable to respond to this. People are find-ing a way to reach back to the source or reservoir of meaning. Nobody buys the whole package—it's 'I love the mass, but not the rest of it'—or some variation on the theme. It has to connect with personal experience. It's like the AA slogan 'Take what you need and leave the rest.'

"The Pentecostal church is popular and growing because it's not creedal—the liturgy is spontaneous, egalitarian, and experience-based. Space is created for the experience of healing to take place—for miracles to take place."

Vivien Cordiner, a Belfast woman who left the Church of Ireland to join a Pentecostal church told me, "Now I see miracles in my life, but I never had them before when I went to the Church of Ireland. In the Pentecostal church they tell you to 'expect a miracle.'"

Despite declining church attendance on the Continent, religious shrines and pilgrimage sites have become the most popular tourist attractions in Europe, from Fátima in Portugal to the tomb of Saint James in Santiago de Compostela, Spain. The great religious shrines of the East continue to draw millions of the faithful, to Varanasi in India, the Hindu "city of Shiva" on the Ganges, to Mecca and Medina, the holy cities of Islam, and of course to Jerusalem, which is holy to Jews, Christians, and Muslims alike. Lourdes, in France, the most famous Christian shrine for healing, was welcoming five and a half million visitors a year in the early 1990s, a million and a half more than came a decade before.

"Perhaps people find religious life too monotonous and want something more intense, more festive, more emotional," Father Michel de Roton, rector of the Lourdes shrine, explained in a front-page article in the New York Times in October 1993. "Perhaps the form our religion has taken today does not respond to peoples' needs."

Today new kinds of pilgrimages indicate that "Americans have become especially efficient in spiritual questing," according to an article in the "Ideas and Trends" section of the New York Times on August 21, 1994. Under the headline "For Today's Pilgrims There Is No End of Holy Grails," Douglas Martin cites pop culture shrines such as Graceland, the home of Elvis Presley, where 40,000 assembled to mourn at the seventeenth anniversary of "The King's" death, and gatherings like the motorcycle rally in Sturgis, South Dakota, where bikers on Harley Davidsons roar each year in numbers that have reached 170,000.

There's a grail out there for everyone. My friend Sara Davidson writes about cowboy poets who gather every year in Elko, Nevada, to celebrate their way of life in sing-song rhymes reminiscent of Robert W. Service and party till dawn at the Stockmen's Motel. For years I've heard friends lament their children leaving home to follow the Grateful Dead around the country, each concert a self-contained ritual, with its own passwords, gestures, food, and clothing bazaars. Veteran Deadhead Tony Mindel took me to one of their concerts at Shoreline, south of San Francisco, insisting that I couldn't write a valid book about miracles without experiencing the group that gave us the song "I Need a Miracle" ("I can't get around and I can't run away / I need a miracle every day"). As Martin observed in the *Times*, "The hunger is for meaning, a sense of place in a land where the wind blows and the radio blares."

That "hunger for meaning," the search for something "more," may account for the current angel craze of books, stories, pictures, images, workshops, and even a movie (with surely more to come) and a television series (*Touched by an Angel*). Angels symbolize the growing search for evidence of—and contact with—another dimension of life beyond the ordinary. Bumper stickers with the legend "Expect a Miracle" advertise the need and desire for belief in some power, force, or influence in the universe beyond the box of conventional Western science, medicine, and mainstream Sunday or Sabbath day religion.

Another factor contributes to the need for meaning, for hope—for the brightness of miraculous healing and empowering transformation—and that is the onslaught of what we call news, which has become a kind of journalistic version of *Nightmare on Elm Street*. We are daily assaulted by true tales of violence, ugliness, death, defeat, and despair. A New York television anchor begins her morning greeting with the line "Here's what we're waking up to" and delivers a laundry list of the drive-by shootings, fires, rapes, car crashes, stabbings, robberies, murder trials, and disease statistics that constitute the latest "news." Who wants to wake up?

As a professional journalist I have always pooh-poohed the whiny lament of unknowing "civilians" (not in the business) who wonder why newspapers don't run front-page headlines about something "good." But in the last decade I have come to think that the "hard news" of disaster has reached a point of overkill, and beyond. Journalism has become a form of assault—on the senses of the audience and the personalities it covers, or rather tries to bury.

I have never seen a lambasting of the lives of a president and his wife as I have with the Clintons, nor until recent years have I seen the exploitation of gore and grossness that was once confined to the supermarket checkout tabloids become the ratings hits of mainstream network television. At the same time, talk of such ideas as "the politics of meaning" is snidely blasted by sharpshooting commentators as idealistic claptrap; while spirituality, if mentioned at all in mainstream magazines, is usually an occasion for sarcasm and satire. (This may be part of the reason behind the birth and growth of so many "little magazines" attuned in a serious and sensitive way to matters of the spirit, like *Common Boundary*, *Tricycle: The Buddhist Review*, the *Yoga Journal*, *Image*, the *Sun*, *Tikkun*, the *New Age Journal*, the *Utne Reader*.

In the world of mainstream media, highlighted by Hollywood crash-and-burn entertainment, life is reflected back to us as bloody, brutal, bizarre, and threatening. We can't turn our back on the fact that much of our culture has become violent and dangerous, yet that is also a reflection of what is seen in the media. We set up mirror images of increasing chaos that keep reflecting back an escalating mayhem. Little wonder there's a search for meaning, for "something else," beyond the blood and gore of the nightly news, the blaze of explosive, big-screen, stereo-sound destruction.

We know—we sense deep down—that there is something real out there beyond the bleak landscape of international and personal abuse. In our nuclear age, in this era of Saturn probes and cyberspace, 83 percent of Americans believe in miracles, according to a Gallup Poll.

A Course in Miracles, a self-study curriculum "transcribed" over a seven-year period by a Columbia research psychologist and atheist who claimed to hear a soundless voice giving her "inner dictation" (the "voice" identified itself as the historical Christ), has become a phenomena of sweeping popularity, not only as a text and workbook but also as the focus of countless multiplying study groups throughout the country. A half million copies of *A Course* are in print, in English and fourteen other languages, and the popularity of guru Marianne Williamson, whose teachings are based on *A Course*, all are further signs of the desire for some sort of spiritual source that is available now, in daily life. The *Course* contributes its own definitions to the search for miracles, calling them shifts in consciousness that "undo the past in the present and release the future."

"Diocese Finds Vision Claims Aren't Miracle"

Miracles are reported with increasing frequency. Even disputing the verification of a miracle can be a news story now, as it was when a draftsman named Joseph Januszkiewicz claimed he had seen the Virgin Mary at his home in suburban Marlboro Township, New Jersey, and the Times reported that thousands of pilgrims came to visit the blue spruce trees in the yard where the visions were said to have taken place.

The pilgrims spoke of their rosaries changing colors, of seeing flashes of light, and finding their camera film exposed in unusual ways; even of being converted to the faith and experiencing a sense of spirituality. Yet a commission appointed by the Roman Catholic Diocese of Trenton concluded nothing had happened "that would require suspension of the laws of nature and could not be accounted for by natural causes. . . . What visitors observed and heard can occur and has occurred without any miraculous cause when people of faith gather and pray."

As Harvey Cox notes in *Fire from Heaven,* "There's a continuing appearance of miracles at the folk level, though the hierarchy is always skeptical of it."

Around the same time as the Marlboro vision, the *Wall Street Journal* reported that in the tiny south Texas town of Elsa, the Virgin Mary "is making a personal appearance on the driver's side rear fender of Dario Mendoza's 1981 maroon Chevrolet Camaro." After Mr. Mendoza washed the car, the image remained, he said, and grew larger. When the local newspaper and a neighboring TV station carried the story, "a small stream of visitors turned into a flood" of pilgrims, including a mariachi band.

Skeptics feel that many of these alleged miracle sights trivialize genuine religious impulses. An article in the *Washington Post* on April 3, 1994, made the point that

> miracles are the foundation of all major religions; those recorded in the
> Bible were indeed grand and perpetual. Lazarus being raised from the
> dead. The waters cleanly parting on the vast Red Sea. . . . But now a
> bizarre banality seems to have supplanted that sense of grandeur. . . .
> Now holy apparitions are said to appear in flour tortillas, in cloud forma-
> tions, in a forkful of spaghetti on a billboard. Places like Lubbock, Texas,
> become pilgrimage sites. A Northern Virginia priest who once rode a
> roller coaster for five days nonstop to set a world record mysteriously
> causes statues of the Virgin Mary to weep.

Humorist Frank Gannon notes in the *New York Times* that "one does hear the word 'miracle' used in a reckless fashion. . . . Consider the Miracle Mets of 1969. Did God really suspend the laws of physical matter 25 years ago?" Gannon adds that no matter how outlandish the idea of miracles may seem, those "nagging, eternal doubts stand next to you and whisper in your ear. 'O.K., Mr. Scientist,' they say, 'How did Pat Sajak ever get his own talk show?' Was that, in the words of Aquinas and my insurance company, an act of God?"

The Reverend James Gill, a Hartford priest and psychiatrist who helps the Catholic church investigate reports of miracles and apparitions, is more of a skeptic than Mr. Gannon. Father Gill acknowledges that through the ages there have been many such claims that, like some today, "seem often quite absurd."

"I mean, how many towns in Europe have got the head of John the Baptist buried there?" he asks. "People want to think that holy people and holy events have been close to where they live and that heaven shows preference for their locality."

The majority of claims he finds without merit: "either an outright hoax or a pathetic bid for attention by the emotionally imbalanced."

Still, so many such claims persist, and increase, one would have to find a large segment of the population to be "emotionally unbalanced" to explain them away. Visions of the Virgin, or "Marian appearances," are being reported with increasing regularity around the world, including some thirty-six places in the United States. More than sixty thousand pilgrims have gathered on a single weekend at a farm in Conyers, Georgia, to hear a message from the Virgin Mary delivered through a former nurse and housewife who lives there with her family.

A thoughtful article on the phenomena by Andrea Young in the magazine *Common Boundary* (which explores the "boundary between spirituality and psychotherapy") cites scholarly and psychological interpretations of the proliferation of visions and concludes that "while everyone brings a different interpretation to apparitions of the Virgin, millions are being transformed: Individuals are experiencing spiritual conversion, the Catholic Church is being forced to reconcile personal experience with institutional dogma, believers are hearing a call to community and world peace."

Nor is this limited to Christian and/or American spiritual phenomena. Around the world, in places urban and rural, people of all races, faiths, and creeds, the illiterate and the highly educated, rich and the poor, male and female, young and old, gather to seek healing, peace, liberation of spirit, the miracle of hope, enlightenment, faith—all that, as Harvey Cox put it, the modern world failed to supply.

"People became disenchanted with pure rationalism," says Rabbi Harold Kushner, author of the worldwide bestseller *When Bad Things Happen to Good People*. "Today people are more spiritually open to the nonrational."

In India millions of Hindus are devotees of Sai Baba, a healer and miracle worker who is called a great avatar.

In South Africa, men in circles leap and thump the earth to exorcise demons and are splashed with holy water and touched by the healing hands of prophets in the rituals of the fastest-growing religious movement in southern Africa, the Zion Christian Church. It has more than three million members.

Buddhists from around the world travel to Rangoon to the Shwe Dagon Pagoda, which rises from the bell shape of a *stupa* (Buddha's inverted begging bowl), surrounded by smaller pagodas, statues, and shrines. Rudy Wurlitzer, novelist and screenwriter of the Bertolucci movie *Little Buddha,* describes in *Hard Travel to Sacred Places* the experience of entering there "a magical Buddha world, a community and promenade of pilgrims and worshipers where everything seems included, from circumambulating monks to businessmen making deals, to entire families chatting and eating snacks, children running in circles, . . . tourists gazing and looking in their guide books, silent meditators."

In our own culture the concept of miracles is now bandied about in all areas of contemporary life, both casually and seriously, from art and literature to medicine and politics, even reaching to that crucial conundrum of modern urban existence, finding a parking space.

"The six of us squashed into one car and parked, in a minor Christian miracle, on Powell Street," wrote *San Francisco Chronicle* columnist Adair Lara. New York art gallery owner Tibor de Nagy, asked how he selects the artists he exhibits, told columnist Leah Garchik, "I expect to be hit by a miracle." A story in the *New York Times Book Review* about author Henry Roth breaking his famous writer's block sixty years after his first novel *Call It Sleep* was published in 1934 ran under the headline "The Long Comeback of Henry Roth: Call It Miraculous." *New York* magazine announced on its cover a "Miracle Cure" for trauma victims.

An update on the life of a woman whose recovery from incurable leukemia as a child in 1952 was declared a miracle by the Vatican and helped the canonization of Elizabeth Ann Seton, the first American saint, was featured as "The Story of a Miracle, and What Came After" in the *Washington Post*. The newsletter of King's Chapel, a church in Boston, quotes a new member as describing their son as their own "little miracle" after fourteen years of marriage. A column by Anthony Lewis in the *New York Times* titled "Miracle with Reasons" declared, "By the standards of today's world the election in South Africa is a political miracle." The Chicago Bulls without Michael Jordan were said to be looking for "a miracle" in their series against the New York Knicks for the Eastern Division championship of the NBA (they got a few, but not enough). "Montana Miracle" was the headline for a game when an aging, battered quarterback Joe led his Kansas City Chiefs to victory over the Broncos at Denver.

So what really *is* a miracle, as defined by what Anthony Lewis calls "the standards of today's world"? Does finding a parking space in downtown San Francisco qualify, or breaking a sixty-year-long writer's block, or discovering the work of a new painter to exhibit?

The new *Random House Unabridged Dictionary* defines miracle as "1. an effect or extraordinary event in the physical world that bypasses all known human or natural powers and is ascribed to a supernatural cause. 2. such an effect or event manifesting or considered as a work of God. 3. a wonder; marvel . . . "

The *Washington Post* story of the woman whose childhood recovery from leukemia was declared an official miracle by the Vatican would qualify under all three definitions; the third (a wonder; marvel) would cover everything up to and including finding a parking space in downtown San Francisco.

I would imagine, though, that what Anthony Lewis means by "today's standards"—for him, appropriately, the standards of the *New York Times* in reporting and interpreting the news of the world—are those without God or any supernatural power, since he goes on to say of the election in South Africa, "But it is a miracle created by human beings."

Perhaps Bishop Desmond Tutu and other religious people would say that this miracle was an example of human beings doing God's work, one of the basic understandings of believers. As Saint Thérèse of Lisieux put it, "Whose hands are God's hands but our hands?" There is fresh appeal now for the teachings of "creation theology," in which humans are seen as "co-creators" with God, a concept beautifully articulated by Hildegard of Bingen, a twelfth-century nun whose works are finding new appreciation today, and eloquently preached in our own time by the visionary priest Matthew Fox.

A useful definition of miracle that could apply to everything from the elections in South Africa to finding a parking space was made by Oxford scholar J. P. Ross when he wrote, "In ordinary usage, 'miracle' denotes a breach of regularity in the functioning of the world."

This helps fill in what seems to be a gap between the *Random House Dictionary's* first two definitions, which require belief in the role of the "supernatural" or God, and the third, which is just plain "wonder" or "marvel." Mary Hesse, a mathematician and philosophy of science scholar and teacher at Cambridge University in England, throws further light on the subject in her essay "Miracles and the Laws of Nature" (in *Miracles: Cambridge Studies in Their Philosophy and History,* ed. C. F. D. Moule):

> *Someone may say "His recovery was a miracle," or, "It was a miracle that a serious accident was avoided." . . . What is pointed to by the use of the word "miracle" is the remarkable, unpredictable, coincidental na-ture of the events, and also, usually, the fact that the outcome was in some way significant and desirable in the context of human purposes. There need, however, be no suggestion that the events are in any way outside or in conflict with the general course of nature and its laws.*

Professor Hesse helps us understand the new, postmodern openness to the concept of miracles on the part of political scientists as well as physicists such as Fritjof Capra (*The Tao of Physics*) and Paul Davies (*God and the New Physics*), when she writes,

Abandonment of the deterministic world-view in physics has made it more difficult to regard the existing state of science as finally legislative of what is and what is not possible in nature. The very fact that what appeared for three centuries to be an absolutely true and universal theory has been shown to be false must cast doubt on all future claims of science to have reached such a universal theory. Science is continually growing and changing, sometimes quite radically. It is far less easy to see it today as a monolithic and cumulative progress toward the whole truth than was the case a hundred years ago. We are by no means sure, even in physics, that existing quantum theories will last many decades. Moreover, we have no guarantee that existing theories will prove adequate in sciences other than physics, and in the sciences of complex systems such as the human psyche and human social groups we have only the bare beginnings of any theories at all.

Many such key theories that held sway when I graduated from college have come under attack and are seen now as outmoded and in decline. Who would have thought that a particle is not one thing, that it can become a wave or a line according to how it is viewed? Yesterday's mumbo jumbo is today's accepted truth. This has been going on since we learned the earth is not flat and the sun doesn't revolve around us—and will no doubt continue.

As we continuously disprove what we *knew* before (for certain!) and discover the next "truth," as those are translated into the way we live and function, yesterday's "miracle" is today's ordinary given, ho hum. My father could remember watching, as a boy in Shelbyville, Kentucky, the first "horseless carriages" take to the streets, with skeptics standing on corners and hooting at the drivers of the sputtering new mechanical transportation, "Get a horse!"

My parents and I were the first on our block to fly in an airplane when Uncle Crawford gave us tickets to go to the New York World's Fair in 1940. The neighbors came to see us off, one of them warning my mother she better not wear that big hat, it'll blow right off up there! Flying from Indianapolis to New York City was miracle enough for people who had seen horseless carriages become a commonplace. Who would have believed me then had I said I would someday leave London at 10:30 in the morning on a plane called the Concorde and arrive in New York at 9:30 in the morning—and hour earlier than I'd left—the same day?

The most helpful and lasting explanation of our constant human amazement at doing what we previously knew was impossible comes from not a scientist but a saint. Augustine long ago pointed out that "miracles do not happen in contradiction of nature, but in contradiction of what we know about nature."

What we know has changed in many areas of life besides physics since I made that miraculous flight to the New York World's Fair (without my mother's hat blowing away). In the area of understanding human behavior, perhaps the biggest switch is the reevaluation of Freud by scientists and scholars that was summed up in an influential essay by Frederick Crews in the *New York Review of Books* ("The Unknown Freud").

"That psychoanalysis, as a mode of treatment, has been experiencing a long institutional decline is no longer in serious dispute," Professor Crews writes, reporting that it has proved to be "an indifferently successful and vastly inefficient method of removing neurotic symptoms." Freudian doctrine, he says, has fared no better: "Without significant experimental or epidemiological support for any of its notions, psychoanalysis has simply been left behind by mainstream psychological research." Yet this was "the truth" when I came of age, the doctrine that at last would liberate humans from illusion and superstition as well as neurosis and set them psychically free.

Fritjof Capra, the physicist-philosopher who wrote *The Tao of Physics,* explains in *The Turning Point* that

> recent developments in psychology and psychotherapy have begun to produce a new view of the human psyche, one in which the Freudian model is recognized as extremely useful for dealing with certain aspects, or levels, of the unconscious, but as severely limiting when applied to the totality of mental life in health and illness. The situation is not unlike that in physics, where the Newtonian model is extremely useful for the description of a certain range of phenomena but has to be extended, and often radically changed, when we go beyond that range.

He also points out that "Freudian psychotherapy neglects the body just as medical therapy neglects the mind."

In *Miracles: Cambridge Studies in Their Philosophy and History* Cambridge University divinity professor C. F. D. Moule says, "Our idea of how things work is based on too narrow a set of data."

Our idea of how things work is being expanded now to claim again what ancient civilizations and philosophers and scientists through the ages regarded as part of the understanding of human experience: the realm of the sacred, the spiritual, the numinous. As Michael Murphy, cofounder of the Esalen Institute, a mecca of the human potential movement, and author of *The Future of the Body*, explained in a recent conversation: "*Miracles* is a term for re-owning, manifesting, or making the Divine explicit."

The *Washington Post* reports that "interest in the power of prayer and divine intervention is clearly growing and even gaining some credibility as an area of scientific study." To document this trend the *Post* noted, "For the first time ever, the National Institutes of Health is funding research into the effects of spirituality. In the fall of 1993 a fledgling alternative-medicine department at NIH awarded a $30,000 grant to a researcher hoping to measure the impact of prayer on the recovery of drug abusers."

The grant was "a sort of landmark thing," according to Larry Dossey, a member of the NIH panel and author of *Healing Words: The Power of Prayer and the Practice of Medicine*. An internist who was chief of staff at a major hospital in Dallas, Dr. Dossey documents the power of prayer in healing, based on more than one hundred studies he considers "scientifically well-designed." He cites studies showing that prayer positively affected medical conditions from high blood pressure to leukemic white blood cells.

The Institute of Noetic Sciences, which sponsors research in fields ranging from mind-body health to cutting-edge theories of new paradigms in business and science, carried out an eight-year study of spontaneous remissions, documenting fifteen hundred such cases of remission of diseases, from cancer to mental disorders, around the world, with categories ranging from "pure remission" (with no treatment at all) to "'miraculous' remission" (those associated with spiritual cures, such as those carefully documented by the International Medical Commission at Lourdes in France).

In *The Future of the Body: Explorations into the Further Evolution of Human Nature,* Michael Murphy brings together a massive body of research and evidence, and argues that

> *by gathering data from many fields—including medical science, anthropology, sports, the arts, psychical research, and comparative religious studies—we can identify extraordinary versions of most, if not all, of our basic attributes. . . . These grace-laden analogues of our normal attributes, which arise spontaneously or as products of particular practices, can be cultivated. Indeed, the evidence assembled here suggests that we harbor a range of capacities that no single philosophy or psychology has fully embraced, and that these can be developed by practicing certain virtues and disciplines and by building institutions to support them. Though every enduring religion has affirmed something analogous to Judeo-Christian doctrines of grace, none has acknowledged the larger spectrum of grace that a collection of this kind begins to reveal.*

Grace? What's "grace" got to do with a comprehensive study of scientific, psychological, and physiological research on extraordinary human functioning and "transformative practices" that Murphy believes can develop such "meta-normal" capacities?

In the living room of his rambling Victorian frame house in San Rafael, California, Murphy explains that "by a sense of grace, I mean something given from beyond the known—so it's *super*natural—and I would apply that to events on a golf course and in bedrooms as well as in monasteries. What we call 'grace' in Christianity is understood in Buddhism as 'the workings of Buddha nature' and in Taoism as 'the Way of the Tao.'"

Murphy's initial understanding of grace came when he was a boy: "The primary vehicle of my awakening was the Episcopal church, around the time I was eleven. My mother was a Catholic, very religious but not a churchgoer, while my father was not particularly religious. His mother—my grandmother—took me to the Episcopal church in the fifth grade; I became an acolyte at eleven, was an acolyte and superactive till I was seventeen and went to college. I became an atheist my freshman year at Stanford and threw all religion over, fired up by evolution. Then came a professor named Spiegelberg, and reading the Indian mystic Sri Aurobindo, and that was it. The spiritual quest has been my compass needle ever since, coded into all my books.

"The great game, the game of games, the story of stories is the unfoldment of the Divine—people like Aurobindo, and Henry James, Sr., understood it. In that context there's a higher order of existence. The universe is re-owning its divinity."

Murphy sees the phenomenon of widespread interest in angels—capped by a cover story in *Time* magazine—as one of the signs of this process of "re-owning" our divinity. "I love it, I believe in it—maybe not many angels have wings and hearts—but it is a rolling thunder throughout the world, these incredible nearnesses.

"As we grow into our 'meta-normality,' what seems supernatural becomes natural. I think its pretty simple—'miracle' is the realm of possibility beyond what we presently know. Scientists will be the first to tell you that. Yesterday's miracles are today's known processes. *Miracle* is a relative term."

Murphy believes that "the concept of miracle is encumbered by the Christian and especially the Catholic view as dispensed by a God who is separate from us. I say this power is both inside and outside. Buddha believed dharma is accessible to us from inside and outside. It's the same in the Hindu Upanishads."

And Jesus, too, I remind him, preached "the kingdom is within."

He nods agreement and says, "I don't believe these events we call miraculous are the results of a capricious Deity. Grace is everywhere and always present—the more you practice, the luckier you get; you can make yourself *available* to grace. Ultimately it's transformative practice. Ramakrishna said, 'The winds of grace are always blowing, but you have to raise the sail.' I would add to that, you have to broaden the sail—you have to have a sail broad enough to catch grace."

As well as his writing and lecturing, Murphy is putting his theories into practice, helping to "broaden the sail" that catches grace. He is giving a course in transformative practices with his longtime friend and colleague George Leonard, the former *Look* magazine writer and editor who was part of the development of the Esalen Institute and became a New Age scribe and workshop leader. With disciplines of diet, exercise, meditation, martial arts, and other transformational practices, Murphy and Leonard have conducted two such courses for eleven months each, with specific physical results they will report in a book on the experience. In the first course, Murphy says, "One woman had developing cataracts stop, and finally disappear. A man with blood in his urine no longer has that condition."

Mystical belief has been part of Eastern philosophy for three millennia, expressed in sacred books such as the Upanishads, the Brahma Sutras, and the Bhagavad Gita, as well as in Vedantic, Buddhist, and Taoist texts. "Great thinkers since antiquity have given paranormal events and mystical truth claims a central place in their philosophies," Murphy points out in *The Future of the Body*.

In the Judeo-Christian tradition of the West, our sacred book, the Bible (both the Jewish Bible, which includes the Torah, or, as Christians call it, the Old Testament, as well as the New Testament), is a story of miracles, a collection of narratives of the human relationship to the Divine, the Other. Our great religious thinkers and philosophers, from Augustine to Kierkegaard, Moses Maimonides to Martin Buber, from William James to Alfred North Whitehead, have explored this connection and its meaning.

The ancient Greeks described the interaction between Gods and humans in great epics like the *Odyssey* and the *Iliad*, great dramas, poetry, and even history. Herodotus, historian of the Peloponesian wars, though he didn't show the Gods in direct interaction with the world of humans, saw them as manifestations of divine power. The coherence of the universe he wrote about depended on both Gods and humans.

When the Persians were defeated at the battle of Plataea, Herodotus reported that no Persian died on the sacred soil of Demeter, which would have polluted it: "I imagine, if one may do so about divine affairs, that the goddess kept them out, since they had burnt her shrine at Eleusis." The Goddess didn't actually appear, but Herodotus assumed natural conditions were influenced by her power.

In the same century, the Greek philosopher and prophet Empodocles was reputed to be a great healer, curing people of pains and illnesses. Appalonius of Tyana was a miracle worker of the first century C.E. in the province of Cappadocia in Asia Minor and was able to drive out demons.

For Plutarch, a contemporary of many New Testament writers (50–120 C.E.), divine power acted rationally within a rational world. There was no such thing as a miracle, since there wasn't a God who made and broke laws for the universe to run on. Instead, Plutarch saw Deity as acting through humans, giving them ideas that lead to action and the courage and hope to carry it out. Deities answered prayers as well, as Plutarch described: "The Goddess did favor Aemylius' prayers, because he prayed for victory with his sword in his hand, and fighting did call to them for aid."

The Jewish historian Josephus in the *Antiquities* recounted miracles as historical events, saying of one "this story, which our fathers handed down to us, is not at all incredible if, that is, one considers the other manifestations of power given by God." Josephus described miracle workers such as Eleazer, who expelled a demon in the presence of Vespasian, a Roman emperor who himself was said to be a miracle worker. Josephus wrote of a Galilean charismatic called Honi who ended a drought by praying for rain. He reported that Hanina ben Dosa, another Galilean, was able to heal someone in a distant place by praying for them—as Jesus was said to do—and as medical practitioners in the 1990s are doing (as described by Dr. Larry Dossey in his book *Healing Words*).

Things are not so simple with modern biblical historians as they were with Herodotus, Josephus, and Plutarch. Today a "Jesus Seminar" of leading biblical scholars puts miracles (represented by tiles) under a magnifying glass and decides by a majority vote—counting the number of red, pink, gray, and black tiles that are put into a common receptacle—whether a particular account of the life of Jesus is true, not true, probably true, or doubtful. A leading scholar of the Jesus Seminar, John Dominic Crossan, professor of biblical studies at DePaul University, writes in *Jesus: A Revolutionary Biography,* "Miracles are not changes in the physical world so much as changes in the social world, and it is society that dictates, in any case, how we see, use, and explain that physical world."

Crossan believes that "the central problem of what Jesus was doing in his healing miracles" comes down to a distinction between "illness" as a psychosocial experience and "disease" as a biological experience, with Jesus, in Crossan's view, "healing the illness without curing the disease." Crossan writes that when Jesus heals a leper, "I presume that Jesus, who could not heal that disease or any other one, healed the poor man's illness by refusing to accept the disease's ritual uncleanness and social ostracization. . . . Jesus heals him, in other words, by taking him into a community of the marginalized and disenfranchised."

Crossan told me in a telephone conversation that he's not trying to sound negative about the healing miracles but rather to shift the emphasis from mind-over-matter healing of individuals to "a change in the social order that *creates* diseases like malnutrition. I'm afraid the emphasis on individual healing undermines how Jesus was trying to alter the social matrix in which disease originates."

In the view of theologian Harvey Cox, however, "All those people didn't come to Jesus because he had a revolutionary social message, but because he was healing people!

"Today there are mountains of evidence of mind-body healing," Cox points out. "The immune system is activated by symbols, voices, signs. The guys who just won the Nobel in medicine are researching the chemistry of external stimuli that changes the composition of nerve cells, signaling activity of the resistance system. Someday we won't need pills to stimulate the immune system. This is a whole new frontier of medicine; these things are happening."

Yet even the most liberal interpreters among biblical scholars, such as Crossan, while acknowledging that "people under stress could be healed immediately" and Jesus could probably heal "stress-related diseases," are cautious in accrediting powers that seem to be fairly well accepted in alternative medicine today and those that are at the medical frontiers. Another leading scholar writing in the *Bible Review* attributes Jesus' healing miracles to hypnotism and "folk remedies" and contends that "to concentrate on these aspects of Jesus' healing is really to miss the point. . . .

The New Testament itself recognizes that others can effect miraculous cures, the stories of Jesus' miraculous cures are intended to convey a religious message." Like the "nature miracles" of Jesus, "we must consider them symbolically."

Students, however, accept miracle stories more readily, says Harvey Cox, judging from his experience teaching a course called "Jesus and the Moral Life" to undergraduates at Harvard.

"When I used to teach my course in Jesus," Cox says, "I talked of Jesus interrupting his treatment of the daughter of the temple in order to heal the woman with the flow of blood. I was making the point that this showed Jesus' 'preferential treatment of the poor,' but the students used to say, 'Wait, what did he *really* do? What made the blood stop?'

"Students now are more receptive to accepting this kind of healing as valid. They're more in tune with the development in today's mind-body healing processes than some faculty members who are stashed away in departments and don't know what's happening in the world outside."

As a layperson and believer, I was naively surprised to learn that leading scholars like Crossan see the nature miracles and reappearances of Jesus after the crucifixion as purely symbolic, literary methods of establishing hierarchy. I asked John Crossan if he had read novelist Reynolds Price's powerful essay on his belief in the literal truth of John 21, the passage after the crucifixion in which Jesus appears on the shore, tells the disciples where to cast their nets, and makes a fire, cooks the fish they catch, and invites them to breakfast. Crossan believes that this appearance and others after the crucifixion are not literal accounts, but symbols: "They are very deliberate images of authority, a 'eucharistic presence,' showing who's in charge."

In charge of what? I later ponder as I re-read John 21. In charge of cooking breakfast? I sympathize with novelist Flannery O'Conner, who was told by Mary McCarthy at a New York literary dinner that McCarthy thought of the Eucharist as a "symbol," and "a pretty good one." "If it's a symbol," O'Conner replied, "to hell with it." She added in a letter to a friend, "That was all the defense I was capable of but I realize now that this is all I will ever be able to say about it, outside of a story, except that it is the center of existence for me; all the rest of life is expendable."

Crossan had not read Price's essay making a case for the literal truth of the story, but he said if Price (and I) believe the literal truth of it, we've been "seduced by a good novelist."

Expressing his admiration for the New Testament writers who created such powerful visual images (ones that people like Price and I take as true accounts), Crossan said, "Those are the magnificent video bites of early Christianity."

Whether historical fact or symbol, Jesus' miracles are an essential part of his teaching (there are seventeen miracles in the first eight chapters of Mark, the earliest Gospel), and they are one of the ways he teaches; his miracles in a sense are like parables manifested in the physical world. In this way they may be unique, yet his audience was accustomed to the concept, for they were raised with a long tradition of miracles.

Biblical heroes such as Moses, Elijah, and Elisha performed miracles, bringing forth water from a rock, feeding multitudes, curing lepers, and raising the dead. In his study *Hebrew Man*, L. Koehler observes, "The Hebrew lives in a world of continuous miracle. Miracles meet him at every step."

Sometimes one gets the impression that we too live in such a world. The "Question Man" column of the *San Francisco Chronicle* asked passersby in a busy section of the city if they had ever witnessed a miracle and got answers ranging from a printing company manager who had an "out-of-body experience" ("I went through the ceiling into the astral. . . . The world looked like a basketball") to a retired welder who gave up his life-long addictions to gambling and alcohol.

Not by any means do all mainstream religious leaders today accept the "new age of miracles" that many people feel we're in, though some find the idea heartening. The subject of contemporary miracles is always a lively topic of conversation and debate in clerical circles. After leading a workshop at a conclave of twenty Episcopal ministers of large urban churches in the United States, I asked them to tell me their ideas about the role of miracles today, in their own churches and in their own faith experience.

Some, such as Rev. Dan Burke of Providence, Rhode Island, felt that the new attention to miracles was "part of the culture of instant gratification. This society is full of people who want a quick hit."

Ed Bacon, from Jackson, Mississippi, said, "The laity has a hunger for understanding these things, and we tend to be careful about our responses. I think a lot of our practice is to protect ourselves from miracles."

Stephen Chinlund, director of Episcopal Social Services in New York City, agreed: "We need to make room for miracles. It makes life spectacular. I think of the miracles that occur in 'the spontaneity of personal choice' where it's impossible to trace in any psychogenic scheme. I know a thirty-five-year-old woman in New Jersey who's going to agricultural school so she can work in Central America and be of use there. She went on one trip there and decided that's what she wanted to do, and it's energized and brightened her life. I keep running into this all the time. How that *zing* comes in and makes someone come alive and do something like that out of the blue—that's a miracle. We are parsimonious about miracles. Just think of your life—what a fountain!"

Frank Wade of Washington, D.C., believed that a miracle was "not a description of an event but a perception of an event, how it came to be understood. Exodus is viewed by the Jews as a miracle, but it was written off by the Egyptians. There's nothing about it in their histories or sacred books. The miracle is in the perception."

Harry Pritchett of Atlanta agreed about different perceptions of the same event: "At Jesus' baptism, when he heard God say, 'This is my son with whom I am well pleased,' there were others present who heard only thunder. Some others heard angels."

A teacher at the Episcopal Divinity School in Cambridge, Massachusetts, Rev. Chuck Bennison points out that "the Bible doesn't use the word *miracle*. It refers to signs, wonders, wonder workers, healings—not as isolated reversals of natural law but as evidence of God's continuing power. Evil can work miracles as well as good."

A minister from La Jolla, California, Blayney Colmore, wondered, "Does one need to be a hysteric to believe that the nature of reality is so much deeper than our perceptions? My mother came to me a year after her death. She appeared. I trust it was real. I saw it. We do the liturgy with the understanding that this is an opening we don't understand—it makes us really nervous."

Sam Eliot, minister of Trinity Church in Boston, said: "It's not about intellect. God is a power, and we've protected ourselves from that power. Religion is energizing when we have access to God's power. It's so scary to a lot of people, it pushes them right out of the paradigm they're living with. We're so careful. The places that are coming alive are really getting access to that power."

Many of the ministers reported that the practice of holding healing services for persons with AIDS has grown into regular healing services for all parishioners, and that these services have become a significant part of the church's programs.

The Reverend George Regas of Pasadena said, "We have a healing service—with laying on of hands—twice a year now. When I describe the laying on of hands, I say, 'Come up if you feel bowed by your failures, come up if you have a broken relationship, come and let God heal you.' It's the most moving liturgy we do—there are people crying at each service. It gives people a chance, gives them permission to believe in miracles."

It is hard to believe in miracles in this century of mass destruction unless one accepts Rev. Bennison's belief that there are evil miracles as well as good. Michael Murphy also believes that as well as the miracle of grace that enables us to do the extraordinary "there is also the demonic—you can't have one without the other. How else to explain some people's actions, the terrible things some people do?"

Surely the Holocaust was a miracle of evil in our time, driven by the demonic power of Hitler and his followers. That wholesale triumph of the demonic shattered the faith of many believers, Christians as well as Jews, and was one of the major factors leading to the theology that declared the death of God.

The perceptive Hugh Nissenson, author of the highly praised novel *The Tree of Life* and a collection of faith-probing stories and journals called *The Elephant and My Jewish Problem*, discussed with me the Holocaust's effect on his own belief.

"I went to the Eichmann trial in Jerusalem to write about it, and I had a loss of religious faith. There was no way any longer I could believe that God operates in human history. I had to look for other answers. I've been wandering ever since. All my work is my own groping to understand—it's the great religious quest.

"My father was a deeply religious Jew, and he struggled to reconcile a merciful God with the twentieth century. He finally surrendered to God, not questioning anymore. I felt that the great miracle of the Bible was the Jews accepting the yoke of the Torah. How is it these nomads take on a moral vision? It's more miraculous to me than 'the burning bush' kind of miracle—that's a beautiful expression of mystical experience. But the idea that this rabble (and there was no attempt to pretty up these people) would accept the Law of the Torah—that's miraculous. And it's miraculous that both Jews and Christians would see David, in all his sins, lust, and arrogance, as a hero. He is a murderer, adulterer, and genius, yet in the Bible he's a hero—and Jesus comes of his stock!

"For me there's been a struggle with depression. The journey inward that the artist makes is always excruciatingly difficult, but it's compensated for by these extraordinary eruptions of resources and playfulness that you get when you're writing. It's happening now as I work on a new novel [*Song of the Earth*]. I've always known that creative power was lurking down there—it's a miracle, and since I was a child I knew it was there."

A Zen Buddhist comes to the concept of miracles today from a different point of view. Rick Fields, author of *How the Swans Came to the Lake: A Narrative History of Buddhism in America* and now the editor of the *Yoga Journal,* explained to me that "by and large Buddhism doesn't put the same emphasis on miracles as Christianity. In Zen, my miracle is 'chopping wood and carrying water'—looking at those acts and saying 'how miraculous!'

"There's a story of the Buddha meeting someone who has practiced meditation for twenty years and can walk on water. Buddha says, 'Why didn't you just pay three rupees and take the ferry across?' That represents the classical Buddhist attitude about miracles.

"In Christianity there's an emphasis on miracles because supernatural acts became proof of doctrine. Buddhism is not dependent on that.

If you have insight, that's what matters. If you're out of synch with the dharma—the way things actually are—you try to get back in alignment rather than do anything supernatural or call on the supernatural.

"There also is, though not as well known, a miracle side to Buddhism. There are eight life events of the Buddha that are like the 'canonical acts'—starting with birth and when he left home. In one of these he performed miracles before a crowd of Hindus and converted them. If you go to India, there are eight sacred Buddhist sites, and one of them is where he performed these miracles. It is one of the four minor sites for pilgrimage—there are also four major sites. The scene is depicted in the carvings of the eight events.

"There's another miraculous act of the Buddha. His mother died in childbirth, and he was raised by a stepmother. He ascended to heaven, where his mother was, taught the dharma to her, and came back down the jeweled steps to earth.

"Buddhism also has stories of Tara healing people [Tara is a bodhisattva, or enlightened being who out of compassion refuses to enter nirvana in order to stay and save others]. The tradition is that in times of despair you can call on her, and she reaches out and comes to the rescue.

"In contemporary Buddhism, in Tibetan Buddhism, there's a miracle in the reincarnation of lamas—when the kid is born it rains milk or six rainbows appear or unexplained sounds of music are heard. A Spanish kid was born and named successor to a Tibetan teacher who died, and now he's being trained in India. There's a story that one of the close disciples of the dead teacher met the successor, who's supposed to be the lama reincarnated, and the boy looked at him and said, 'You've gained weight.' [The reincarnation of lamas was the subject of *Little Buddha*, a feature film directed by Bernardo Bertolucci, starring Keanu Reeves.]

"Tibetans talk about the death of His Holiness the sixteenth Karmopa, head of the Karma Kagyu order, who died in Illinois on a visit to America. After his heart stopped, his body remained warm. Nonbelieving physicians attested to it and were astounded."

I asked if contemporary Buddhists—those in America as well as in Asia—regarded this as miraculous, and Rick said, "Yes. Tibetans buy it and tend to be impressed by it." He smiled and added, "Even the ones in New York."

A white frame Victorian house on San Francisco's Baker Street flies an orange flag with yellow stripes that look like rays emanating from the sun. At first I think it's Japanese (the house itself was once a Japanese Buddhist temple), but the flag is not the emblem of any nationality. Rather it symbolizes the power of meditation taught here at what is now the Brahma Kumaris Meditation Center by the "Daughters of Brahma," an order of Hindu nuns.

Sister Chandru, a gracious woman wearing a long white robe with a white sweater over her shoulders (the sisters wear only white) greets me and leads me to a seat in the high-ceilinged living room that features a black and white photo of Brahma Baba, the founder of the order. Sister Chandru stresses he is not a "guru," believing there should be no intermediary between humans and God.

When I ask her about miracles in the Hindu tradition, she says, "I am not a scholarly expert, but in my own study I find all of our Scriptures are full of miracles—visions, encounters, legends, and myths. The whole Hindu religion is based on miracles, philosophy, and ritual.

"Miracles are still happening. I am not talking about the kind like those of Sai Baba, making dust appear between his fingers when he rubs them. I don't mean the kind where people claim they are providing miracles.

"I am talking about the miracles of Divinity and transformation, spiritual enlightenment. We consider *that* to be miraculous, based on truth and belief—on faith.

"It's up to the individual how one can see that as a miracle. We understand miracles never happen unless one deserves it. It's like hitting the jackpot, but you have to prepare to bring yourself to this point. You cross many milestones, but it happens when you aren't expecting it, and it seems sudden. You don't *wait* for a miracle; you come to the point gradually, and then it appears, something clicks, and everything changes, so in your life it seems a miracle.

"I've seen many miracles in my life, coming through faith and good deeds. The self-healing power of meditation plays a very good role in it. Your spiritual contemplation has to do with transformation—the transformation of life, controlling the devil, healing the wounds (not physical but emotional wounds) as well as illness.

"I've seen many people pass through here going through that process of miracles—alcoholics have changed, some have just stopped. People say it's willpower, but I call it a miracle—it's God's grace, and it's the last source. You try everything else and at the last thing, people go to God."

The controversy over miracles stemming from the Western science-religion split suddenly seems bizarre rather than commonplace when viewed through another cultural lens. Dr. Khalid Siddiqi, director of the Islamic Education and Information Center in San Jose, California, points out that "science in the West suppressed miracles, the supernatural. Now it's coming to the surface again. In Islam we never separated science from religion. Whatever helps humans is religious. In Islam nothing is secular—science *is* religion. It's a religious duty to do work that helps humans. We have many scientists, as well as religious scholars. From the Middle East came astronomers, mathematicians, engineers. The basic sciences were developed by people in the Middle East." An intense man with glasses and a jet-black beard, Dr. Siddiqi sits at his desk in shirtsleeves, informal but highly focused, frank and open in his responses. When I ask if he has seen any miracles himself, he answers without hesitation, "I've seen evil spirits released from a person by reading passages of the Koran. I've seen people with sickness cured. I've seen a drought ended.

"We don't have the word *miracle* that you have in English. In Arabic we have *ayah*, meaning 'a sign' [plural, *ayaat*]. Anything supernatural is a sign of God in Islam. It's given to selected people, prophets and messengers—like Moses, Jesus, Abraham, Isaac, Solomon, David—down to the last and final prophet, Mohammed.

"The prophets Jesus and Mohammed both did supernatural works, and there's historical evidence. These miracles are of a number of types, both spiritual and physical—such as Jesus walking on the ocean or trees leaving their place and moving toward the prophet Mohammed.

"There are two types of *ayaat*. One is performed as supernatural, as evidence of a prophet or messenger. These are limited to their time and presence. But the last *ayah*, the Koran, is not limited to time, for it is still the most updated version of God's message and is good up to Day of Judgment.

"Miracles continue to happen, but these have a different name. If something supernatural happens now to a righteous person, following the prophets, following the message of God, it is called *karamah*. It can happen at any time, any place.

"If something supernatural comes from evil it is not karamah. It's what you would call black magic or sorcery. It's not a miracle unless it comes from God. No *person* has the power to do miracles, it is only God's power coming through them, as with Jesus in the Koran. When he causes recovery from sickness or brings the dead to life, it is with the permission of God.

"We believe every person has two angels, one on each shoulder— even nonbelievers. The one on the right is good, the one on the left is bad. They whisper to you, tempting you or inspiring you. A basic part of our faith is in the unseen—God himself, hellfire, paradise, angels. All these are unseen, they are part of faith."

I am reminded of an oft-quoted line of a Western classic, Antoine de Saint-Exupéry's *Little Prince:* "What is essential is invisible to the eye." The wisdom of this popular and revered story is perhaps made acceptable by its guise as a parable for children. As P. L. Travers astutely noted in a review of the book when it was first published, "All fairy tales are portents."

Biblical scholars may tell us the miracle stories are fairy tales, and devout believers may have their doubts and concerns about the "sightings" of saints in backyards and apple orchards. Many Christians agree with Buddhist Rick Fields that using miracles as proof of doctrine can be a dangerous and misleading process. Emilie Griffin, a perceptive writer whose book *Turning* is a classic look at the conversion experience (including her own conversion to Roman Catholicism), explains, "I don't like the idea of miracles being 'supernatural'—people who are coming out of the old theology are looking for proof that God exists.

"The old 'zap from heaven' way of thinking about the miraculous—the intervention of a powerful God into ordinary life—that's the old Cecil B. DeMille kind of miracle, and it's dangerous to think in those terms. Thomas Merton says his friend Robert Lax was so close to God but was waiting for a bolt of lightning—and that let him off the hook.

"I experience what probably is miraculous all the time—the person you most needed to talk to turns up; or someone raises the hardest questions when that was just what I was wrestling with—like you coming to ask about miracles right now. When someone close to me was ill and the worst problem on my mind was death, I saw a TV interview with Billy Graham just back from Korea talking about resurrection—and it was wonderful. That sense of synchronicity is amazing to me. The answer is there, and the person who gives it to you doesn't even know you're asking the question!

"That's the kind of 'miracle' I'm talking about. I felt that way about my conversion experience. I felt that way about having children."

Emilie's husband, William Griffin, a former Jesuit who is now an editor and writer of books on religion (including a biography of C. S. Lewis), recalls that "one summer Emilie and I took a crash course in religious studies at Loyola on Matthew, Mark, and Luke. It was three hours a night for five weeks. The professor said at the outset that the New Testament is 'figurative' writing—this shocked a priest from New Guinea who said he'd been taking it literally and preaching that way, and it worked just fine. It all comes down to 'Did Jesus do this or that, or didn't he?'—and only God knows for sure.

"It dawned on me that the more convincing the professor was intellectually, the more I realized the fellow couldn't recognize a miracle if it was tattooed on his arse. He rendered himself a totally imperfect observer of human existence. *What writers realize and others don't is that something can be literal and figurative at the same time—that is, something may really happen and may also be a symbol or metaphor for something greater; but that doesn't necessarily mean it didn't happen.*

"I have no doubt that miracles happen; also I don't feel I have to see one to believe they happen. Those theologians who emphasize humanity over divinity—I feel they wouldn't know God if he ran them down in a car. It's part of faith. Can God do a miracle? I think he can. He doesn't have to put the magic show on, and I don't think I have to ask him for one."

The debate about miracles—those who experience them or believe them, those who deny them—began at the dawn of human history and will surely continue to its end. Perhaps the best, most practical advice about it came from Albert Einstein: "There are only two ways to live your life. One is as though nothing is a miracle. The other is as if everything is."

Choose.

Chapter 2

IN SEARCH OF
MIRACLES

Istand naked and shivering as two men in blue aprons place a black garment over my chest that reaches to my waist—it looks something like a bulletproof vest—and tie it in back. The garment is icy cold and wet and prepares my body for the shock of the dunking to come in water of just such temperature. Blue-aproned attendants on each side of me hold an arm, guiding me to the steps of the marble bath that is fed by a spring discovered in 1858 by a fourteen-year-old shepherd girl who claimed she was led to it by a vision of the Virgin Mary. The water was said to be healing, and Lourdes—a French village in the Hautes-Pyrénées near the Spanish border—became world-famous as a place of miracles. Millions come every year to pray, visit the grotto shrine, walk in torch-light processions, drink the water from the spring, and take the baths, as I am about to do.

I step in, gingerly, sucking up a deep breath, and the attendants say a brief prayer, make the sign of the cross, then lead me to the front of the rectangular pool and dip me backward, down into ice-cold water for three seconds of full immersion, and pull me back up, dripping. I've not heard voices, seen visions, or experienced a miracle, but I feel braced, exhilarated; at least I'm not frozen. If anything, I feel warmed by the spirit of the place, projected by the caring concern of the volunteer attendants.

Memory brings back the baptism I sought as a boy of eleven at the Broad Ripple Christian Church in my Indianapolis neighborhood, where in white shirt and pants I was dunked by the minister in a water-filled tank behind the pulpit, to the tune of a hymn whose words I found disturbing rather than reassuring: "*Have thine own way, Lord, have thine own way; Thou art the potter, I am the clay.*" I wanted to have *my* own way, shape my own destiny, which I then envisioned as future sports editor of the *Chicago Tribune,* a sort of modern-day Grantland Rice, the Homer of the Golden Age of Sports, or successor to Red Smith, a wry stylist of the sports pages. How much I controlled my fate can be glimpsed by noting that fifty years later my work on a book about miracles led me to a dunking in the baths at Lourdes—a long way from Wrigley Field.

The men smile and help me out—not to the warmth of a waiting towel, though, for the practice is to let the water dry naturally. Damply clothed, I shake hands and thank the men—one Italian, one French— who have used their vacation to serve the pilgrims at Lourdes.

The Italian says he's from Milan, and noting his bushy mustache and big smile, I imagine him a jolly baker or chef (pasta maker), but in fact he's a copywriter for a public relations firm. People of all ages, nationalities, colors, and backgrounds—army generals and PR executives, graduate students and factory workers, novelists and farm laborers—come here to search for healing, of body, mind, emotions, and spirit. Many come as volunteers and find their own healing of spirit and reaffirmation of faith through unselfish service.

As a pilgrimage site Lourdes is more popular than Jerusalem, Mecca, or Rome (and drew more than double the number of believers who attended the games of the San Francisco Giants, my adopted hometown team, the last complete season before the baseball strike). The promise of miracles in the sense of extraordinary physical healing is now deemphasized. Gone is the wall of crutches that were said to be cast off by crippled pilgrims who walked away when healed. Sister Mary Patrick, a nun who has worked at Lourdes since the late 1940s, says the crutches display was "a distraction" to the "spiritual healing" that is emphasized now. Such healing might come through prayer or the ritual of a bath in the spring Bernadette was led to by her vision (a kind of new baptism for some). The healing might stem from caring for those infirm and disabled pilgrims who require others' help to be there at all.

Such service itself can have a transforming effect—at least on mind and spirit, which now we are coming to recognize has a powerful effect on flesh and bone as well. The idea that attitudes, behavior, and beliefs have a bearing on health has gained new validation with the growing awareness of the mind-body connection in Western medicine.

Since stress reduction by lowering heart rate and blood pressure through meditation and breathing methods was pioneered by Dr. Herbert Benson in the 1980s at Massachusetts General Hospital, a growing number of mainstream medical practitioners report the effectiveness of mind-body work. Dr. Dean Ornish, director of the Preventive Medicine Research Institute at the California Pacific Medical Center in San Francisco, has statistically demonstrated effective results of meditation, diet, and exercise in lessening the risk of heart attacks and reversing arterial blockages. Dr. Jon Kabat-Zinn, director of the Stress Reduction Clinic at the University of Massachusetts Medical Center at Worcester, uses meditation and "mindfulness" techniques to reduce chronic pain as well as stress. Bill Moyers's TV series "Healing and the Mind" heightened public interest in the subject.

The power of prayer and spiritual belief has been examined at Lourdes since 1858, when Bernadette Subirous, while gathering firewood, saw in a grotto a vision of a lady in a white robe with a blue sash who told her to return the next day. In a series of apparitions, during which Bernadette fell into a trance, she was guided to dig at the site of the spring and told to go drink and wash in it. The country people set up a crude shrine, bringing flowers and candles, and though civic authorities scorned the visions and closed the shrine as fake, more pilgrims came, and miracle claims began. A blind man who washed his eyes in the spring regained sight; a neighbor of Bernadette dunked her dying baby in the waters and it lived.

The bishop of the diocese established a commission to investigate and in 1862 declared some cures at Lourdes miraculous, defined as "contrary to all known biological laws and medical science." (Bernadette entered a convent, died at age thirty-five, and was canonized as a saint in 1933.) Emperor Napoleon III declared the shrine open to the public after his son claimed a cure, and the crowds swelled. Hotels sprang up in the town—it now has more than any city in France, after Paris—and no doubt the first souvenir shop followed.

Skeptical medical authorities called the healing claims "self-hypnosis" and "autosuggestion," and the patients "sentimental neurasthenics." The dean of the medical faculty at Bordeaux University branded Lourdes "exploitation of human stupidity." Ongoing criticism as well as fraudulent miracle claims (people who faked cures) led the Catholic church in 1885 to approve a doctor living on site to verify healings.

Charges of quackery continued, but a new kind of medical validation was given in 1893 when the famous French neurologist Charcot (a precursor of Freud) wrote his interpretation of miracles at Lourdes as "The Faith Which Heals"—perhaps the first modern Western medical recognition of the mind-body connection. In 1903 a skeptical young doctor named Alexis Carrel went to Lourdes and wondered at first if he was hallucinating when he watched a tubercular woman's abdominal tumor disappear in minutes; when he presented that and other cases he witnessed as authentic, he was booted off the medical faculty at Lyons University and joined the Rockefeller Institute in New York, where his research won a Nobel Prize in 1912.

No kind of verification will satisfy committed skeptics, though. The great French author Emile Zola, a pronounced atheist, wrote a novel called *Lourdes* in which he took well-known case histories of Lourdes pilgrims but falsified the accounts to end in death rather than healing. When reprimanded by a doctor of the medical board, Zola wrote back, "My characters are my own. I shall do whatever I like with them." He offered the real-life "characters" money to leave France and live abroad, but they refused. The novel dramatized Zola's own point of view: "Even if I saw a miracle, I couldn't believe it."

The very idea of a miracle is anathema to many, and some go to great lengths to disprove any such claim. A case in the medical records of Lourdes documented by Dr. François Leuret, president of the Medical Bureau from 1947 to 1954, tells of a woman who took the baths and claimed the miracle healing of an anal fistula (a duct leading from an abscess). She assumed the Lourdes doctors wouldn't examine such a private area; when they insisted, they found no affliction. The woman admitted she was sent by an antireligious organization to show that the Lourdes medical board certified healings without examination.

The resistance to claims of miracles—the very idea of miracles—comes at least in part from rationalist thinkers who fear that "proof" or acceptance of such phenomena invalidates their own worldview, their understanding of life, human nature, even their own experience. It's easier today to accept mind-body explanations because they are being verified by medical science. The word *miracle* carries the suggestion of God, and religion to the atheist is like the red flag to the bull. Religion stokes passions in nonbelievers as deeply as in the faithful.

None of the controversy over miracles has quelled the crowds that continue to grow at Lourdes, a village of eighteen thousand in the southwest corner of France, six hundred miles from Paris, ninety miles from the Spanish border. From my room at the Hotel Christina I look down at the flowing green Gave de Pau River and across to the foothills of the Pyrénées, a vista pleasant enough for any vacationer. The scene is pleasing to the pilgrim as well as the tourist, but the open souvenir shops I pass that line the hilly streets of town are disillusioning to some believers and feed the antireligious sentiments of scoffers (both groups complain of commercialism). For sale is everything imaginable with emblems of Lourdes—from crucifixes and coffee cups to Bernadette dolls and statues of Mary and Jesus (some with blinking lights).

But once past the gates of the high iron fence that surrounds the *domaine,* or grounds, of Lourdes (the *Cite-Religieuse*), I'm relieved to see no hint of souvenirs or any form of trash; the walkways, paths, and grounds are spotless. Light and space surround the high white statue of the Virgin Mary with her blue-painted sash (as Bernadette envisioned her), with white roses growing in a circle at her feet, ringed by a fence where pilgrims stick fresh bouquets. To one side is the grotto where Bernadette saw her visions and, beyond that, a long row of faucets where people run water from the spring to splash on their face or take home in bottles. At the end of the long esplanade is the Upper Basilica, a magnificent church with soaring spires, built against the riverbank; beside it and below is an underground basilica that holds twenty thousand worshipers. Except for candles on sale for placing at the grotto shrine with prayers, everything is free—the daily pilgrimage tours during season with guides; the baths, water from the spring, masses and processions, blessing of the sick, a video of Bernadette's story.

This whole enterprise began with claims of miracles more than a century ago, and I wonder how officials of the Lourdes Medical Bureau explain such phenomena today.

Roger Pilon, an immunologist with a degree in internal medicine, is president of the Lourdes Medical Bureau. He tells me, "In every disease there is a psychological part—any doctor will tell you that someone who wants to be cured is a better patient and has a better chance of recovery than one who gives up. Even more reason that at Lourdes a sick person receives help.

"Coming here gives people hope, maybe not a physical cure, but hope in a better life, no matter what their condition."

A trim, energetic man with close-cropped gray hair and shirtsleeves rolled up as if ready for action, Dr. Pilon sits in his small office on the domaine of Lourdes beneath a fluorescent light, a carved wooden figure of Bernadette in prayer, a cross, and a wood plaque of Madonna and child. He makes forcefully clear that his job at Lourdes is not to determine miracles. "For us, as doctors of the Medical Bureau of Lourdes, there are only 'cures,' and 'unexplainable cures,'" he says. "Miracles are a spiritual matter."

If a case passes the Medical Bureau, it is reviewed by the International Medical Commission of Lourdes, two dozen specialists from throughout Europe; if verified, it is passed on to a canonical commission in the diocese of the claimant to determine the theological basis for a miracle. Before going to that stage, a number of rigorous medical criteria must be satisfied, and Dr. Pilon ticks off the main considerations, leaning forward at his desk and tapping an index finger against his palm for emphasis.

"The cure must be from a serious disease, an organic disease; there must be laboratory proof, such as X rays, biopsies; the patient cannot have received any medical treatment for it; the cure must be extremely quick, if not immediate, and come without convalescence; it must be a definite cure, followed by a waiting time—five years with no return of cancer, for example. The bishop may wait another five years to see if the patient can give witness to the cure as a good Christian. For declaration of a miracle, the bishop must determine if an unexplainable cure is a sign of God's love—a miracle."

Since medical verification began at Lourdes more than a century ago, only sixty-five cures have been authenticated both medically and spiritually, the last one in 1982. Among those verified by an international medical board as well as a bishop of the church were cures for tuberculosis, peritonitis, complete remissions from ulcers with gangrene, spinal sclerosis, multiple sclerosis, abdominal tumors, sarcoma, and blindness of cerebral origin. Of more than six thousand claims of miracles submitted to the Medical Board over the years, two thousand "unexplained" cases passed the medical criteria but did not receive religious verification as a miracle from the Roman Catholic church.

Contemporary medical researchers use the terms *spontaneous remission* or *spontaneous regression* to categorize reversals of cancer and other diseases for which there was no known scientific explanation. In 1993 the Institute for Noetic Sciences, a research and educational foundation, published an annotated bibliography of more than thirty-five hundred case histories of spontaneous remission of a range of diseases from 830 medical journals in more than twenty languages. The volume notes that since cures validated as miracles at Lourdes must evidence a spiritual element as well as physical recovery, a miracle might be described as "spontaneous remission held to a higher standard."

Belief in the unexplainable is always difficult, and reading case histories seems remote. Sister Mary Patrick, an Irish nun who was in Lourdes when some of those events took place and knew patients whose cures I read about, speaks of them in a personal way that makes such phenomena feel more immediate. She serves at Notre Dame, one of three "hospitals," which are really hospices where *malades* (invalids and ill people) stay.

"In April of '52 a Swiss-German pilgrimage came to us," she tells me. "It was a long journey, and they arrived late. There was a Christian Brother, Brother Leo, who was an invalid, at the last stage of multiple sclerosis, and I had to try to feed him. He had a beard and was dribbling the food—he couldn't swallow. The next day he was taken to the procession of the Blessed Sacrament, and he came back walking and talking."

In Brother Leo Schwager's own words, after taking the baths twice his legs no longer felt numb or heavy, and while praying that day as the

Sacrament was brought toward him, "All at once I felt something like an electric shock and immediately got out of my wheelchair without knowing what had happened to me." His paralysis of five years, and numbness, headaches, and backaches were gone. The "instant and extraordinary cure" was verified without relapse after six years and proclaimed miraculous in 1968.

"I see Brother Leo every year," Sister Mary Patrick says. "He became the Swiss-German pilgrimage leader. He's in his eighties now."

Just as spontaneous remissions happen without medical explanation, I'm sure such cures have occurred at Lourdes, and I suspect they were triggered by the influence on believers of the powerful atmosphere of faith, prayer, and the healing history of the place. Christian Brother Leo Schwager's remission was surely a Lourdes phenomenon, less likely to occur for a monk in a Paris bistro or at a soccer match.

Dramatic as such accounts of sudden, unexplained cures may be, sixty-five "miracles" among millions of pilgrims in 136 years is not very encouraging to one seeking a cure. Ruth Cranston, a Protestant who spent years in residence to research *The Miracle of Lourdes,* uses a higher estimate of cures but warns readers, "Only one out of ten thousand of the sick is physically cured. True, you might be that one. The chances are 9,999 to 1 that you would not be."

So why do people come to Lourdes in increasing numbers? Sister Mary Patrick says, "Everyone who comes has their own miracle—they're transformed in some way, even if not physically healed. The emphasis now is on spiritual and emotional healing."

Dr. Pilon thinks people return because "they discover another dimension, a spiritual dimension to life. We have 'the heart's cure' here, but you won't see it—it's different from an objective physical cure."

Brid Clancy, who teaches math and the Celtic language at a secondary school in Limerick, Ireland, and volunteers here on her vacation, says, "People are amazing—they come here and have a change of heart. They find greater peace internally."

"I'd like to meet such a person," I say.

"Come then," Brid says, "I'll introduce you to Brendan."

Brendan Crehan has just arrived with a pilgrimage from Brid's diocese in Ireland and is waiting for the evening procession to begin. He's a former football player and looks it: a big man with a broad chest and shoulders, a ruddy face topped with reddish hair. His massive frame is confined to a wheelchair, legs and left arm paralyzed. He wears a pin-striped suit, white shirt, no tie, and talks fast and loud, as if announcing a ballgame.

"After my playing days I was a referee twenty-eight years, and I collapsed on the field. At the hospital they gave me an injection of a drug I was allergic to—I went into coma for nine days. They said I only had another day to live. My son called in the parish priest, who prayed for me, and I regained consciousness next day. They said it was a miracle.

"When I came out of hospital eleven months later, I was paralyzed. My priest brought me to Lourdes, and I've been every year since. I'm a fighter—I've seen plenty worse here than myself. This is my sixth year, and now I bring others. People back home ask me, 'Why do you want to go back to Lourdes? You've already been.' I say you don't get anywhere else the kind of peace you get around the grotto—that inner peace and tranquillity. It recharges your motor, gets you going again."

Brid says later that she remembers Brendan "the first time he came, in '89, not talkin' to a soul, tears in his eyes. There was resentment at first, then a total change of heart—a big part of it was what he got here."

Part of what Brendan and others get here is pageantry, on a grand scale, which they don't just observe but participate in, like the candlelight procession. Every evening during the season (Easter to November), as dusk falls, from five to twenty thousand pilgrims from around the world gather for a ceremony.

A hush of anticipation and awe descends as people of all ages and nationalities gather around the banners of their diocese or travel group. Flags of red, gold, green, white, and blue proclaim the origins of pilgrimage: Pellegrinaggi, Diocese Bergamo, San Marino, Manchester, Koine, Bayern, Anjou. Looking for an English-speaking group, I walk to a banner that reads "Parish of the Resurrection, Bayside, Dublin," where I'm welcomed with smiles and handshakes. A family comes over whose mother asks in a brogue, "Are you Irish? Can we go with you?" and they too are welcomed.

Candles are lit and the procession moves forward in harmony, of music and goodwill and spirit. Some of us are walking, others pushing wheelchairs or being pushed; women, men, and children, lame and whole, sighted and blind, invalids and athletes, children and octogenarians, joined in a sea of light from the thousands of candles and the sound of voices in a chant song to Mary, the Madonna. The words are in French, which isn't my language; the prayers, which are translated into English, Senegalese, Italian, and German, are Roman Catholic, which isn't my faith. Yet I'm moved by the beauty of the spectacle and the sense of quiet power of the place, its history, the emotions it stirs, the hope it offers.

There's an awesome feeling in being part of such a sea of humans gathered from around the globe in hopes of healing and in homage to something beyond themselves, whether it be the faith of Bernadette or simply service to others. Many are able to be here only with the help of intimate and constant care, from bathing and feeding to dressing and being taken to the bathroom.

The festive air of the procession is different from what I'd expected, as is the whole ambience of Lourdes. I had braced myself for a sad display of the lame and the halt, with noble types gritting their teeth to aid the poor souls. Instead I find smiles, good humor, mutual respect, and the joy of being in a place where aid and access is given to all. As the doctor of an Irish pilgrimage puts it, "Lourdes levels the playing field."

I see no one rise from a stretcher as a beam of light shines down. But the day after the procession, I walk beside Pat Fisher, a mother of six from Columbus, Ohio, with "stage-four fallopian tube cancer and coronary artery disease," and as volunteers push her wheelchair to a mass, she tells me, "I still have hope," and puts her hands in prayer form, smiling. When I wish her well and add that I'll say a prayer for her, she thanks me and says, "I'll pray for *you*."

Caring for others is the spirit of Lourdes and perhaps its most enduring miracle. Time and again while here I meet people whose lives have been transformed, not from limbs restored or illness cured, but eyes opened to new visions of life through serving those not as fortunate as themselves.

Mike Campbell and his wife, Kathleen, gave up their respective careers in England (she was an optician, he an overseas sales manager for a telecommunications company) to move to Lourdes permanently three years ago as directors of Hosanna House, a nonprofit facility of the Handicapped Children's Pilgrimage Trust, a British institution that sponsors disabled young people from all over the world on five-day pilgrimages to Lourdes.

"Before I came to Lourdes, I feared it was all sort of gloom and doom," Mike Campbell tells me. "But it was joyous, and it had a tremendous effect on me—to see there was a caring side to life. I knew things would be different from then on."

Kathy Campbell says, "The disabled people give so much more than you could ever give them, our work seems almost selfish. They don't realize what they give you—it's a source of inspiration."

It's also hard work. For nine years Renia Stawski, a medical research analyst for a pharmaceutical company in Nottingham, England, has been coming to Lourdes on vacation. She says, "This year's not as taxing as some. I looked after a girl who was brain damaged, and it took six of us to care for her. She was doubly incontinent and needed feeding. The worst part is I never got through to her, she could never communicate her needs. It's not always so. I looked after a young man who was blind, deaf, and mentally disabled, but I got through to him—he could convey what he needed to me."

I ask Renia if she thinks the brain-damaged girl really got anything out of her trip to Lourdes.

"No, I don't think so, but her family got a great deal. She had brothers and sisters. For one thing it gave them a rest."

I mention that Frommer's 1994 guidebook to France warns tourists that they may be discouraged by "the sight of ill or deformed people who have spent their life savings to come for a cure and go home not only unchanged but broke."

Mike points out that pilgrims to Hosanna House are paid for by the trust, and most of the diocesan pilgrimages raise money for the ill and disabled to come. But I still wonder: Aren't some bound to be disappointed when they don't find a cure?

"Even though some might have an idea of a miracle when they come, they go with a change of spirit," Mike says. "You will always see someone worse off than you. There's a change—there's not one that regrets coming."

"The disappointment comes at the end of the week here," Kathy explains. "You can't bear to leave those people—there's a post-Lourdes depression."

Three recent college graduates from West Auckland, New Zealand, who've known each other since childhood and are "checking out the rest of the world before we settle down," have stopped at Lourdes to work as volunteers at Hosanna House.

"Awesome" is how Rachel Hogg describes their experience.

Jody Gill says, "We had no expectations—we didn't have a clue. Our attitude has changed. Now people in wheelchairs aren't even strange. There's a boy they feed through a tube. The only normal thing is his face, and he smiles—we got him on a bike and he was thrilled."

Rachel, whose straight blond hair gives her the look of a California surfer, says, "We used to say, 'Oh, we're ugly'—we look in the mirror, we don't suit ourselves—but there's nothing really wrong with us, and yet we're moaning and complaining. It makes you realize."

Craig Dunford says, "I was doing management before—that's fine if it's what you want in life. Now I'll go into something more service oriented rather than have my goal be to succeed and rub shoulders with bigwigs."

People of all ages are moved by being at Lourdes. Claude Jeanneau Astrachan, a French sculptor, remembers coming to Lourdes as a child with her mother, Madeline, and her father, the late Gen. René Jeanneau. Claude's parents were married at Lourdes and came every year after the general's retirement on the Pilgrimage of Rosary, sponsored by the Dominicans. These trips, her mother told her, provided "a deepening of our own faith."

Madeline says they attended discussions at Lourdes, and at one of them, the general, "who was usually silent and very discreet," spoke up to a very unhappy man and said, "Sir, read Saint Paul—maybe that will help you find your path." Madeline said the general told her later, "It was as if the Holy Spirit came to him, gave him those words. Next day the man was transformed, happy. He said he spent all night reading Saint Paul, and 'I can understand much better.' It was like a spiritual healing."

Flannery O'Connor, the southern novelist whose Roman Catholic faith was crucial to her work as well as in her life, contracted lupus in

1951 and went to Lourdes at the urging of an elderly cousin in 1958. She was not very impressed. She wrote to a friend that "Lourdes was not as bad as I expected. I took the bath. From a selection of bad motives, such as to prevent any bad conscience for not having done it, and because it seemed at the time it must be what was wanted of me. . . . They pass around the water for '*les malades*' to drink and everybody drinks out of the same cup. As somebody says, the miracle is that the place don't bring on epidemics. Well, I did it all and with very bad grace." She wrote to another friend about Lourdes, "The supernatural is a fact there but it displaces nothing natural; except maybe those germs."

The prolific and proudly Catholic novelist-columnist-commentator William Buckley wrote after going to Lourdes in 1993 of the "buoyancy experienced on viewing the great processions. . . . The spiritual tonic is felt. If it were otherwise, the pilgrims would diminish in number, would, by now, have disappeared, as at Delphos, which one visits as a museum, not a shrine."

Some former faithful feel Lourdes has become too commercialized. Mary Apodoca, wife of a retired U.S. military officer, went to Lourdes in 1952 and says it was a quiet little village, a beautiful place to be, but after returning in the 1980s complained, "It's so commercialized it's like a circus now." Frommer's 1994 guidebook to France warns tourists of the "tawdry commercialism" of the place. (Nevertheless, if after that warning, you still want to go to Lourdes at the peak of the tourist season, the guidebook recommends that you "nail down your hotel reservation.")

"I didn't realize it was so commercial," says Paula Halloran, a twenty-three-year-old from Greenwich, Connecticut, who has come to Lourdes as a volunteer. "All those awful souvenirs—there's even a blinking Jesus for sale. After being on a plane for eight hours, I saw that stuff and thought the apparitions had already started."

Carol O'Dwyer, a recent college graduate who arrived from Tipperary a few days before, is also upset by the "blatant commercialism." She feels many pilgrims must be disappointed: "If I were ill, I'd expect something, like 'God'll give you a push.'"

The other young people I've met are inspired by being here, and I wonder if these new arrivals will feel differently at the end of their two-week stay. I hurriedly scratch my address on a sheet of paper I tear from my notebook and ask them to write if their impressions change.

A month or so after I return home, a letter arrives from Carol O'Dwyer. She identifies herself as "the Irish skeptic" and writes of her experience at Lourdes:

> *After the two weeks my whole outlook had changed. . . . My work in the Baths has made me appreciate my good fortune as I witnessed people in coma, on a stretcher or with only one leg. The faith of the people in the nightly procession stunned me—especially when everyone raises the candle to Our Lady singing "Ave Maria"—similar to the raising of glasses at a feast. A nun said that at Lourdes everyone experiences their own private miracle. Lourdes has answered me, in the fact that when I go to mass, I now go with my head held high, and gone is that sense of embarrassment. . . . So yes, it's true, my opinion has changed.*
>
> *It's a pity I had to go so many miles to find my faith—but it was worth everything. . . .*
>
> *Yours faithfully,*
> *Carol O'Dwyer*
>
> *P.S. So miracles do happen, after all.*

But are those the only kinds of miracles that happen now—restorations of faith rather than health?

I ask the Campbells, who operate Hosanna House, if they've ever witnessed a physical healing. They haven't, but Kathy says, "A few years ago we brought a baby with a split chromosome disease—the brain doesn't work, and she was very disfigured, a deformed face and head, bulging eyes, no nose, webbed hands and feet. At first it was difficult, but by the end of the week everyone's attitude had changed—you knew her then, and you couldn't see an ugly child, she was beautiful. She didn't have a healing miracle, in the sense of a physical alteration; but she changed in everyone's perception of her, the way they saw her. She didn't live to her fourth birthday."

In Ireland two priests whom I met the summer before at a conference on ministry tell me they often take people to Lourdes on pilgrimage, and I ask what miracles they have witnessed.

"For years I've gone to Lourdes and never seen the physical healing kind of miracle," Father Frankie Murray says. "But I saw different things happen. It's so common to see someone who goes and becomes reconciled, to illness, disability, whatever it is they bear.

"You always see the sickness of a person in a wheelchair—but there's greater woundedness of people whose wounds you can't see. The more hurt they are, the more they seem to hide it, yet the more they seem to need healing."

Father John Cullen, a priest from the town of Roscommon, nods agreement and adds, "We start out as a group going to Lourdes, not knowing each other, and by the end of five days something happens. A bond is formed, and all these isolated people who are anxious and suspicious become trusting of one another—that kind of veil is taken away."

Such changes of heart are touching and meaningful, but I keep on wondering if "real" miracles—visible, tangible, physical healings—still occur at these holy places that are pilgrimage sites. Do the lame and dying no longer rise up from their stretchers and walk, with a whole new life? Are the physical healings only stories from the past? And if they don't happen today, mustn't we wonder deep down if such things really ever occurred? I explain I'm writing a book about miracles, and I feel if I'm going to use the term I have a true account of such occurrences in the present.

Fathers Cullen and Murray look at each other and say, "He's got to meet Marion."

"Who's Marion?" I ask.

I learn she's a woman in their parish who experienced such a physical healing at a pilgrimage site in Ireland called Knock. They hadn't mentioned her before because they thought I was interested only in things that happened at Lourdes. Knock is Ireland's most popular pilgrimage site, "the Irish Lourdes."

Father Murray explains that "Knock became a holy site when a woman went out one August evening in 1879 and saw what she thought were statues. The priest got there and saw figures—the Virgin Mary, Saint John, Saint Joseph. And fifteen or sixteen people came by and saw these figures. It wasn't one special person who saw this, it was totally democratic. It happened during the famine years in the poorest part of Ireland."

"Before Marion Carroll went to Knock," Father Cullen says, "I saw her on a stretcher. She'd come to a healing mass. She was paralyzed from the waist down, and she was doubly incontinent. She'd been paralyzed for three years."

"At Knock, she got up off her stretcher and walked," Father Murray says. "She's been fine ever since."

A friend with me says, "That's a biggie."

Father Murray laughs and says, "I think all miracles are the same size."

"Would you like to meet her?" Father Cullen asks.

Yes—I was going to leave for Dublin the next day, but if I could talk with this woman, I'd postpone the trip and stay on.

Father Cullen gets up from our table at the restaurant where we're having dinner in the town of Athlone and goes to a phone. He returns to say Marion is leaving for England the next morning to go to a wedding, but she's going to have a good-bye drink with her husband and son at the Prince of Wales pub tonight, and we can we meet her there.

Marion is a short, plumpish, lively woman, with bright eyes, wearing a white skirt and green sweater. Her husband, Jimmy, is with her, a quiet man with glasses in a blue T-shirt; he's a sergeant major in the army. Their son, Anthony, is with them, and they also have a daughter, Cara.

A rock band is blaring at the Prince of Wales, and Marion and I go sit in a corner in hopes of hearing each other. She speaks loud and clear in a lilting Irish brogue that manages to transcend the heavy bass and boom of the live rockers.

"In '89 I wanted to go Lourdes, but we couldn't afford it. But a friend asked me if I'd like to go to Knock for a day. In '78 when I was diagnosed with MS, we went down to Knock, on a Tuesday. It was deserted, rainy, and I thought, 'This has to be the most miserable place on earth.' I got back in the car with the promise I would never go to Knock again the rest of my life. I said I'd go this time only 'cause I'd go anywhere to get away from the four walls—and so Knock was planned."

"The Friday before I was to go to Knock for mass on Sunday, my kidneys got worse, and the doctor came out and told me I had to go to the hospital. I told him about Knock, and he said to go ahead, but be ready for the hospital on Monday. That Saturday I knew I'd come to a cross-roads in my life. I knew I couldn't go forward, couldn't go back, couldn't go sideways. I knew I was goin' to die, and I had been prayin' to Jesus and Mary to let me live long enough to see my daughter and son out of their teen years. But now I knew it wasn't goin' to be. I didn't want to go to Knock now. I just wanted to stay and be with my family. But my friend had made all the plans, and I didn't know how to get out of goin'.

"Jimmy got me ready on Sunday mornin' and put me into an ambulance from Athlone Hospital. When they brought me into the basilica at Knock, first they were goin' to put me to the right of the altar, then they were goin' to put me to the left, then they decided center—right under the statue of Our Lady of Knock, and I realized this is where I wanted to be. Here I was under her altar, and when I looked up, I thought it was the most beautiful and friendliest statue I ever saw in my life. I prayed to Our Lady, not for a cure, I knew I was goin' to die—I was just worrying about what would happen to my children. All I said to her was, 'You're a mother, too.'

"Then I heard this kind of whispery voice telling me to get up, to open the stretcher. I tried to laugh it off.

"I remember thinkin' to myself, 'Hold on now, Marion, you've more sense than gettin' ideas like that.' I wasn't goin' to tell anybody, keep my dignity, I'd just go home and tell Jimmy. They took me back to the place to have tea, where the ambulance would come take me home, and I heard the voice again.

"The wife of the doctor on the pilgrimage that day started talkin' to me, and I said to her, 'Would you think I was stupid to believe if that stretcher was opened I could get up and walk?' She said no, but she didn't know what to do. She called to one of nurses from Athlone Hospital—nurse Maureen Rafferty—and Nurse Rafferty opened the stretcher, and as she told me later, 'I only opened it to peace-ify you.' But when she opened the stretcher, I lifted my legs over the side, and they went out straight. I wasn't even stiff after all those years. I'd been seventeen years with MS, and three completely paralyzed.

"I was holdin' my head myself without the collar, and I was usin' my arms and hands, and my speech was perfect.

"When I stood up at Knock, it had nothin' to do with walkin' or movin'. Right in front of me I seen my own heart, and it was so full of joy and peace, I was so shy it was like lookin' directly into the sun. And then the rheostat controlled me and I got them gifts of all that joy and peace and great love. Mrs. Koin, who founded Handmaidens of Knock, asked, 'Can you read?' I said no. She handed me a book. A page opened. It said, 'Why is the rosary so powerful?' I could read all the small print. I said, 'That's a prayer for my home and family,' and I knew Our Lady had kept her promise, 'All those that pray our rosary I will take care of.'

"I sat up straight the whole way home in ambulance. I said, 'We'll say nothin' to Jimmy, we'll surprise him.' I was walkin' down the steps of the ambulance, and Jimmy came out the front door with the wheelchair and said, 'Well, Marion, how was Knock?'

"'Ah, it was all right Jimmy,' I said. 'But why would anybody bother goin' down there?' He didn't realize I was walkin'. I got into the wheelchair, and Jimmy opened the patio doors. I stood up and said, 'Look, Jim, I can walk!' He said, 'Oh God, Marion!' I never seen a man cryin' like that. He got down on his knees and started thankin' the Lord. My daughter came in and seen her daddy cryin'. I had never really held my children, I was afraid to drop them.

"My greatest thing was puttin' my arms around my child, feelin' my child in my arms.

"The doctor came and said, 'What do we do now?' This had never happened to him before. I stayed in bed readin', but by Tuesday I got fed up, jumped out of bed, and said, 'Look, Doctor, I can walk.' He told me, 'Throw away the wheelchair.' The morning I went to Knock, the muscles were mostly wasted in my legs, and when I come home they were perfect. That morning I took my drugs, and I haven't taken any since. Two weeks later the nurse said, 'I'm goin' to take out the catheter.'

"My cure and my healin' does not belong to me. This is a special gift to people from Jesus and Mary to let them know they are there. We're so human we need to feel, touch, and see God's love—my cure was that instrument.

"I was only three months' married when I got sick. Before that I worked in a factory. I'm still the same person. But when I stand up to talk, it doesn't matter if it's two people or a million, I have no worries. I know the Lord will give me what to say. I have a deep inner peace.

"I've been to Fátima, Lourdes, Jerusalem. People want to go to a place of miracles, but they only have to be open to the Lord. They don't need any of those places. He's here, he's in our churches, and he never lets you down. The only time he doesn't heal a mortal illness is when he calls people home to protect them.

"I went to Medjugorje in February of '91. We went as a family. While I was there prayin', my hands got a glow in them and a feeling, like pulsin', like a single heartbeat in each hand. I thought to myself, 'You're hallucinatin'.' I went to confession and told about it, and the priest said, 'Will you pray over me?' I didn't know what to do, so I closed my eyes and put my hands on his head and counted to four, and prayed.

"Then things started to happen. I started doing healin', mental, physical, and spiritual healin'. When I came home from Medjugorje, I didn't want to join every Tom, Dick, and Harry who claimed to be healin' people, so I went to our bishop. The bishop listened and told me to go ahead. Every move I make I tell the bishop. That way I'm not being exploited or exploitin' my gift. I believe in obedience.

"I travel around world now for mass if I'm invited. I do mental, physical, and spiritual healin', and family healin'. I can go into a family situation. I guide them, and I follow it up, to see how they're doin'. When I pray for them, that's not me, it's the Lord workin' through me. I'm only an onlooker. When I'm speakin', it's like I'm outside myself lookin' in on myself.

"The ambulance driver who took me to Knock, he and his wife never could have children of their own. They had two adopted children, and I asked Our Lady to bless them, and they had a baby girl.

"I had a trip to Rome comin', and I told Jesus I'd love to get near the Holy Father when I was there, if he could help me do that. Well, a sister got me a general audience with the Holy Father, so then I asked the Lord if he was happy with what I was doin', and I told him if he was, he could confirm it by allowin' me to get Holy Communion from the Holy Father personally. That's the way I chat him up—that's the way I've always chatted the Lord. When I got there, word came I was to have that Holy Communion from the Holy Father, and I did. That was a miracle too.

"Every single night when I go to bed, I'm like a child on Christmas Eve. I'm wonderin', 'What great thing is he goin' to do next?' His work is happenin' *now*—it's fantastic—like when he walked among us."

The visions at both Knock and Lourdes, which produce such miracles and draw such large numbers of pilgrims, occurred in the nineteenth century and might be pigeonholed as part of the belief system of a past era. Yet another powerful apparition with similar results took place on June 24, 1981, in the small village of Medjugorje in what was then Yugoslavia, a few hours north of Dubrovnik. An apparition of the Virgin Mary has been reported every day since that original vision was seen by six children, two boys and four girls, and continues to appear to them around 6:30 to 6:45 every evening.

By 1986 there were some 250 to 300 reports of healing there, according to Father Slavko, a Franciscan monk with a Ph.D. in psychology who served as the children's spiritual director. A woman from Milan who had been diagnosed with, and treated with all known medical resources for, multiple sclerosis arrived in a wheelchair. She was in a room with the children when they were having the apparition experience. Feeling a sudden movement through her body, she stood up and said, "I can walk, I am healed!" The priest simply told her to kneel down and pray, which she did.

This case was reported by the late Brendan O'Regan, who was vice-president for research at the Institute for Noetic Sciences and coauthor of its comprehensive *Spontaneous Remission: An Annotated Bibliography.* O'Regan went to Medjugorje and was in the room with the children for one of their daily experiences of the apparition. Though he did not himself see the Virgin, he reported that, "It was as though there was this incredible wave of feeling throughout the room that hit one in the solar plexus—an incredible kind of sadness that made people cry. It was a very intense thing that quietly takes hold of you. I was not told about it in advance, and I was sort of taken aback by it. . . . When the apparition left the children, everyone outside began spontaneously singing the Ave Maria in all these different languages with no cues from those inside the room as far as I could tell. So it's a strange feeling, but you get the sense that something very, very intense is happening there. . . . It's a very deep experience. You come away feeling, well, if there are conditions of prayer and spirit and mind that can be conducive to healing, then surely this is a good place for them to be expected. In a paper called "Healing, Remission, and Miracle Cures," O'Regan reported that he was in Medjugorje when the cloud from Chernobyl blew over it, but no one was aware of it because they were cut off from the news. He later found out that a Boston researcher had gone there to measure radioactive levels, and when the apparition was appearing, his Geiger counter went way above normal. This researcher also measured the electrostatic field in the area when the apparition was appearing and found that it rose by seventy thousand volts.

I have talked to several Americans who have been to Medjugorje and are anxious to return, but like many potential pilgrims around the world, they are prevented by the war that has torn that part of the world asunder. Like O'Regan, they also reported powerful emanations from the place and experienced a deep sense of the spiritual simply by being there.

Sacred places have always been part of the spiritual landscape of the world. "If we got in touch with the earth, we'd see that every place is blessed," says Father Gerry O'Rourke, a priest of the diocese of San Francisco, "but there are special spots that remind us of that, remind us the earth is holy.

"There are holy spots of Ireland, pre-Christian, that Saint Patrick was smart enough to acknowledge as sacred places. The holy wells of Ireland were there before the Christians, such beautiful wells of water. They're so magnificent they're seen as holy and were places of worship before Christianity. The place where I was baptized, in north County Roscommon— St. Lassar's Well, named for a local saint—is known as a place of healing. People left crutches there; you can see fragments they left behind.

"Of course Ireland doesn't have the only holy sites," Father O'Rourke admits with a smile. "There are even some right near where I live now in San Francisco! The Native Americans says Mount Tamalpais is a holy mountain. I have no problem with that—something about it makes it a sacred place. Mount Shasta is another place sacred to Native Americans. Why it is that Mount Tam is sacred and Mount Diablo is not? I don't know—but I can feel it."

Rick Fields, the Buddhist editor and author, told me that another American place of healing is Chimayo in New Mexico, an hour from Santa Fe.

"You go up a road and there's a beautiful church. In the back of the church is a dirt floor, and if you take the dirt and put it on you, you can be healed. The place is filled with crutches and canes and testimonials of people who have been healed there. People go there—I go there myself—

because it has quite a good feeling about it. In fact I've picked up some of the dirt and put it on myself."

The new wave of pilgrimages to holy places of healing is in fact a return to older practices. We've already noted the miracle healings of the West that go back to Elijah and older Jewish healers such as Hanina ben Dosa and that became the center of Jesus' ministry. Beyond that, in the Middle Ages, shrines of saints and martyrs became like spiritual hospitals, and lists of miracle healings recorded by monks have been called medical journals of medieval life.

In "Faith Healing in Medieval England," historian Ronald Finucane writes of paralysis, blindness, broken bones, leprosy, epilepsy, gout, and mental derangements cured at shrines. Michael Murphy in *The Future of the Body* compares these knights, yeoman, craftsmen, and poor people of the Middle Ages to twentieth-century pilgrims at Lourdes: "Like many who are healed in similar circumstances today, they felt they had contacted a transcendent wholeness, a presence or energy beyond their ordinary functioning that restored them in a manner that seemed miraculous."

The church of Our Lady of Perpetual Help is huge and ornate, like a European cathedral, and it seems out of place in the Mission Hill section of Roxbury, a poor, innercity neighborhood in Boston. Built in the nineteenth century when this area was a wealthy suburb, the church looks as if it's been put in the wrong setting, like a baseball stadium in Times Square or a fancy night club in the middle of a prairie. What is it doing here in Roxbury in the nineties? And why are these busloads of people coming here?

This is not simply a congregation assembling from the neighboring community for a Sunday service. People from across the United States and down from Canada, several thousand men and women and children of all races and nationalities stream into this church on a Sunday afternoon that isn't even a holiday or any sort of special occasion or celebration. It's the routine biweekly healing service on the regular schedule of the church's pastor, Rev. Edward J. McDonough, a Roman Catholic priest.

Inside on the walls hang crutches of those who came crippled and rose to walk away, symbols and testimony of the healing power evoked here. After the service begins with hymns, prayers, and Scripture readings, people who were healed here speak of their own miraculous recovery from pain, blindness, arthritis, cancer; diseases and injuries and conditions said to be incurable, inoperable, hopeless— all of them cured or made whole, they say, by God, through the healing touch of Father McDonough.

This Father McDonough, I expect, is a powerful man, a charismatic figure whose voice and presence inspire with eloquence and passion. Soon, I think, he will come forth to the pulpit, replacing the aging little Irish priest who's been leading the prayers and reading the Scriptures in a dull monotone. But it finally becomes clear that the anonymous-seeming priest *is* Father McDonough.

How can this man heal anyone, or be the transmitter of healing? He speaks in a virtual monotone. He *drones*. He is the epitome of ordinary— or a little less, at least in stature. He affirms that impression. He says he has no magic; he preaches only the Scriptures, and whatever he does comes not from him but from the word, of Jesus Christ, of God. He is a priest of the church, a servant, that is all. I believe him. But why are all these people here to see him?

Father McDonough asks that all those who want to be healed of ailments or problems that are not of a life-threatening nature stand up and come to the middle aisle. They form in rows, and church members trained to assist in this procedure come forward and stand beside and behind them. Father McDonough comes down from the pulpit and moves toward them. Speaking his prayers and blessings in the name of the Father, the Son, and the Holy Ghost, he touches a man on the forehead and the man falls backward into the waiting arms of an assistant. The priest moves along the rows, touching each person's forehead—not pushing, merely touching with outstretched fingers—and the people, men and women, large and small, tall and short, thin and heavy, fall backward.

The falling is different from any I have ever seen. The people touched by Father McDonough do not simply crumple or slump to the floor like people I've seen faint or pass out. These people go down like trees being felled—stiff and straight, as if struck by lightning, into the waiting arms of the assistant, who's been trained as a "catcher." Most, if not all, make this fall at the touch; some simply move backward as if shoved (though there is obviously nothing so strong as a shove, only the featherlike touch). They are temporarily unconscious, some for only a few seconds, some for nearly a minute or so, and then they rise or are helped up and return to their seats. Afterward some come forward to testify of the experience, those who have had some ailment healed or lifted.

There is another call to the aisles for those who have life-threatening illnesses that they wish to have healed, and again the aisle is filled, again the priest moves along them, touching and felling. I did not see anyone throw away crutches or rise up from wheelchairs, though afterward in the testimonials some people spoke of sight being improved or returned, of ailments or illnesses cured or gone into remission as the result of the touch.

When I saw this for the first time in 1982, I had only a year or so before returned to church and begun a long climb toward recovery of faith and the effort to follow a spiritual path, and I was not so much awed by this as I was wary, even frightened. Was this legit? Was it appropriate for me to experience it? Would my going to the aisle simply be an impulse to have what looks like literally a quick hit of the spirit, a zap of proof of the power of God, and therefore basically sacrilegious?

I worried that my own faith at that time, which still seemed new and fragile, might be somehow undermined or compromised or even shattered by such a powerful but unknown experience, outside my own church and faith community.

When I talked to my minister, Rev. Carl Scovel of King's Chapel, he nodded as I described the tree-felling phenomenon and explained that this process is called "slaying with the Spirit" and is part of the charismatic healing tradition.

At that time, the notion of healing through prayer, faith, and the laying on of hands seemed spooky to me—a bit off the map of mainstream practice, of intelligent, contemporary knowledge of the world, even for people who declared themselves Christians and belonged to a church—and I'd guess it seemed that way to most of my fellow parishioners as well. I couldn't have guessed—nor perhaps could my own minister at the time—that only four years later our own church would be offering a healing service.

"This church is more than three hundred years old, and there have been many different kinds of services held here," Reverend Scovel told the congregation assembled that historic night. "We have had services for weddings, funerals, and baptisms, services for holidays, feast days, secular holidays like Thanksgiving, services for induction of new members, even services for blessing a new governor of the Commonwealth who was a member of this congregation. The one kind of service we have never had until tonight is a healing service."

It happened because of AIDS. The churches in Boston had pledged to take turns holding an AIDS healing service for the whole community once a month, and our church was one of the first to do so. After a sermon, hymns, and prayers, Reverend Scovel, his associate minister, Charles Foreman, and our seminarian, Pamela Barz, each accompanied by two volunteer lay leaders of the congregation, stood behind the altar rail to lay hands on any person who wished to come forward and say what healing was desired, and a prayer would be said in blessing for it. Reverend Scovel urged everyone to come forward, not only people who had AIDS or were HIV-positive but also those who wished to be healed of another physical illness or infirmity or a mental, emotional, or spiritual problem.

The original idea of that call was to protect people with AIDS from singling themselves out—declaring themselves as carriers of the dread disease—by walking up for healing. People without it would walk to the altar rail with them, would also kneel and receive a blessing for whatever healing they wished to take place.

The next day many parishioners called Reverend Scovel to say that they had been moved by the experience of being prayed over for their own healing. They didn't have AIDS and had simply wanted to show their support and fellowship of those who did. The first healing service at King's Chapel proved fulfilling to so many people that the minister called for a gathering of those who would like to meet on a regular basis to look into the role of the church—our church—in healing. Out of those meetings came a regular weekday healing service at the church, in the downtown business section of Boston, open to all.

With the AIDS epidemic, spiritual healing has come out of the closet and taken its place in the liturgy of mainstream churches of many different denominations throughout the United States Synagogues as well are reviving traditional Jewish healing practices.

Sha'ar Zahav is a small, frame temple (the building was formerly a church and looks like a New England meetinghouse) painted a light brown, with a modest-sized stained-glass window and a belfry. It stands on a corner of a residential neighborhood in the Castro district of San Francisco. I am sitting with fourteen men and women of assorted ages, scattered in the first four rows of wooden pews at six o'clock on a Monday evening for the bimonthly service sponsored by the Jewish Healing Center.

On the raised platform in front of us is a table with a white cloth and blue letters in Hebrew, on top of which sits a bowl of water for ritual washing, a single candle, and a small vase of flowers. In a chair next to the table, facing us, sits a dark-haired young woman in her thirties, wearing a print dress. She is Rabbi Nancy Flam, and when she fixes her dark eyes and her concentrated gaze on one of the people asking for prayer for relief of pain or disease, physical or mental, you can almost see her connection to the person as a tangible force, bridging the space between her and the person who is speaking.

A man in the pew behind me says, "Andy will have a procedure on Monday and wants us to include him in our prayers. His Hebrew name is Avram. Doug also wants our prayers."

Rabbi Flam leans forward, nods, and asks gently, "What does Doug need now?"

"He needs to let go, he needs resolution. His parents are here now. Pray he may go on to the next world in peace."

A woman in front of me says softly, "I learned today I have uterine cancer. I see it as a way of getting things resolved, making a new beginning. I'm glad to be here."

Rabbi Flam listens to other concerns, of those present and others they speak of who can't be present. She says little, gives acknowledgment but not advice, and engages with complete involvement in what she calls the ministry of presence—listening fully, being totally present to the other person's feelings.

Someone asks for prayers for "a man who was dumped out on the street. He's forty-eight and had three brain tumors. He came here to our service once but didn't like it. He's part of the community of our hearts."

"I've had a healing with my mother," a young woman shares. "I didn't think it was possible—it makes me see there's always an opening for healing, there's always an opening . . . "

When everyone who wants to speak has had a chance to express themselves, Rabbi Flam says, "Let's center ourselves by chanting a Jewish tune to deepen our awareness and wake ourselves up. This is called a *nigun,* sung over and over like a mantra."

She closes her eyes and leads the musical chant, the sound becoming the focus of the room, of attention.

"*Ya la li, la la, ya la li, la la . . .* "

When the chant is finished, the rabbi asks people who wish to do so to come forward for a ritual washing of their hands in the bowl on the table.

"Water is purifying," she says. "The water symbolizes washing your hands for mikvah—it's a method of transforming from one state to another."

People get up one at a time, go and wash, and return to their seats.

The rabbi asks for prayers said aloud of thanks to God, saying, "Place it before God, and in community, which gives it a holy dimension. That's what we live for."

Worshipers share aloud the miracles for which they are personally grateful. "Blessed is the source of life," each person sings, then inserts his or her own sentiment.

A woman gives thanks to God "who brings Nancy's words to open our hearts, so we'll see and be in new ways." The woman who has just discovered she has uterine cancer thanks God "for giving us new opportunities . . . the will to learn . . . may such blessings be in our consciousness." A man facing his third operation for prostate cancer the next day gives thanks for "the richness of this place, which has helped sustain me, making me aware of the richness of everyday life."

The rabbi leads us in a study of the Book of Ecclesiastes (in Hebrew, *Kohelet*), passing out photocopied quotes for us to consider.

"This is part of the Wisdom literature of the Bible," she explains. "It's different from the rabbinic literature. The message of Kohelet is 'When the sun shines, seize it, enjoy it—that's all we have.' It's the idea of being in the present, doing it now—praise God now, for there's no praising God in the other world. Do it here."

She suggests we read Kohelet like a notebook or a journal of the author and elicits comments and questions from us on the text. It almost feels as if we were a family sitting around a fire, discussing a good book, one that raises the deepest questions, hints at answers, and offers humor, sometimes cynicism, leavening the wisdom.

In closing, the rabbi prays, "God, help us to shed more of the crippling self—the judgments we schlepp around. We have a screen of unworthiness. We need to get rid of it and have a closer living sense of the Creator. Let's try to see ourselves as entirely beautiful and entirely worthy."

After one service Shifra Raffel, who suffers from a painful wrist condition, told a visitor, "It's not that my troubles have gone away—it's just that I feel much stronger, recharged." A man with AIDS said, "I feel like I'm opening myself to God."

I learn that the healing service grew out of a similar service that members of Sha'ar Zahav, San Francisco's Reform synagogue with outreach to gays and lesbians, offered for AIDS victims. As often happens (as it did in my church in Boston), the AIDS service here led to healing services for all, regardless of their illness or need.

The healing services now are sponsored by the Jewish Healing Center, which, Rabbi Flam explains, is "an organization that started three years ago, with five women, three of them rabbis, to help meet the spiritual needs of Jews living with illness, dying with illness. We're an education center and are retrieving ancient texts and creating new ones. We just had an eight-week study group on Judaism and spirituality. We do hospice work and public education and have a library and research program. We don't offer or provide physical healing. We undertake to minister to the mind, body, and spirit."

Services like the one provided by the Jewish Healing Center bring about healing and reconciliation in more ways than expected, for Jews and Christians alike. The ministers at the Episcopal conference where I led my workshop said the practice had positive effects they had never thought about beforehand. William Tully, minister of St. Columba's Episcopal Church in Washington, D.C., knew that the presence of well-known people of government and the media at services sometimes is daunting or off-putting as well as intriguing to visitors, especially prospective parishioners.

"We have a healing service every Sunday now, and, aside from the main point of healing, it turns out to be a healthy antidote to those who come and think we're elite or that our congregation is too successful for them. When they see people kneeling down, it changes the image."

These "side benefits" are real, as if the very practice and intent of healing moves outward into other areas of life, bringing healing of different kinds. Still, it is not only "side effects" that result from prayer but true healings that defy scientific and medical knowledge and predictions—healings, recoveries, and remissions that are indeed miraculous.

Chapter 3

MIRACLES
OF HEALING

❧

If all of us at this table get sick and God picks out John and cures *him*, and the rest of us die, what kind of God is that? A capricious God?"

Father Frankie Murray looks around the table at a group of friends having dinner in Athlone, Ireland, and we're silent, pondering one of the greatest conundrums of all.

"A friend of mine died last week," Father Murray goes on, "and before she died she said, 'The miracle is not necessarily the cure. The miracle may be accepting the illness, even accepting death.' "

Accepting illness or disability seems hard enough, but accepting death even more impossibly noble and wise. Yet I hear accounts of such quiet miracles.

Marie McGuiness, a school principal in Dublin, tells me, "I took my father to Lourdes when he had cancer. He was only thirty-six and he was angry, but at Lourdes he came to accept it, he found peace. When he got home he called us all together and said, 'I've never harmed any man. I have my bags packed, and I'm ready to go.'

"He made two last requests—that he be put in a nursing home, because my mother had been ill for a long time and he feared that she'd die if she had to take care of him. That's very unusual for an Irish man, to ask to be in a nursing home instead of his own home, for any reason. The second request was that we take my mother to Lourdes. We did, though she never found there what he found."

Acceptance of illness and even death is its own kind of miracle certainly, but it leaves unanswered the question "Why me? Why must I die or be ill—or why should I get well and live—while others don't?"

A woman in Georgia who is thankful for her daughter's survival of a near-fatal accident tells me: "We don't flaunt our miracle. What do you say to those people who don't have one, whose children will be in a hospital the rest of their life? It's not fair."

I was in a prayer group with a woman who had a physical disability. Since childhood she had prayed for a miraculous healing. She read the Bible stories of miracles over and over. She prayed and prayed. No healing happened. It made her doubt, question her faith, and despair. The idea of miracles disturbs her: The stories of them in the Bible are so inspiring, yet she can't make one happen in her own life. I wonder how many people in her situation become bitter and angry.

I asked Father Gerry O'Rourke of San Francisco how he explained such things. How would he respond to the woman in the prayer group?

"What miracles in her life did she not acknowledge?" he asked. "There's the miracle of being able to contribute to life in the face of disability—the inspiration to others as she lives and praises God. No matter how sick and deprived we are, to the end of our lives we can show and manifest God's patience and love in the world. We've met people who have ungrudgingly taken on their deprivation and inspired us."

When I later asked Marion Carroll, the woman who experienced the miracle cure at Knock, how she understood God's failure to heal the millions of others who go to such shrines, she told me, "Illness is a ministry. A person in a wheelchair can be seen by another person who suddenly realizes his own blessings and says, 'Thank God for my health.' It makes him aware."

I think of Lloyd Kantor, a Vietnam veteran who lost both arms, both legs, and one eye in a land-mine explosion and considers himself "luckier than most people" because his girlfriend still wanted to marry him when he returned from the war. They determined to have a whole life together, and they do, including world travel.

I think of Reynolds Price, the novelist who was stricken with cancer of the spinal cord in 1984, which gave him intense pain and left him confined to a wheelchair for the rest of his life. He has used that catastrophe to serve as a greater focus for his work. He works more productively creating novels, plays, and poems since his illness than he did before it struck.

"In ten years since the tumor was found, I've published thirteen books—I'd published a first twelve in the previous twenty-two years," he reports in his powerful autobiographical work *A Whole New Life: An Illness and a Healing*. As a writer of courage and spiritual faith, Price is an inspiration for many, including me. Hearing the story of his recovery at his sixtieth birthday party, the physician wife of one of his doctors exclaimed, "But that's miraculous!" Price's doctor looked at her, grinned, and said, "You could say that."

Only recently has it dawned on us in the West that we can learn from the healing practices of other cultures. With parochial arrogance, we had assumed we knew the best and latest of everything (a popular American assumption). There is now, even on the part of some American Medical Association doctors, a fascination with and serious interest in learning from the East. Chinese medical practices were featured on Bill Moyers's TV series on healing. Dr. Deepak Chopra has brought the Ayurvedic medicine concepts of India to a growing audience in the West. We are beginning to become aware—belatedly and inadequately—of the wisdom of Native American healing traditions.

Other healing practices, close to our own borders, have been overlooked or neglected. Just to our south, a rich and powerful tradition of folk healing is carried on in Mexico. A different attitude toward miracles also exists there, not only a willingness to accept them but a desire to document such occurrences by photographing them.

In a book of photographs and text about the followers of a Mexican healer (*Nino Fidencio: A Heart Thrown Open*), the folklore consultant Kay Turner explains that among such healers and their followers the camera seems to have become "an adjunct instrument in healings, marking the historical moment of a miracle and making it demonstrably real."

There are many documentary photographs of a healer in the act of curing, Turner reports, "especially removing tumors [a visible manifestation of illness that can be easily photographed]." Current healers are "keenly aware of the camera's availability to them as an instrument for recording events," Turner writes. "These image-documents become part of testimonies of belief." One healer takes snapshots of each person she heals and frames the photos in a collage that provides a record of her healing.

Awareness of this openness to miracles in a neighboring culture has been brought to us by freelance photographer Dore Gardner in her powerful book of text and photographs on the Mexican healer Nino Fidencio. Gardner's discovery of healers and their practices, as well as her own healing, is a fascinating example of how the spirit—or what some may call the life force or the power of creation—moves us to where we need to go. Her journey began, as many do, with a longing for something lacking in her life, which she sensed was the experience of faith.

JOURNEY TO HEALING
Dore Gardner

Dore Gardner's photographs have been published and featured in the *Boston Globe, Common Boundary* magazine, and other newspapers and periodicals. *Nino Fidencio* was her first book, and she is now working on another. She has taught at Marblehead High School in Massachusetts and received foundation grants to support her work.

"I was brought up in a Jewish family in Canton, Ohio. I couldn't relate to Judaism, nothing clicked for me. In Canton I wasn't exposed to any other religions. It was a small, inbred Jewish community, and I wasn't allowed to go out with men who weren't Jewish. I went to Ohio State and then did graduate work at Lesley College in Cambridge. I hadn't yet studied photography.

"I got a job integrating arts into the classroom at Marblehead [Massachusetts] High School. I saved my money so every summer I could go to a different country. I started taking photos. They had power to them. I took a photography course at the Mass College of Art. I photographed the Wonderland Ballroom in Revere. I wanted to show how people transcended their daily life. They were blue-collar workers who cleaned up after work to be kings and queens of the ballroom. I interviewed them and got their stories. That was my first thing published in the *Boston Globe*.

"One of my high school students was a gospel singer. I went with her to take photographs in gospel churches—in Georgia and South Carolina, black Baptist churches, big tabernacles with black priestesses. I didn't know that kind of faith, but I wanted to. It seemed remote, beyond my experience.

"My first leap of faith was when I asked for a leave from my job. In 1984 I quit. I went to Florida, to South Beach in Miami, and photographed old Jewish people. Then I traveled with a circus and photographed. Next I photographed Elvis impersonators. That, too, was a way for people to transcend their ordinary lives. They were saying Elvis healed them. People go to all-night vigils at Elvis's grave, bring flowers and notes, like people do at the shrines of saints. They use Elvis to connect to the Other.

"I was back in Cambridge, and one Thursday night when it was raining hard, I ducked into the Harvard Film Archives. I decided to watch whatever film was playing, hoping that when it was over the rain would have stopped. It was a film on El Nino Fidencio, in Spanish. I was totally mesmerized, even though I didn't know the language, and the film was old and shaky thirties images. Fidencio felt oddly familiar. I immediately wanted to know about him and to go to his hometown, where his followers go on pilgrimage. I called the filmmaker in Mexico, and he told me the faithful gather in March and October at Espinosa.

"That Christmas I had a break from a part-time job teaching photography at a private school, and I drove west to San Antonio and then to Laredo, where, I had heard, some of those who healed in Nino's name performed their work. I spent two and a half weeks hanging around in cafés on the border, asking about healers, but I wasn't getting very far. Then a cab driver said to see a healer he knew across the border. We saw a lot of different healers, but I knew from the film that the 'spirit of Nino' healers looked a certain way, dressed a certain way, and I hadn't found any of them yet.

"It was getting dark and I thought maybe we should go back, but there was one more to see, so we went down this dirt road with deep ruts. Just as I was thinking, 'This is silly; we should go back,' a woman came out of a house. She had hair to her waist and was wearing the Nino robes with a heart on them. She took me into the house. There was an altar with an image of Nino.

"Outside again, as I prepared to leave, I asked in my broken Spanish if I could attend a healing service she said she was holding the next day at two, and the woman said, 'I'll ask Nino.' She went back into the house, went into a trance, came out, and said, 'Nino says you're supposed to be here. Welcome.' I wondered if Nino knew I used a flash.

"Everywhere I went I got messages from him, and people opened their lives to me. It was special that they had opened that way to a white woman.

"I went to Espinosa for the first time the next March on a dusty train. There I was, a Jewish woman from Marblehead, in this dusty, remote town that's not even on the map. I felt so drawn to Mexico. My family is from Lithuania and Russia, but those places seem unlike me. When I got to Espinosa I was smiling—I felt I was home. No one had told me how to get there.

"The day after I arrived, a woman came up to me and said, 'Nino has a message for you. He says you worry too much. He has chosen you to do his book.' I hadn't even thought about a book at that time.

"At the end of a day when I was feeling restless and tired, a healer came up to me and said, 'I bring you a message from Bertha.' That's the name of my grandmother. It isn't even a Spanish name. How could she know?

"At another time, another woman approached me and said, 'Nino has been coming to me in my dreams. He told me to help you.' After that we traveled together and she translated for me, in Espinosa and across the border, in the Mexican-American community in El Paso. I dedicated the book on Fidencio to her—Alma Martinez.

"I manage to have deep relationships with people I photograph—not like people you meet at parties where you just chatter. Also I feel enriched by them, and I can give something back to them in my photographs. I wrote to invite both the people I'd met in the town and the healers to the opening of my show on Fidencio at the Houston Center for Photography. All these Mexican women drove thirteen hours from the border to be at the gallery opening. They took their books around and had healers autograph them. The healers wrote across the chest of their pictures like movie stars. They pasted mementos in the book. They thanked me for telling their story and telling the truth.

"After the book came out, Alma Martinez came up to visit me. One day during her visit I looked out and saw her in my yard with squirrels sitting around her. I started to go out and shoo them away, to warn her they might bite. But I realized she was perfectly comfortable with them, and they with her. She came from a culture where miracles happen. Now we in the United States are being reintroduced to something that was taken away from us. When my grandparents came from Europe, mystery and magic was part of them. They threw it all away to come to this country; it was stripped away. This whole idea of mystery and miracles is new to us— we're shocked by it. But Mexican people from traditional culture find it natural. Unlike us, they don't need to be hit over the head to notice things.

"During this time of working on the Fidencio photographs I was trying to understand faith. A year after I started this project I got deathly ill. It had been coming on for a few years. My symptoms were exhaustion and nausea. I was going to all sorts of doctors, but no one could say what it really was. It got so bad I couldn't move. Finally I went to a doctor who was a specialist in environmental medicine. He said I had developed a sensitivity to photo chemicals—it's called a type two allergy. He told me to dismantle my home darkroom. I couldn't believe it. I was doing this project on healing, and not only was I sick, I was sick from a part of the project. The doctor said I could think of myself as being healed, since, due to my body's violent reaction, it had been possible to catch the illness in time. Some people who continued using materials they were allergic to ended up with lymphatic cancer.

"I didn't know if I could go on with the project. I got some worker's comp and applied for grants. I no longer used a darkroom. I'd lost my health, lost my income, lost my way of being a photographer—I thought I'd give up. But I continued, I got grants. I kept returning to Espinosa.

"Once when I was down there and had swollen glands, which were a symptom of my allergy, I went to one of the healers for help. He said prayers over me and went into a trance. The next day I was fine. I can't say that my illness was cured directly by Nino or his healers, but I know a lot of people with this kind of chemical allergy who got chronic fatigue syndrome and never fully recovered. I'm back to myself again. The project on the healers was going on concurrently, and I think doing it gave me whatever I needed to come back fully.

"Doing the book elevated me in my personal and creative life. I didn't have to relate to faith in a religious way—I could have faith in my ability to keep moving forward. I'd never done that before, without 'security.' I think there's much more for us to draw on than we usually imagine.

"I fight the miraculous. I say, 'See, that's nothing.' But after years I see it's *not* nothing. It's like something Joseph Campbell told Bill Moyers: When the hero starts on a path, invisible hands come out to help. Bill said, 'It always seemed that way to me.' When you put yourself out there, you aren't alone. When I decided to go to Mexico, people tried to warn me off. They'd say things like, 'Be careful, Mexicans steal.' People's fears hold them back from everything wonderful in the world.

"I still get afraid. There are periods when things don't seem to be working out, but I want to be out there, learning and seeing. I find myself praying now. I feel connected to something. I didn't before."

When we think of miracles, we most often think of healing, of accounts like that of Marion Carroll, who rose up off her stretcher at a shrine of the Virgin Mary, serving as a kind of contemporary archetype. Just as Doubting Thomas needed to put his hand in the wounds of Christ to believe, so it is that physical proof, changes of flesh or bone we can see and touch, are the most specific, or concrete, kinds of miracles and thus seem most authentic as well as dramatic.

The stories that follow describe such experiences. None occurred within a traditional religious, much less a traditional medical, framework. The hand of a pianist and the arm of a quarterback are healed, and they are able to continue their professions. A woman is spared an operation advised by a specialist when an informal group of experimenters heal her without even touching the injured flesh.

These things happened.

A HAND RESTORED

Nancy Rosanoff

An inner voice gave Nancy Rosanoff the answer to a difficult dilemma and led to a career of lecturing, writing (her book *Intuition Workout* was published in 1991), and giving workshops on how to use your intuition, for corporate and adult education audiences. It also took her on a path to the physical healing of a debilitating condition, enabling her to play the piano again.

"I was studying music at the University of California at Berkeley to become a concert pianist, when a severe case of eczema on my hands made playing not only difficult but painful. The eczema was so severe that my hands were cracked and bleeding and oozing. I went to doctors, did everything they told me, but nothing helped.

"I was very discouraged. I dropped out of college after my second year and moved with my first husband to a house in the woods without plumbing or electricity. There were unexpected problems there, too.

"One day my dog ran off and didn't come home, and I found out some neighbors had the dog tied up at their place because she'd killed twenty of their ducks (they raised these ducks to sell). They said, 'When dogs do this, kill animals like this, they can't be trained, so we shoot them. We have a gun and we want you to come and shoot your dog.'

"I went up to their place and found twenty dead ducks and my dog. They handed me the gun. I pointed it to my dog's head, but then I couldn't do it, I couldn't shoot her. I said to the neighbors, 'Give me two weeks to train her, and if it doesn't work, I'll bring her back.' Over the next two weeks I tried everything I heard about dog training, and nothing worked. The two weeks were up, and I went for a walk and asked for help, somehow. A voice in my head said, 'Get a bell.'

"I did and tied it around her neck. When she went to chase animals, the bell jingled and warned the animals. The thrill was gone for the dog, and she lost interest in the chase. I got some chickens to use as a test, set them out by the house with the dog, and the dog just lay down. I took her back to the neighbors' and she lay down in the midst of all these ducks. The problem was solved.

"The miracle wasn't the voice in my head that told me what to do, but it pointed me in the direction my life was going to go in. I'd dropped out of studying music at Berkeley and wanted to retire from the world, to live in the woods the rest of my life. I'd had it with civilization. A couple of years later, though, we moved to a small town in northern California—Garberville, in Humboldt County.

"I went back to school at Humboldt State University and took up music again. While I had lived in the woods, the eczema had calmed down; but when I went back to school and started studying music again, it came back with a vengeance. My right hand was ugly, and playing the piano was painful. I kept trying cures, but still nothing helped. My friends told me to go to some psychic healing classes.

"The psychic gave me a reading. She told me she got images of a past life—it was a gory story—and she said what happened then created the fear of expressing myself creatively in front of other people. It made sense to me, but I didn't feel the skies had opened or anything. I had no special feeling at all until the next morning. When I woke up, I was completely healed. The eczema was gone. I knew that things had shifted in a lot of other parts of my life, too. I was able to play the piano one hundred percent. My teacher suggested that I study with this guy in New York, so I did.

"I was going to stay in New York for one year, but during that year my life changed again. I realized after six months that I wanted to teach people how to tap into this source of information and vitality inside them. And I wanted to find a non-scary, non-weird way of teaching it. This seemed more important than playing the piano.

"I'd done other things to make money, and they all had failed. I'd got to the place where the third endeavor failed, and I was desperate. I went to the beach, it was Fire Island, in June. I sat down and said, 'What will I do now? What do I want?' I said to the inner voice that everything was gone in New York, and I didn't know what to do. The voice said just to go back and teach some classes.

"I studied with a psychic for six months, who told me the basic way to work with some of these things. I started developing stuff on my own, teaching classes, practicing, listening to the inner voice.

"The first class was almost all men—seven—and met in my apartment. I started telling people what I wanted to do, and from there it just developed. I made some calls and had twenty people in the next class, and from there on it was success after success, opportunity after opportunity."

I met Nancy at the Omega Institute, a center for holistic studies in Rhinebeck, New York (I think of it as the Esalen of the East), on eighty acres of lawns and trail-marked woods in the Hudson River valley. Both of us were leading workshops that week, mine in spiritual autobiography and hers in intuition. I attended an evening lecture she gave and participated in intriguing and helpful exercises in using your intuition. On the porch of the snack bar she coached me in how to use intuition to decide on an offer I couldn't make up my mind about. After those exercises I realized I couldn't make up my mind because I was thinking that I should do it, but I didn't want to do it. I went home and politely declined the offer. I've never regretted the decision. I found again that people "on the path" can help you on your own path.

"I WAS THROWING LIKE I WAS TWENTY-ONE"

John Brodie

John Brodie was a star quarterback for the San Francisco 49ers and is now a professional golfer on the senior PGA tour. He has been one of the most articulate professional athletes in describing experiences in the action of sports and has coauthored articles (with Michael Murphy, in the *Intellectual Digest*) and a book (*Open Field,* with J. Houston).

"I had a miracle happen with my arm. I was gone, as far as being a player. The most respected doctor in the field took X rays of my arm that showed calcium and all kinds of stuff. He said no movement in the arm was possible. I was taking a lot of drugs to relieve the pain, and you can get hooked on them in the process. That codeine can feel real good.

"I consulted this very creative guy in Scientology, and he put me through two hour-and-a-half sessions in three days. After the first session the pain was gone. I said, 'What's going on?' It was a process they have in Dianetics of relieving the incidents that caused the problem. There was a trauma with a history in a certain part of my arm. A suggestion exists in the unconscious, and you try to recollect it.

"During my session, we got to one big incident from '62. I had run into a tree in an automobile. The ambulance driver had said, 'It doesn't look like this s.o.b. is ever going to throw again.' When I recalled that, when I saw it, it was like a pop! I could throw again.

"I went in for more X rays. They showed nothing at all—no calcium, nothing. My arm never got sore again. That was five years before I finally quit. The players on the team with me can attest to this. When I was thirty-four I couldn't lift my arm, and I'd become addicted to codeine. After this process, I was throwing like I was twenty-one. I played much better than I had before. And I became drug free.

"I felt I gained a considerable amount from the Dianetics technique. As for Scientology, the organization itself, I let it go—we parted in a friendly way. I gained a lot from them.

"The experience gave me an awareness of things of that sort—I was willing to experience anything. I recognized the spiritual nature of miracles. I don't pretend to know how they occur.

"Playing on the golf tour now, I've had messages I'm prone to listen to. Every once in a while I've got the kind of calm that came over me at times when I was looking for a receiver in football and the line was coming at me but everything seemed to slow down.

"Meditation is about getting in to present time, and when I compete in golf, in preparation, I try to improve my ability to be in present time. You can create a calm, a space of freedom."

"The more I practice and work, and the more I live life in a way that I'm satisfied with, when I feel good about what I'm doing, the more that happens. In that state, everything improves—not just your golf but your family, everything. To the degree that you apply yourself in the direction you approve of, in your whole life not just in sport, you create that experience."

THE BURNS WERE GONE

Marcia Seligson

Marcia Seligson is a journalist whose work has appeared in many national magazines. She now specializes in lecturing and writing on issues of women's health.

"I was visiting my family in London in 1978 when an entire pot of boiling coffee spilled onto my leg and foot. I had third-degree burns and was told I would have to have a skin graft. When I got back home to Los Angeles, I went to see a famous 'burn doctor'—he was known for treating burn cases of movie stars, and he was going to do the skin grafts and surgery.

"Before it happened, a friend of mine called who was part of a group of doctors and other people in medicine and psychology who met once a week to experiment with alternative healing techniques. They loved to have a live guinea pig, and my friend, who was a psychologist, said, 'Let us work on you,' and asked me to come to one of their meetings. I had nothing to lose, so I went with her to meet with this group in Malibu one evening.

"They put me on a table and said they were going to use 'energy techniques.' About ten of them stood over me around the table and waved their hands in the air. No one touched me. It was very quiet, and it took about an hour and fifteen minutes. When I got up, a lot of the pain was gone. I'd been in almost constant pain before that. I stayed overnight at my friend's house, and when I got up the next morning, the burns were gone.

"I went back to the doctor, the burn specialist, and showed him my leg and told him what happened. It made him crazy. He said there was no way it could have happened. It flew in the face of his 'paradigm.' He was very upset."

We earnestly hope and pray for others to be healed when medical science offers little hope of cure or assures us no cure is possible. Our hopes and prayers are especially intense and heartfelt when children are involved. As we know, miracles don't often happen, even for the innocent; but when they do occur, it seems especially marvelous. It is also humbling, as a mother learns when her daughter is in a near-fatal accident and specialists say there's no hope of recovery, yet her church and community determinedly pray for healing. A grandmother gathers prayers for her yet-to-be-born grandson, whose sonogram shows a spinal malformation. A pregnant woman who is told by specialists her child can never come to term calls on a spirit for help. Powers unseen come into the lives of these people and the children they love. Faith is deepened, but questions are also raised for those who are blessed and confront the mystery of why some receive such healing power when others, as worthy and as innocent, do not.

"THE DOCTORS TOOK AWAY OUR HOPE"

Carter Morris

The Reverend Chuck Bennison, whom I met at an Episcopal conference in New Orleans where I gave my workshop, told me about a healing regarded as miraculous experienced by a member of the church he pastored in Atlanta before he went to teach at the Episcopal Divinity School in Cambridge, Massachusetts. I spoke with Carter (Mrs. Hampton) Morris, and she told me the story of her teenage daughter's recovery from a near-fatal accident.

"On May 11, 1992, my thirteen-year-old daughter, Heyward, was at a friend's house roller-blading in their neighborhood in Atlanta. They were being lookouts for each other as they skated out of driveways into the street, but somehow the system broke down, and Heyward sped out of a driveway and hit a passing car. She was unconscious, in a deep coma, and luckily her father, Hampton, was nearby. He raced her to the hospital, where they said she had suffered a TBI—traumatic brain injury.

"The doctors took away our hope. They said that based on what they knew of other such conditions, she would be in a permanent vegetative state. There was one doctor who seemed more positive or optimistic than the others in his attitude, and I went to him and said, 'Give us your best hope. What's the best thing we can hope for her?' He said maybe someday she could feed herself. That was the brightest outlook, based on medical evidence and knowledge.

"The word of our daughter's injury had got around the community, and people poured their hearts out. There was a vast network of Christians and non-Christians praying for her. We're not a high-profile family. My husband is an attorney, and we belong to St. Luke's Episcopal Church, but we're not high profile religiously or in the community. Still, the word spread like wildfire. We were deeply moved by the outpouring of prayer and compassion from people we didn't even know. It made us feel that people are good. There were Bible study groups from other churches, there was a group called "prayer warriors," there were people from all over, praying their hearts out. At one point I felt there was so much support that the hospital itself could have been raised off its foundations by prayer. My brother and his wife prayed over her for a week, and they said at one point they sensed a warmth from her hands and body.

"Our daughter goes to a nondenominational school, but there's an Episcopal chapel service, and they asked if we'd allow them to have a prayer service for her every morning. The kids were so frustrated—this allowed them an avenue to feel that they were able to do something. First they just prayed for her to recover, but then they wanted to pray specifically, not just for her to get well, but for some specific thing to happen. On the eleventh day of her coma they prayed that she would open her eyes. That was the day she started to come out. It was the day of the spring performance that she was supposed to be in, and the kids sang to her the song 'Tomorrow' from *Annie*. We taped it and played it for her in the hospital. She now says she thinks she has a vague memory of hearing it.

"One of the doctors looked at her when she came out of the coma and said 'Don't you even have a headache?' She said no. When we asked the doctors if they had any explanation for what happened, they said 'You're very lucky.'

"After she came out of the coma, she was taken to a rehabilitation hospital for two months, and now, two years later, she's fully recovered. Everyone truly felt it was a miracle. When they see her walking through the halls at school now, the students think of her being back as a miracle of God, and that they contributed to it.

"I think it helped the clergy, too. The clergy get so burned out from hearing all the problems people have, the things that have gone wrong. This gave them a kind of renewal. I feel that a ripple effect of good things has come out of this.

"We feel very humble now, very appreciative of each morning. We don't take anything for granted. We sent thank-you cards to people, with a joyous picture of Heyward. People still have it pinned up. Heyward is an acolyte at church. One woman said when Heyward walks past her, 'I feel closer to God.'

"We're pretty low key. There wasn't anything in the papers. We gave one speech about it—that's it. We focused on our family—we're staying focused on keeping our ship afloat.

"You hear the word *miracle* a lot now. I don't use it lightly. So many people don't get one. When Heyward was still in a coma and we didn't know if she'd ever recover, people came and told us their miracles of a child recovering, and I felt like throwing something.

"We don't flaunt our miracle. What do you say to those people who don't have one, whose children will be in a hospital the rest of their life? We visit people now in rehab who may be there for years or permanently. It's not fair. I know, there's a way of saying some good comes out of everything, but it seems like turning lemons into lemonade. Some are still bitter. I guess it's all in the attitude.

"I do think that the way our experience has helped the people who helped us with their prayers may mean there is a higher purpose for the whole thing."

THEY COULDN'T EXPLAIN IT

Norma Kay

Norma Kay was browsing in a bookstore when she saw a title that looked interesting—*Accept the Gift*. She read a few pages and found them wonderful, bought the book, and took it home, learning it was made up of excerpts from *A Course in Miracles*. This led her to doing the course, which she has studied and followed the past five years. She has worked in the home all her life as a wife and mother and is now a grandmother, living in Merced, California.

"Our son, Randy, and his wife, Renee, were expecting a baby last winter. The doctor took an ultrasound sonogram of the baby a little less than four months into the pregnancy. He also took a video of the sonogram. He was very concerned, as the baby's spine had a spot that looked like a hole. He spoke of the possibility of spina bifida. The sonogram was done late Friday afternoon, and Randy and Renee could not get in to see the specialist until Monday morning. (The specialist didn't consider this an emergency.)

"Of course we were heartsick to hear of this. Some of the family talked about abortion to Randy and Renee, but they said a definite no. Randy said, 'I believe in miracles but not abortion.' I called my friends and family and asked them to pray for the baby. Randy and Renee did the same. I also called our church's prayer line in Missouri and asked them to pray for the baby. In my prayers for the baby I always tried to visualize him as perfect.

"Monday morning Randy and Renee went in to the specialist for another sonogram. Three specialists examined it and said the baby's spine looked perfectly normal. They looked at the video of the first sonogram and said, 'We can't explain it.'

"Last month Ryan William was born—a beautiful, healthy baby.

"Every time I get upset or worried about something, I stop and remember that miracle. I try to live in a state of gratitude. I don't say I do that perfectly, but I'm working on it."

"I WAS LIFTED OUT OF MY BODY"

Tama Bass

Tama Bass lives in Mill Valley, California, where she formed a nonprofit corporation, the Children's Channel, to provide classes in alternative health care, vegetarian cooking, the martial art of aikido, storytelling, and other subjects in an after-school, PTA-supported program in the Marin County (California) public schools.

"I got pregnant in February of 1971, and the pain started in May. One night I was in a lot of pain and went to the emergency room at the Alta Bates Hospital in Berkeley. I was diagnosed as having two fibroid tumors that were growing and would continue to grow. The doctors said there would be a time when they would suffocate the fetus—a full-grown fetus could not develop. They said they couldn't operate, there was nothing to do. Eventually the tumors would contract, and I would deliver prematurely at around five months.

"I heard what they said, but I wasn't tuned into it. I had another way of seeing life. I was on a more spiritual path, and I believed I had the ability to transcend what appeared to be programmed to happen. I wasn't negating the information they gave me; I knew it was entirely valid.

"I was in and out of the emergency room constantly with pain—when the tumors contracted, the whole uterus would contract. I was taking painkillers and muscle relaxants that were fed intravenously. No one paid any attention to what was happening to the baby, since they felt it would never live, so they just tried to keep me out of pain until the premature birth.

"I had a strong desire to have a child, a strong motivation to be a mother. I started doing things to get healthy, like carrot juice fasting, because I felt I needed to purify my body and make friends with these tumors.

"I was living and working at the One World Family Commune, and I went to the man who was the spiritual leader, Alan Michael. He wasn't like a guru with devotees—he preferred to stay in the background, let people create their own way of life, let people have their own independence, their own interpretation of his ideas. He said he wanted to attempt a psychic healing. It was not something he ordinarily did, but I said it was all right, that we could give it a try.

"We lay down next to each other, with ten other people in the room. He channeled a force. It was not him, but he was the agent of a higher force, what seemed like a Godlike energy.

"I was lifted out of my body and could see it as a 'physical vehicle.' I saw that the tumor situation was serious, that having the baby seemed impossible. A white light came into my spirit, and it was clear that this was my karma, it was all true and real, and there was no way to overcome it on that level. But this introduced a shift in my reality, and I saw that I could make the healing happen on a higher level. I didn't have to have that karma; I could work it out on another level.

"I saw that it wasn't too late, that I could change in midstream. That was the result of this psychic healing. It wasn't like the psychic surgery I've heard about, where someone is physically healed right there. This just gave me the ability to go somewhere beyond myself, and it let me draw my own conclusions.

"The man who did this for me saw what was going on, and he didn't think there was much hope. His interpretation was negative.

"The pregnancy went on, but now when I was in pain, instead of going to the hospital, I'd get into meditation, I'd try to draw the white light down on me. I did yoga and meditation. I was careful with my diet, trying to stay pure. I did a lot of juice fasts, which doctors at the hospital said was airy-fairy stuff and that I'd weaken myself, I was not giving my body enough nutrition.

"I was seeing my own doctor regularly, and he never knew what to say. He'd tell me, 'I don't have any idea what's going on, but keep doing whatever it is you're doing.'

"I also knew that no spirit had entered my body; she didn't come until she was sure I took this to another level.

"When I got to seven and eight months in the pregnancy, the doctors were amazed. They kept telling me, 'You've taken so many drugs, we have no idea what will happen to the fetus. It could be deformed or mentally retarded. This could be a disaster. Maybe it would have been better to have aborted.' They never gave me anything positive.

"I had made radical changes in my life. I'd been lifted into an understanding about service—that 'love is service done'—I found what my destiny, my mission was.

"I made the choice to leave a beautiful, peaceful home for a chaotic commune, taking kids off the street, operating Schools of Experience, putting them in 'love service-ships.' I was in the front line in the vegetarian restaurant run by the commune, serving rice and beans to people. The Berkeley riots were on, there was a lot of chaos, but I felt the energy was healing for me.

"I went into labor in the middle of the night and went to the hospital in the morning. They found distressing signs—a black fluid was coming out. They hooked me to a machine recording heartbeat and contractions, said maybe a Caesarean was necessary—there was alarm that something was drastically wrong. I was in labor five to six hours, and all of a sudden I felt an energy come right down through my head, through my body, and fill my body and speak to me, saying, 'I've arrived, I'm here, you've done well. Now you can relax, you've done your job. Now I'm here to take over.' She'd been waiting in the wings to see if I could fulfill what I needed to fulfill.

"Suddenly the cervix was being pushed open, and I said I'd deliver immediately. The nurse said it was impossible, I wasn't dilated. I dilated in five contractions. The doctor took me to the delivery room and practically caught the baby as she came out—I didn't do a thing, she just moved herself out.

"The doctor said, 'I have no idea what you did. There was some primal energy or force in the room—I didn't do anything and you didn't do anything.'

"He and I played no part, and out came a perfectly formed, beautiful little girl.

"After I delivered Celise, they wanted to remove the tumors. I said no, and I stayed in my lifestyle, kept my diet very clean, became pregnant with Michael, and the tumors, which had been as big as grapefruits, were all gone. They had disappeared in that year-and-a-half period. My next child was a home delivery. The tumors never showed up again.

"After that I began to be more trusting, more expecting of miracles. They weren't even 'miracles' anymore. Miracles became an everyday event. I was raised to another level. I saw I could control my life destiny, that there was a whole other way of doing things, of being creative with your life. I don't go to the doctor anymore."

Sometimes physical healing is not enough. Sometimes flesh and bones are healed but the mind and spirit are left disturbed, as an actress learns when she's able to walk again without pain in her body but seeks some further resolution. One person's need for physical healing may act as a healing force on other levels to the people around her. The idea voiced by Marion Carroll and Father O'Rourke that "illness is a ministry" is demonstrated by the experience of a young woman pastor of a small church in Maine.

LEAVING THE PAIN BEHIND

Kathy Baker

Kathy Baker, an outstanding actress who won an Emmy for her performance in the CBS drama *Picket Fences*, costarred with Michael Keaton in the feature film *Clean and Sober* and has won praise for her roles in the theater both on and off Broadway. I was so taken with the warmth of her performances as Jill, the doctor, wife, and mother she portrays on *Picket Fences*, that I wrote her a fan letter. I was delighted to get to meet at her at the wedding of my friend Michael Pressman, a movie and TV director who is an executive producer of *Picket Fences*, and the actress and drama teacher Lisa Chess. At the wedding dinner Kathy told me about her own experience of healing, while I took notes on the back of my wedding invitation. Her story illustrates how more than physical healing is necessary to become whole again.

"I was born with a deformed hip socket. Five years ago it started giving me trouble, and in the last three years it really got bad. I was on the set of *Picket Fences* with a cane and crutches. I shot fifty percent of my scenes that way, though you couldn't tell—nobody knew except the people on the set. I was forty years old when the pain got bad, and I thought I'd be that way the rest of my life—I'd be like an old woman the rest of my life.

"I'd had two surgeries that weren't successful. Then a year ago I had a hip replacement operation, and it worked. I was without pain for the first time in years. Still, I didn't feel completely healed. The whole experience didn't seem to be in the past yet.

"I grew up in Albuquerque, New Mexico, and all my life I'd heard about the church at Chimayo where people went to be healed. It's supposed to be like Lourdes, in France. Six weeks after my hip replacement operation, my husband and I went back to Albuquerque to visit my family, and I wanted to stop at Chimayo.

"The church was so small and beautiful. As soon as I went inside I could feel that it was a special place. I felt this deep emotion—it was like letting go of all the pain, all the surgeries, all the hospitalizations.

"There were crutches on the wall that people who'd been cured had left. I had a walking stick I'd been using since the operation, and I wanted to leave it there. It was a nice one, and new—my husband had just given it to me. I told him I wanted to leave it, and he understood. It was part of leaving the pain behind. After that I felt the whole thing was over, I was finally healed—I felt I was whole again."

PEOPLE WERE GALVANIZED

The Reverend Pamela Barz

The Reverend Pamela Barz, a valued friend of mine who's the minister of a church in Saco, Maine, was thirty-one years old, and in seemingly excellent health, when a doctor's checkup revealed she had Hodgkin's disease, a cancer that attacks the lymph system. She was told she had a fifty-fifty chance for recovery, but when a CAT scan showed that the disease had spread into the lungs, and exploratory surgery found it below her diaphragm, the percentage of her chances for recovery went down. She would have to undergo chemotherapy treatments for eight months. I was part of a group that prayed for her.

"It became increasingly important to know that others were praying for me, especially after the chemotherapy and the drugs I was taking sapped my energy," Pam said. It felt like that blocked my inner connection to God."

I wrote and called Pam over the coming months and was pleased and impressed to hear how the congregation of her church had mobilized to help her.

"When I was first sick, my doctor had suggested that I might want to go live with my parents in New Jersey for the course of the chemotherapy treatments. I told him, "The only thing to do in New Jersey is be sick," and I wanted to keep working. The church members made up schedules for volunteers to drive me to and from chemotherapy sessions, to cook for me, clean my apartment, sit with me, answer the door and the phone when I'd just returned from treatment and needed to rest.

"This was hard for me to accept. While I knew intellectually that one had to receive as well as to give, I hadn't really put that into practice. To practice it, I had to give up a lot of what I thought was important. With my loss of control went some loss of privacy and independence as well. I found they weren't as important as I had held them to be.

"Before the eight months were up, they found that the cancer was gone, and I was able to end the chemotherapy treatments a month early, right after Thanksgiving. It was a joyous holiday season, and in the new year I was able to work full time again.

"Someone in my congregation told her teacher that she went to my church, and this teacher, a Catholic, said, 'Oh, that's the church with the miracle minister!' I don't think my own healing was a miracle—except that it happened faster than anyone thought it could. The miracle I see is what happened to the church. This church, which was divided and exclusive, is now a community that's united and reaches out to strangers.

"When I announced I was going to have chemotherapy and I'd have to cut down on my hours of work, I thought it would be a dead time for the church. Instead it was a creative time, especially in the way people in the congregation responded to my illness, to my needs and others' needs. It galvanized people, and they realized what was important. It surprised me.

"There had been a distrust of an 'in' group at the church, and people worried about offending anyone. All of the sudden they got a sense of what's really important—we learned to trust each other more, not worrying about stepping on toes, feeling we're all in this together much more. There's more a sense now that everybody's a minister—I'm ordained, but they're all ministers.

"By letting people minister to me I made them free to minister to each other. We have induction of new members twice a year. There were more in December than any other year since I've been there—we'll have doubled this year the number of people who have joined.

"When a minister gets sick, it's not always this way. One church I know about didn't react that way at all. It went downhill. We've come together."

The scourge of AIDS has raised our consciousness, forcing us to search not only for new medical and scientific knowledge but alternative ways of healing and new or deeper commitment to the spiritual quest. A woman learns her husband is HIV-positive less than a year after they are married and goes with him to follow every trail of hope, medical and spiritual, as they are led to a Navajo reservation in Arizona and take part in Native American healing ceremonies. An Emmy-winning TV news producer who has AIDS turns to the religious roots he has ignored, learns Hebrew, and reads the Torah in the original, finding that his spiritual search "outweighs all the stuff I did on TV."

A FULFILLING AND
EXTRAORDINARY LIFE WITH AIDS
Michelle Dunn Baker

Michelle Dunn Baker is a writer of short stories and nonfiction. She lives with her husband in Hollywood, Florida, and is writing a book about living with AIDS.

ॐ

"In May of 1987, ten months after our marriage, a life insurance company denied my husband, Steven, coverage and informed him that his blood test had come back HIV-positive. We went immediately to the National Institutes of Health Center at the University of Miami, and two months later he entered the first testing of AZT for HIV-positive asymptomatic patients. Unfortunately, his body could not accept the toxic drug, and five months later he was disqualified from the study and shut off from the only possibility for help that the medical establishment had to offer.

"Forced to find an alternative to conventional medicine, we began to read, travel, and gather information about holistic healing, making significant changes in our diets and lifestyle. We were writing our own recipe for survival.

"Steven decided to treat his condition as a chronic disease, not a terminal one. There was no way I found to eliminate the fear of losing him, but I believed that if I participated in his efforts to heal, if I loved him enough, he would have the strength to go forward. We stopped reading the gloom and doom reports in the newspapers and began creating our own reality.

"It was important for me to be involved in the process, so whatever had to be done, we did it together. Not everything worked. We flew out to San Francisco to meet a doctor who had written about natural healing, but we found out Steven's body couldn't tolerate megadoses of vitamins. We visited a chiropractor in Santa Fe who charged $350 per appointment, insisting we come daily. When we ran out of money, she pronounced our treatment complete.

"We settled into a lifestyle that included a combination of preventive Western medicine, including antibiotics to guard against infections, and non-Western alternatives to promote a healthy immune system. We eliminated red meat, white flour, refined sugar, and dairy products. Steven called me the medicine woman as I prepared health foods and brewed medicinal teas from Chinese herbs, barks, and roots. Steven received acupuncture and deep healing massage.

"In 1989 he contracted Kaposi's sarcoma, a form of cancer, which changed his status from HIV-positive to AIDS. It was his Chinese health-care practitioners who strongly suggested he seek further conventional medical care. The fear-mongers were saying there was nothing out there in the way of help.

"Dr. Bernard Siegel says that if you can't hug your doctor, find another doctor. This became a standard for us. A Boston physician involved in AIDS research had prescribed Steven's antibiotics and followed his case. We trusted him. When we asked him what he would do for Steven's health, he said 'Whatever it takes.' We were on the same track. With his T cells (healthy cells that fight the virus) at a count of 160 (complications usually arise below 200), Steven entered Dr. J.'s first phase-one study for the new antiviral DDI. The requirements included reporting twice a week to the clinic in Boston, so we commuted from Florida.

"The drug looked promising at first, but less so as time went by. When the study ended after two years, Steven was only one of two participants still living from the original thirty-two. The drug was not what they hoped, yet Steven's lesions had gone into complete remission, and his T cells had risen to 375.

"Steven decided to pay more attention to spiritual matters. He studied movement of his life force, practicing Chi Gong and Tai Chi daily. Through Taoism he found harmony and the connection between simplicity and physical well-being.

"Something was happening: time was passing. We celebrated our fifth wedding anniversary. Steven renewed his driver's license for another six years. While we had once hoped with all our hearts for a child, we were now grateful for what we had. It was a fulfilling and extraordinary life, and it had everything to do with my husband's having AIDS. Sometimes he said he treated his disease as a gift, and people looked away uncomfortably, as if witnessing something too intimate.

"We watched helplessly as AIDS claimed the lives of loved ones, a best friend, a famous person, an unknown from a newspaper story. Each one of them left us with something valuable. The day. Our love. The support of family and friends. The knowledge that there are no such things as problems, only challenges.

"Three years ago Steven began to read about Native American culture. We planned a trip to the Southwest, not exactly sure what we would find. A friend was related to a Navajo elder by marriage. He introduced us by letter, and the elder offered his son as a guide.

"Steven and I embarked on a journey through the deserts of Arizona to places on the reservation where most Anglos are never permitted entry, our guide acting as interpreter. Our first medicine man was a diagnostician, called a stargazer. He used crystals, eagle feathers, and a hollowed-out eagle bone that he played like a flute to perform a healing ceremony on Steven on a rainy summer night. He told us we would have to go farther, though we would experience some immediate results.

"Several days later we met an old medicine woman who sent us out on the plains for hours to look for a rare plant. Later she sat with Steven in the dry dirt, drawing figures on the ground with her gnarled fingers, the sun winking off her silver and turquoise rings. She chanted and waited for guidance from the spirits. She told us we needed to come back and find a man to do a sacred Navajo ceremony that lasts for eight days. In her trance she had seen us in a big wind and asked if we had ever been in a storm together.

"When we returned home two things happened: Steven's T cell count reached 450—the highest since he'd had the disease—and we survived Hurricane Andrew as it swept through south Florida.

"We have returned to the reservation three times since then. Before last year's trip, Steven's T cells had gone back down to 350. After the eight-day ceremony, they reached 499. That was a new high. Again, in the year that followed, his T cells went down to 250, and we got alarmed. We returned to the reservation, participated in a three-day ceremony, and got back home two weeks ago. Yesterday we got the results of his blood test, and the T cells were back up to 450. Whatever is happening in these ceremonies is no fluke. This is a bonafide miracle.

"We continue on the journey. We know we are blessed. Each morning, my husband opens the window shades to the light and reminds me that today will be the most wonderful day of our lives. I awake to a sense of awe, to his enduring energy. He looks well, not at all like a man with a life-threatening disease. He carries on at his job, working regular hours, earning his salary. When people ask him how he's doing, how he feels, he says, 'I'm the healthiest person I know, other than a touch of AIDS.'"

"IF YOU HAVE AIDS, YOU'VE GOT TO BE RESILIENT"

Rob Hershman

Rob Hershman was a producer for the CBS news department, producing stories for the prime-time television programs *West Fifty-Seventh* and *48 Hours*. He has been nominated for the Emmy Award a number of times, the last for his segment on AIDS for *48 Hours*. He has also won television's Peabody Award. He now lives in Los Angeles.

"I came back to Judaism through the Episcopal church. My lover, Ron James, was dying of AIDS in 1988, and he found solace in the Episcopal church. I went with him to services at his church, St. Ignatius, on Eighty-eighth Street between West End Avenue and Broadway, and I became close to the priests there.

"I saw that across the street was a synagogue, B'nai Jeshurun, and the rabbi was Marshall Meyer. I couldn't believe this was the same rabbi I'd met in Argentina when I was doing a story for CBS News on 'The Disappeared.' The Marshall Meyer I knew in Argentina had saved so many lives that Jakov Timmerman dedicated a book to him. It was the same man. I started going to services there before I started to feel ravaged by AIDS myself. Ron and I went to services on Saturday at B'nai Jeshurun and on Sunday at St. Ignatius.

"I started to study Hebrew and the Torah, and the idea that I was learning and growing at the same time that my body was disintegrating was really helpful, really sustaining.

"It's always helpful to know that people have been reading this work for a long time—it must be true in all religions. The cycle of worship is increasingly comforting and empowering. Reading the same passages in the Torah every day is powerful, knowing it's been read for two thousand years. And now it's available to me.

"I've learned enough Hebrew now to read the Torah in Hebrew. I'm so proud of that. My accomplishments of the last two years in this spiritual search outweigh all the stuff I did in TV.

"I made a commitment to read the Torah every day, and I hoped I'd get through all of it at least one time. Now I've gotten through it twice, and even if I get through it a third time, I'll continue to read it.

"I've been blessed that in Los Angeles there's a plethora of great rabbis. The renewal movement in Judaism has great teachers, and they give a real context to Judaism. Our parents and their generation were the 'guardians' of Judaism, but they didn't know why it was so great, they didn't know it was *theirs*. Now that the next generation is secure, it can open that storehouse of riches.

"Jewish meditation always existed, but many in Reform Judaism seemed embarrassed by it, and it got dropped. We're finding the content of Judaism now and celebrating it. I'm in a Jewish study and meditation group that meets every week. I'm also in a support group for people with AIDS that meets once a week, and it ends up that both groups are about the same thing. The issues of the support group are essentially spiritual— the people in it have been through hell. One member is in the process of dying right now—it will be in days or a week. Coming to terms with that, he is talking spiritually.

"This week we were studying the story of Abraham. In one incident a 'priest of the Lord Most High' blesses Abraham. The priest is not a Jew, yet Abraham accepts the blessing. The story is a paradigm for being open to the blessings that come to you.

"People with AIDS die one of two ways—either with a glow or so angry. The ones who are angry can't find a spiritual context for what is happening to them.

"Without the healing element of this spiritual work, what I'm finding in Judaism, I don't think I'd still be around now. If you have AIDS, you've got to be resilient. You think you can accept one level of pain or break-down, but then you get hit again with something else.

"You need to have some place to pray. I can't imagine getting through this without prayer."

Chapter 4

MIRACLES
OF RECOVERY

ॐॐ

P eople who have never been hooked on booze or drugs find it hard
to understand why those who are addicted can't "Just say no."
(Sounds easy enough, doesn't it? N-O. No. See? It's only one syl-
lable!) A friend who has never been down that road asked me why I
thought "just" getting off alcohol, for instance, was any kind of miracle.

I'll attempt to speak only for myself, since everyone's experience is in
some ways unique (and in many ways common).

If I had met you before 1980 and you asked me to tell you something
about myself, I would have said I needed to have a drink every day. I
wouldn't have admitted to being "an alcoholic." No way. I was simply a
guy who had to have a drink every day—in fact, a lot of drinks. That's the
way I'd been getting through life since 1956 (that was nearly a quarter
century), and I saw no reason to continue otherwise.

I might not have changed course (and might not have lived to be
writing these words) had I not been given a warning by my own body
that something had to be done, something different and drastic, or the
course wasn't going to last a whole lot longer. A panic-rate "resting pulse"
of 120 led me to a program of stress reduction through exercise, then
diet, which brought down my pulse to 80; and finally a month without
any booze at all, as the doctors predicted, lowered it to 60.

It was still another three years before I stopped altogether, part of a
general "turning" that started with exercise and diet and temporary absti-
nence that led to church, prayer, meditation, Tai Chi, "controlled drink-

ing," and then the controversial est training in the last year it was given (before becoming a new and gentler program called the Forum), which blew me open in a liberating way and brought an epiphany that "lifted" the desire to drink, something I could not have previously conceived as possible.

Though many people have asked me if I'm "a friend of Bill Wilson," I have to say I'm only a friend of his friends; I did not do the AA or any other twelve-step program, though I fully support, endorse, and admire them. I believe that as well as providing the most widespread and long-lasting relief from substance abuse and addiction in this society, twelve-step programs have brought a spiritual awakening and a sense of community that give hope for the transformation of the culture as well as of the individual. I agree with Kurt Vonnegut that when later historians look back at America, they may well judge that our greatest contribution to Western civilization was Alcoholics Anonymous.

Perhaps my own disagreement with AA, or maybe just many of its followers, is that it is often presented as "the only way." Though it is surely the largest and most successful system of recovery in this country, I don't believe there is an "only way." I think the stirring stories to come show that the miracle of freedom from addiction may come in many ways, from AA to "a voice from the canyon."

I don't think my own "way" is the only one, either; in fact I don't know anyone else who had that particular result from the program I did, nor do I recommend it as treatment for that problem. I can only say what any of us can say of our experience: That's what happenend to me. It may not happen that way for you or anyone else.

Some people, like the writer and columnist Pete Hamill, are simply able to stop, period, as he relates in his stirring memoir *A Drinking Life*. After a while without booze, he found he had replaced the habit of drinking with "the habit of not drinking."

One of the most frequent miracles of the Bible is the casting out of demons. I think being possessed by the compulsion to numb ourselves with drink and drugs—and the myriad other habits that dull our senses and our spirit—is a modern analogy to that experience. When I first went back to church, I found myself drawn back time and again to the stories of Jesus expelling demons, knowing I had my own demon in the daily need for alcohol. I prayed with those Scriptures, asking that it be exorcised, even as I was still feeding it, indulging it. That prayer was answered.

Recovery is a spiritual experience, which sometimes isn't so clear and sometimes is blazingly obvious. It is the theme of a man who tells us here of his recovery from heroin addiction, which led to his own lifelong work to help addicts. It is powerfully demonstrated in the case of the great jazz saxophone player and composer John Coltrane, who in the agony of his withdrawal from heroin prayed that he would live through it and survive and pledged that if he were so blessed, he would devote himself to God. He did make it, and he carried out his part of the deal, composing inspirational, spiritual music with religious themes such as "A Love Supreme."

He said toward the end of his life that he wanted to be a saint, and some of his followers declared him one, opening the storefront church of St. John Coltrane on Divisadero Street in San Francisco, where his music is played for the first hour of every Sunday service.

Drugs and alcohol are only one kind of addiction, only one way to numb the feelings. One man tells here about his release from tobacco addiction, which I know is as powerful as any of the others. I've seen two friends in the past few years die in the agony of emphysema, breathing and speaking through oxygen tubes at the end. I smoked a pipe every day for more than twenty years, which made my gums sore and my teeth brownish-yellow. I didn't think I could write anymore if I stopped, but I was able to throw away my pipes and take up Stimudents (wooden sticks like toothpicks) after seeing a friend who had had a lung removed hack and cough until he went into paroxysms of agony yet was still unable to stop.

Gambling, mindless sex, uncontrolled spending, and many other habits can grip people in a helpless compulsion that destroys the spirit and wrecks the fabric of family life and fruitful work. Even work can become an addiction, as a former businessman relates here in his own story of transformation from despair and denial to feeling, joy, and contribution. A woman who never had a drinking problem tells how Al-Anon helped her overcome her addiction to codependence and prescription tranquilizers that made her "stark-raving sober."

Latter-day critics of twelve-step programs have snidely put them down as another kind of addiction, since people keep returning to the meetings for support and inspiration. In the same sense exercise is attacked as an addiction, and no doubt regular prayer and meditation will be (if they haven't already been) condemned as compulsive behaviors. This is ludicrous. Repeated behavior that enhances life, that makes people healthy in mind and body and spirit, is a blessing, not an addiction.

In hearing the stories of others' miracles, we may find the seeds of our own.

To move from a life of numbing feelings and destroying relationships, kidneys, liver, and mental processes—a deadly way of existence from which there seems no escape—into the experience of freedom, choice, and fullness of feeling is indeed a miracle. The joy of emerging into such a new kind of existence is expressed in a buoyant line from *The Crown of Columbus* by Louise Erdrich and Michael Dorris: "I was lost, but now I'm living in a daily heaven of an unexpected life."

Skeptics of miracles dismiss such extraordinary events as belonging to a dead past, an ancient era when humans could explain their world only by making up tales of Gods and Goddesses or even one God, the Jehovah of the Bible. In those old tales, people believed they heard voices from beyond, like the Bible stories of God speaking to his people, giving them warning, advice, guidance.

It still happens.

The modern world associates hearing voices with delusion or madness; if it occurs, it is seldom admitted or talked about. I was surprised and inspired by the number of stories told me by perfectly sane, responsible, intelligent people who heard "a voice" that turned them from a downward path toward health and recovery. A newspaperwoman hears a voice from a canyon that turns her toward a new path of life. A man driving home alone from dinner at a country inn hears a voice tell him that he will give up a health-destroying habit. A prisoner gets up at dawn to speak to God and is answered. A woman whose life is in a shambles hears a message in a dream that gives her the courage to do what she needs to do.

Of course the voice alone, no matter what the message, does not bring about the miracle. The people must respond, must "obey" the voice, and carry out difficult and challenging changes in behavior in order to bring about wholeness and healing. The process is an illustration of how we are co-creators with God or the life force—rarely are we passive recipients of psychic lottery jackpots.

I admire the courage of these people in recounting their experiences and am awed by the mystery of it, which seems to me testimony to the forces of light and life in the universe.

A VOICE FROM THE CANYON

Sylvia H. Lang

Sylvia Lang is a special sections writer for the *San Jose Mercury News.* Her favorite pastime is "mountain bagging"—climbing mountains. "That's where I get a lot of my spirituality," she says.

"During my college years I lost my faith. I also lost a vision of heaven.

"I wondered how I could achieve heaven here on earth, and I turned to booze—spirits, as it were. The booze sometimes sent my brain soaring into ecstasy, only to slap me to the mat the next day. So it was heaven, then hell, day after day.

"I sought new vistas through travel. In 1978, on a vacation from Minnesota to Arizona, I decided on a whim to take an excursion via a small tourist plane from Phoenix to the Grand Canyon. As the plane floated and dipped over this colorful, sculpted, natural work of art, I gasped, and my heart jumped. I felt as though I had been transformed into an eagle; I longed to leave the plane and glide in and out of the rock formations and dive for fish in the Colorado River below.

"When the plane landed, the other tourists and I took a limousine ride along the canyon's south rim. As I sat staring at the cathedral-like spires, a hundred feet or so away from the other tourists, I heard a voice echoing out of the canyon shouting only one word: *Grow!*

"I turned around to see if someone was there speaking. But there was just the canyon. With tears in my eyes I looked into the canyon and responded, 'I will.'

"After this trip I bought backpacking gear—tent, backpack, boots, stove—and began taking long and short hikes through Minnesota's wilderness and beyond, including Arizona, Tennessee, Pennsylvania, and Montana. I also returned to the Grand Canyon and walked to the bottom—covering twenty-six miles, all in one day, from my motel to the frozen rim above the canyon to the warm desert bottom a mile deep below and back. I came the closest I have ever been to death, from hypothermia. Nearly unconscious, I managed to get to my motel room. I fell asleep and dreamed of geologic wonders for the next eighteen hours before I woke again.

"In 1982 I gave up drinking alcohol, mainly because I was having trouble hiking from what this poison was doing to my body. I discovered I could find spirits in other places—beyond the bottle—and most particularly in California. At Mount Shasta's sprawling base, I found Mother Nature's arms, which consoled me after my mother's death. At Sunset Beach near Santa Cruz, the Pacific Ocean sent soothing waves toward me, empathizing with me upon the death of my father. At Lassen Volcanic National Park, I became a Native American, running (naked, in my mind) swiftly through the trees, freer than I had ever felt, leaping and jumping along the ridges.

"Discoveries beyond nature nurtured my soul as well. One day, during a session with a psychotherapist, my body suddenly became cold as death and shook uncontrollably for an hour. The therapist covered me with one blanket, then a second, a third, and a fourth. When I stopped shaking, I began to know who I was.

"During another psychotherapy session, a week before undergoing a hysterectomy, I released rivers of tears about the children I never had, the many relationships I had lost, and the other tragedies that were part of my life. Once the tears were shed, I was able to accept the hysterectomy more as a birth of a new me than as the death of a part of me.

"I know there is nothing wrong with me as long as I have faith that when I am not in control, I am most alive, freest, least empty, least lonely, most open to glory and joy."

"I HEARD A VOICE SAY, 'THIS IS YOUR LAST PIPEFUL'"

Bill Tewell

Bill Tewell, a hospice volunteer in New Hampshire, took my workshop in spiritual autobiography and wrote me about his release from tobacco addiction.

"A fellow member of AA and I took two young ladies in the program to dinner in a country inn near Woodstock, Vermont. We were celebrating their AA anniversaries. About eleven P.M., after the dinner party, I was driving back to Hanover, New Hampshire. I was alone in the car. As I drove along I refilled my pipe with tobacco. I then heard a voice say, 'This is your last pipeful. You will not smoke again.' I didn't feel fear but seemed to have no will to argue. I finished the pipe, tossed it out the window, reached into my glove compartment for two other pipes, and tossed them. My tobacco pouch followed the pipes. No human could have induced me to give up something as important to me as tobacco. I did not and do not follow orders well. I had not even considered giving up.

"I haven't smoked since that episode more than twelve years ago. I had few withdrawal symptoms and really lost the desire to smoke. I had been a heavy smoker. I had a pipe or cigarette going during all my waking hours. I smoked before I got out of bed in the morning and before I turned out the light at night. I usually took a bath instead of a shower because I could smoke in the bathtub but not the shower.

"About three weeks after that episode my last remaining wisdom tooth began to cause trouble. The dentist pulled it out, but the area refused to heal. Mary Hitchcock Hospital diagnosed cancer of the mouth. A three-by-five centimeter tumor growing in my neck had reached the tooth. The cancer was so advanced I was eligible for an experimental program. To get into the experiment I was required to sign a statement that I realized I had but a 15 to 20 percent chance of living two years. That was twelve years ago, and I'm still here.

"It was obvious my body, someone, or something knew about the cancer long before any physical symptoms or discomfort appeared.

"I spent most of the winter of 1982 in the hospital. There I learned what AA's twelve steps really mean—especially turning your life over to a Higher Power, as you understand it. I had known, intellectually, that the steps describe the traditional mystic way. It took cancer to induce me to make a serious attempt to live those steps—to take the trip.

"I also learned the value of living one day at a time. I would wake up each morning and admit to myself that someday I would die, as would the doctors and nurses attending me. I would assure myself that it was most unlikely that this would be the day. Unless, of course, I forgot to look both ways before I crossed the street or a stray bullet came along. Cancer was not an excuse to not look after myself. I remember laughing when I realized that for the first time in my life I was buckling my seat belt.

"I knew I had a close call with death and decided that I should try to come to terms with it. I took the hospice training and have been a volunteer ever since."

WHY THE TREE DOESN'T SUFFER

James Allen

James Allen is the director of the Addicts Rehabilitation Center in East Harlem, which houses five hundred people who are in the process of getting off drugs. He received his B.A. degree in sociology from John Jay College in New York.

❧

"*Miracle* is just a label people apply when they don't realize that God can do anything. Anything is possible through God; it doesn't need a special label.

"I grew up in Texas and Louisiana and went to California, where I smoked reefer for seven years, going up and down the coast from San Francisco to San Diego. Around 1948 I came to New York. I became addicted to heroin and slept in the streets for ten years.

"In 1957 I went to the federal narcotics hospital in Lexington, Kentucky. I went because my wife kicked me out of the house, and it got to my ego. I wanted to show her I could get off drugs. That was the only place to go for treatment in those days.

"At Lexington I met a lot of religious people. I met Muslims and Christians. I started thinking of my grandfather, who was a sharecropper and who always had a smile on his face. The only time I had a smile was when I was prostituting my feelings with heroin. I started taking a second look at God. That's when I saw that God was real. I thought if I really came to him and asked, I'd get help. I spent a lot of time in the library there reading the Bible.

"I started getting up very early in the morning to talk to God. I didn't want the other men to see me talking to God, so I got up before anyone else. I was in the presence of God. One morning I was looking out the window, and I said, 'Lord, when I get back to New York, I want you to help me. I don't want to sell dope anymore, but my car's got old and I want to sell just enough to get a new car.' He said, 'If you get a new one, then the new one will get old and you'll be back in the same place.'

"I was looking at a tree, and I said, 'God, why doesn't that tree standing there suffer? You created that tree and you created me, and I suffer but that tree doesn't. Why?'

"God said, 'The tree doesn't suffer because it obeys the purpose of its creation. You don't have the sense of a tree.'

"Well, after that I was ready to go back. He'd made his point. I told God, 'I'll do anything you ask me, even if you ask me to walk down the street naked. But I won't be pious, I won't be righteous. I don't want to be delivered from all my sins.' I had to be honest.

"I had thought if you ask for God's help, you had to square up, you had to do everything right. But it's not like that. He'll help anyone if you just ask him for help, if you want the help.

"I left the hospital at Lexington after twenty-five days. You were supposed to stay four months and fifteen days, but I knew I didn't need to be there any longer. When I left, a social worker gave me a card and said, 'Go see this man when you get back to New York.'

"The name on the card was Norman Eddy, and I presumed he was a black man. The world I lived in was black, and here was the address of this man in East Harlem, so it never occurred to me he wouldn't be black. Imagine my shock when I saw this tall white man with blue eyes! He had the kindest eyes I had ever seen—so I stayed and talked. He had this Bible study class for people with drug problems, and I started going to it. That's where my spiritual life really took root.

"I was living in West Harlem, though, and I went to a church over there. The first day I went, the minister said an addict had come to him and asked if God loved dope fiends, and so he was interested in starting a group for addicts. I became part of that group. That's how the Rehabilitation Center here got started. At one point the church lost the building we were using, and we were able to buy it. Now we have buildings on Madison and also on Park. We house five hundred people. Now we're starting a program for people with AIDS.

"When I got off drugs, I worked as a clothes presser to make a living, and I went to John Jay College and got a degree in sociology.

"A lot of people call me Reverend and think I'm a minister, but I'm not. I'm the same old unrighteous guy. I don't give any lectures. My lectures are in what I do."

A HEALING DREAM

Nancy del Guidice

Nancy del Guidice is an acoustic singer-songwriter who recently had her first CD released. She lives in New Hampshire.

"When I landed at the state hospital after attempting suicide for the third time, I was so fragmented I couldn't even remember my phone number. I had five or six psychiatric diagnoses and a prescription list that looked like it was meant for six people. I had totally given up hope for the future, and my sense of myself as a human being was so painful that I could see no point in living.

"The doctors at the hospital decided that in order to diagnose me properly they would have to clean out my system first. Seven weeks later I left there drug-free and whole, and in the three years since, my life has been transformed.

"The change began about ten days into my stay at the hospital when my mother inadvertently dropped a bomb over the phone. She told me that my psychiatrist related to her a confidential matter without checking with me. Apparently I woke briefly after the last drug overdose and informed a nurse that my father had once molested me. This was an issue that had been part of my therapy for several years because my therapist, the 'expert,' had long insinuated that there must be some huge repressed memory to account for so much misery. He had long pegged my relationship with my father as being pathological, and I am not surprised that I came up with that vindicating little vignette in a semiconscious state. The power of suggestion between a therapist and a vulnerable 'client' can be a very destructive force, as I have learned from this experience. Without even telling me, he shared this with my mother, who could not possibly discuss it with my father—he had died a year before. What if my mother hadn't told me? I knew that I was on my own. I no longer trusted the man whose words I'd valued above anyone else's for the last two years.

"My husband broached the subject of a divorce. He would have custody of our three little daughters. My life was in a shambles.

"Then I had a strange dream. In the dream I heard the words *Nothing real can be threatened*. I woke up and wrote it down. This comforted me in a deep, warm way. It meant that if I knew I was going to be all right, it didn't matter what anyone else thought. I began to meditate and take long walks. The staff treated me kindly and respectfully, and I faced the withdrawal from Xanax as a challenge. A quiet resolve grew inside me that my life from then on would depend on the wisdom deep inside, my connection with a Higher Power (to use twelve-step language), and I nominated myself the only living expert about me.

"When I left the hospital, it was time to fight for my marriage and my children. The battle was won inside me when I let go of my anger, my list of betrayals, and trained myself to live in the moment. I came to recognize that it is easy to love others when we take good care of ourselves. My husband and I found a way to build a loving connection, far more real than the original one.

"Forgiving my therapist may have been the most difficult and critical piece of what makes me feel so whole today. I prayed for many months that I could somehow forgive him and go on with my life. When it finally happened, it seemed so huge; I could never forget even the smallest details. It began while I was being tested on my CPR training. Suddenly I had a flash of sensing what it might be like to be that man who had tried to change the shape of my soul. I could feel his intention. I could feel his fear of my suicide. I felt him as a human being, and a light flooded me. It overwhelmed me and lifted me. All the way home the tears poured down my face as I felt the real article of freedom. I swore to myself that I would teach other people what I know about this.

"I began writing songs. Some of them flew away and brought back trophies with them. Last year I was one of 40 songwriters chosen from 627 nationwide to perform in a showcase of emerging songwriters in Kerrville, Texas. Talk about miracles!

"The bad news is, things are much worse than we think. The good news is, our expectations aren't anywhere near high enough! *We need to expect miracles.*"

Sometimes only the prospect of death awakens us to life. Sometimes those who abandon all hope find resilience when they hit the bottom. Maybe it seems natural that someone would choose life over death, but that is not at all guaranteed. We all know people who hit bottom and simply were unable to change course, to find the strength or meaning to fight for survival. They gave up and sank into death.

It is easy to give up trying to get well when medical authorities tell you your case is "hopeless," as they informed a distinguished professor of English. He found his own miracle when he faced the choice between death or sobriety. A Native American who was on the verge of suicide met a man who knew exactly what he was thinking, and he wanted to live to find out the secret. Both of these men, of different backgrounds and life experience, turned from the edge of self-destruction and went on to create works of insight and hope for others.

"A 'HOPELESS' ALCOHOLIC"

Roger Forseth

Roger Forseth is professor emeritus of English at the University of Wisconsin in Superior and founder of the journal *Dionysus: A Tri-Quarterly of Addiction.*

❧

"I started drinking at an early age. I recently went back to Aberdeen, South Dakota, where I grew up. I was telling my wife I did a lot of hunting there as a boy, and when we passed the tavern, I realized a good deal of the 'hunting' I did in high school was actually drinking.

"In 1963 I went home to South Dakota for Christmas and was drinking heavily and taking amphetamines and tranquilizers. I decided I'd stop drinking the day after Christmas, and I did, but then I started having seizures.

"My father took me in an air ambulance helicopter to the University of Minnesota Hospital, and they put me through a lot of neurological tests. After they got the results, they told me I was 'a hopeless alcoholic' and gave me a prescription for Dylantin.

"Since they told me I was 'hopeless' I figured there was nothing I could do about it. I thought, 'Gee, this is a free ride!' I kept drinking for the next twelve years. Once during that time I went for a medical checkup and my doctor said my liver didn't look too good, and if I didn't stop drinking, it was going to fail me. I stopped drinking for six months, and when I went back to see the doctor he said, 'OK, your liver is fine right now,' and I started drinking again.

"At no time did any doctor tell me to go to AA or give me a single insight about my alcoholism.

"In 1975 my wife and I got our eldest son into a fine treatment center for alcohol in Duluth, and my wife and I went into its family therapy group as part of our son's recovery. After the therapy group meeting was over, my wife and I would go to a nearby bar and drink to relieve the tension from the therapy meeting. As we sat in the bar drinking, we could look up the hill and see the hospital and the room we'd just been having our therapy meeting in. We realized this was crazy.

"I went into the treatment center. One counselor looked like a Paul Bunyan lumberjack kind of guy. He said if he caught any of us drinking, 'I'll throw you out the fourth floor window!' That was pretty good therapy.

"The miracle came when I was sitting in one of the groups and realized I had no way out—it was either stop drinking or die. That was the epiphany. It sounds very ordinary to the outside world, but for me it was a miracle.

"When I got out, my wife had stopped drinking and had stopped taking Valium, without any treatment. That we did our recovery together is another miracle. That was nineteen years ago, and we've had a wonderful life since then.

"Here's another kind of miracle, if you want to call it that. I taught at L.S.U., at Southern Illinois University, and at the University of Wisconsin at Superior, and I was boozing the whole time. I got my Ph.D. and became a tenured full professor at age forty, and I was a drunk the whole time. Not one of the deans or university presidents or department chairmen seemed to notice."

CHILDREN OF THE UNIVERSE

Tom Thunderhorse

Tom Thunderhorse is a Native American with both Apache and Cherokee bloodlines. He is author of *The Voice of Many Waters,* a collection of his essays, prayers, and poems, published by the Native American Press of Santa Rosa, California. He has worked in the maritime service as an engineer, and now he writes, "plays with computers," plays the organ for the elderly people in his community, and is a spiritual adviser for the Eagle Vision Educational Network.

"When I started in school, I wasn't aware of my heritage. I was shielded by my mother from knowing I was one of the hated people of earth. When I got older, I got hooked on cowboys and Indians in the movies, and I wanted to be a cowboy—the good guy—when my Cherokee grandmother told me what I was. Well, I was an Indian, and the Indians were the losers.

"I believed that garbage. I had a loser attitude, a miserable attitude. I became a full-blown alcoholic. I can't imagine how the Great Spirit took care of me.

"I'd been working in the maritime, but when I was thirty-nine, I came home and took sole care of my mother, who was ill. When she died, I lost it. I became a vagabond. When I was forty years old, I was going to stick a shotgun in my mouth; but before I did that, I had to say some good-byes. When I told one of the friends I went to see what I was going to do, he said, 'Do you mean you're sick and tired of being sick and tired?'

"Well, I was moaning 'Oh, woe is me' and feeling sorry for myself, and this friend read me like a book. In fact he seemed to know so much about me, I got curious. Instead of wanting to kill myself, I wanted to find out how he knew all this!

"He was in a twelve-step program, and I went with him to a meeting. I've been in the fellowship for fourteen years.

"When I was a kid, I was led to spiritual things, but for a long time I shut it off. Now kids come and talk to me, and I tell them to get real. I caught one kid in a lie and told him so. He said, 'Oh, when you told me that, I got a rush.' That was no 'rush,' I said, that was just getting real. If they're thinking about starting the twelve steps, I tell them they have to want it. If they don't want it, they don't get it.

"I don't pretend to be some big-time prophet, guru, or teacher to any one people, but I certainly believe that we all have the power to communicate with the Great Spirit and to receive his wisdom while walking the path of life under his direction.

"No matter who you are, or whether or not you believe in a Deity, the flow of universal wisdom will no doubt cross your path. As it was written long ago, the wisdom of the universe is written in the hearts and minds of all, even of those who seek it not. We are the children of the universe, no less than the trees and stars."

There are more ways to numb ourselves into lifelessness than with drugs and alcohol. The key to turning off is to disconnect from our feelings, like pulling a plug. Some people do it by stuffing themselves with food, others become workaholics and are rewarded by society, some become codependent and focus totally on tending to others. A woman who never had a drinking or drug problem went to an AA meeting with her sister and saw how the people who spoke there were connected to their feelings in a way she was not; she was able to reconnect through twelve-step programs and by writing her own poetry. A man who learned how to be successful in business found he'd become addicted to his wheeling and dealing, using the hyperactivity to avoid his feelings. In personal growth programs, he learned to open up, to give back to society, and to find a fulfillment he had never known.

"I WAS STARK, RAVING SOBER"

E. J. Miller Laino

E. J. Miller Laino works in recovery counseling for the town of Reading, Massachusetts, and has written curricula for insurance companies on drinking and driving for young people. She is also a poet whose work has appeared in such literary magazines as *Poetry East,* the *Massachusetts Review,* and *Prairie Schooner.* I was proud to publish a poem she wrote in my workshop, "An Open Letter to God," in my book *The Story of Your Life: Writing a Spiritual Autobiography.*

"Thirteen years ago my sister begged me to go to an AA meeting with her even though I was not an alcoholic myself; I never had a drinking problem. I just went to be a good sister, and I found myself listening in fascination to an eighty-year-old man speaking. He had been on skid row, he was twice given up for dead and taken to mortuaries. He started recovery when he was seventy and became mayor of his town.

"The story was interesting but I thought, 'This has nothing to do with me.' I was in a room with people who seemed like the kind of people

I always prayed I'd never have to be in a room with! For some reason, though, I felt safe there. The people weren't cool, they weren't intellectual, like me—but they could speak the truth! They were talking about things that it's 'not OK to talk about' with most people. They were hooked up with their feelings, connected to how they really felt.

"I didn't even drink, but I was what they call 'stark raving sober.' That really described me. I was nuts. You must know alcoholics who live with people who are even crazier than they are—these are the codependents, and they keep marrying alcoholics. That was me. I was the one who took care of everyone when I was a kid; I was the 'hero child' in the family. I was still as an adult trying to make everyone behave. To keep doing all this I had to disconnect from my feelings. I didn't drink, but I numbed myself with hyperactivity and prescription drugs—tranquilizers and sleeping pills. I didn't abuse them; I only took what was prescribed, but it did the job.

"I had to recover from codependency. I had to recover my own feelings. I went to Al-Anon and Adult Children of Alcoholics. In college I was an English major, I wrote poetry, but I stopped writing after college. About five years ago I took your workshop, where I wrote a poem. People liked it. Then four years ago I signed up for a course at the Boston Center for Adult Education on 'How to Write the Greeting Card and Start Your Own Greeting Card Company.' My sister and I thought we'd write recovery greeting cards and start our own company. But the course was canceled, and they told me I could take any other course that met that night for half price. I'd already planned to go, I had a baby-sitter, so I looked in the catalog and decided to take a poetry workshop.

"I found I could say things in poems that I'd never talk to anyone about, and it was all right. Through the poems I was able to reconnect with my feelings. I wrote one poem about a painful experience and had no trouble with the writing, but when I read it to the workshop, I only got to the seventh line and I started sobbing. I felt like my wires had been severed a long time ago, and now they were being connected again. I could feel.

"I loved the poetry of Sharon Olds, and I read that she was giving a workshop in Squaw Valley, so I signed up. I planned our family vacation out there, bought airline tickets, and rented a condo. Then I was told I had to be *accepted*—there were more than three hundred applicants and only thirty places. When I said I'd already spent all this money, the administrator asked, 'How long have you been writing poetry, and where have you been published?' When I said I'd been writing for a couple of years and I'd never been published, she sighed and said, 'Too bad, honey,' explaining that I didn't have much of a chance.

"Then I heard I was accepted. It was great! Since then I've had twenty-five poems published, and I'm working on the manuscript for a book. Through the poetry I reconnected with myself. To me this was a miracle."

"I FOUND OUT I HAD A LOT OF POWER"

Bob Smith

Bob Smith is a volunteer teacher in San Francisco, where he coaches the women's softball team at Mission High School and teaches history at Delancey Street, a halfway house for former prisoners.

"Seven years ago I was divorced and lost. I sold all my businesses. I had two marinas, a shopping center, a home-building company, a road-building company, and a newspaper. My life was chaotic. Business can be an addiction just like alcohol, and when I had all those businesses, I was going from one to the other and keeping up this chaos to shut out the pain.

"I left New Jersey and went to Nevada, to Lake Tahoe. I decided I wouldn't have a drink or a date for a year, but the night the deal had closed on selling my businesses, I went to a bar to celebrate by getting drunk. I knew the bartender, and she wanted me to meet someone. This woman who was a friend of hers came over and started talking to me about some kind of program called Life Spring, which was supposed to help you get it together. Before she could even start selling me on it, I said, 'I'll do it. Whatever it is, I'll do it. How much is it? Here's a check.'

"They had you write down what you wanted to get out of the course. I wrote that I wanted to be able to talk in front of a group of people. I was full of fear. Next thing I knew I was up there talking to the group. I found out I had a lot of power. I found out we all have power.

"That program was a springboard for me. I opened myself up. I started a quest to find myself. I did everything. I went to Adult Children of Alcoholics; I took seminars in 'higher consciousness' with Ken Keyes; I joined a spiritual group at Lake Tahoe. Now I was beginning to feel again, and I had to deal with my feelings.

"I went back to college as a freshman at the University of Nevada at Reno and studied anthropology. Then I found out that my daughter had cancer, and I went back east to be with her. I was with her the whole time until she died. My goal was just to be there, and I did that. She lived nearly a year. She died before she was thirty.

"I was full of anger. I took a workshop from John Bradshaw, and he said, 'If you don't forgive, you never grow up.' When I heard that, I committed myself to getting rid of the anger, to growing up finally. I spent a year working on that. I did a program called Lomi, which uses massage to integrate body, emotion, and spirit. I worked with Richard Heckler, a former All-American track athlete and author of *The Anatomy of Change*, who helped develop the program.

"I started teaching in prisons in Nevada. I taught those guys how to get up in front of a group and talk. I told them how they had a lot of power, that anyone could transform himself, even in prison. It was great to see them change. You could see it happen when they got up to speak.

"I met a woman in San Francisco, Elaine, and I moved to the Bay Area and rented a houseboat in Sausalito. I teach American history at Delancey Street, a halfway house for ex-prisoners. I coach a girl's softball team at a high school in the Mission Hill district. I take a yoga class. I'm having a great time. Elaine and I are going to get married.

"It's all gravy. I never expected any of this. In high school I was told I wasn't college material, but I went anyway. I graduated from Seton Hall. Sometimes when people talk about reincarnation, they say, 'Oh, don't tell me I have to come back to earth again.' How come they say that? Why wouldn't you want to come back? This is great!"

The key to enlightenment in most of the great religious or spiritual traditions is surrender. Give up the ego, the absorption in self, the self-will that wants you to be the master of the universe. It is also a key point in recovery, the first step in AA, admitting one is powerless over alcohol and/or drugs. Bill Tewell recognized that the twelve steps describe the traditional mystic way. It's miraculous that this way has been interpreted for our time, for masses of people, giving them the power to carry on their lives without drugs or alcohol. Surrender is part of that path, the path of the spirit.

For a novelist, surrender meant getting down on hands and knees to pray. A minister realized that the most important confession was to admit, "I need help." A former political candidate and adviser who became a minister found he had to give up his last vestiage of "macho male pride" in order to surrender and begin the road to recovery. All fought this giving up of ego control yet found relief and new life in finally letting go to a Higher Power.

"BETWEEN THE IMPULSE AND THE ACT"
Ivan Gold

Ivan Gold, a friend since we were students at Columbia in the 1950s, wrote a brilliant novel, *Sams in a Dry Season,* about a boozing writer who goes into Alcoholics Anonymous. He has also spoken publicly about his own recovery through fifteen years in the AA program, as well as his finding release from a twenty-year writer's block to finish *Sams.*

"You learn that there's an interval between the impulse and the act. It was like a revelation. There's a moment when you can consider all the variables, the result of the act, and decide what to do, and make a choice. That's freedom.

"Stopping drinking is the least of it. The main thing is how do you put a life together sober when you've been dependent on drinking for so long? It's terrifying. People continue drinking because they are too frightened by the idea of living without it.

"The change comes when you're willing to do what AA tells you to do. They said to get down on your knees and pray. I said, 'I can't do that, I'm a Jew, we don't do that.' About a week later I was down on my hands and knees in my living room, trying to pray. You're willing to try anything to manufacture a life without alcohol. In the early slogging you gotta be open to anything—and that's a miracle. You know how closed I was when I was young, how arrogant I was.

"God is a relief. The idea that it's OK to believe. You spend your youth pushing away the God of your fathers, so you're left with nothing. AA gives you the opportunity to rethink that—to rethink your relationship to the cosmos."

THE POWER OF THE GROUP

Dan

"Dan" is a retired minister in one of the mainline Protestant denominations. He worked for racial justice in the 1960s, took part in the human potential movement in the 1970s, and helped manage shelters for homeless people in two large cities in the 1980s. He says he has experienced suicide in his family, the near death of his son, a divorce, and other personal and vocational traumas, but "through it all I've been sustained by a great mother, great friends, and great music and literature."

"To say that my sobriety of well beyond three and a half years is a miracle is an assertion of faith; that is, it cannot be proven in purely naturalistic terms, as one could prove that the light is on in this room right now. Miracle to me points to that Mystery in which all of our lives are enveloped, which manifests itself in pivotal moments as inner peace, strength, and unexpected motivation. Unexpected: Grace is no longer grace when it ceases to surprise us.

"I was (and am) a minister of the gospel, and I was a closet drinker at home. Throughout many years I was really helping lots of people in various kinds of need through my presence, preaching, and priestly ministry. I was also increasingly in bondage to alcohol and could not, would not, find a way out. After some twenty-three years, I hit bottom, which was the stark fear that I would have to enter a hospital detoxification unit. By the time I was tested, I had detoxed myself during an agonizing three days and nights and was ready to get serious about my condition.

"Looking back, I can see that my disease progressed from rather little drinking to compulsive swigging of white wine. Drinking contaminated my first marriage by exacerbating unresolved anger in times of stress with my then wife. In my second marriage alcohol worsened my periodic depressions. My ministry suffered because of chronic guilt and decreased efficiency. I knew I was in trouble when my morning drinking came to include a couple of swigs of Chablis before I went to church to lead the morning worship. Finally, after some 'talk' in the church, I was confronted by some of my peers from the extralocal church structure and pressured into an outpatient rehabilitation program, which proved to be a great experience.

"Sometime during my first year of sobriety I told my sponsor that I wished for an overwhelming spiritual experience, such as I had read about in the *Big Book* of AA. He said such a simple thing: 'Look at the results.' What? Oh, I noted with interest, I am not drinking. Somehow the miracle had happened. Quietly, powerfully, I had been freed from that terrible obsession.

"Having spent my life in the church, and thus seen, heard about, participated in many noble and vivifying events, I wondered why there could not be more deep and honest sharing of what was really going on in our lives, such as I had seen in the rooms of AA. I know that kind of honest sharing does happen here and there in the life of some Christian communities. But there is also a lot of pretense and hostility. And then the thought came to me: In AA we are a community of need. We come together confessing, 'I need help.' How can help come if need is not admitted? The help does in fact come, to innumerable men and women who, in their dereliction, ask for new life. It comes because of the power of the group and the miracle Spirit, 'which bloweth where it listeth.'

"I think it is not widely understood that stopping drinking is only the beginning of the AA program. The twelve steps are a program for life, for change and growth in one's attitude and behavior. Incredibly, the change happens; you see it in the lives of members of the fellowship and in your own. The grace of God does come, as simply perhaps as the rain that falls."

AN ANGRY PRAYER

Roger Cowan

Roger Cowan is minister of the First Unitarian Church of North Palm Beach, Florida. He has been a candidate for Congress and was state chairman for the presidential campaign of Senator Eugene McCarthy in Tennessee. Three times he served as president of the Florida Unitarian-Universalist Ministers Association. His books of sermons include *Inside Out.*

❧

"After waging a daily, lonely, and private civil war for almost two decades, I gave up trying to control my heavy drinking by willpower. It took the loss of family and job and the shattering of every last vestige of macho male pride for me to surrender. In a detox in Knoxville, Tennessee, I despairingly prayed this angry prayer: 'Goddamn it, God, you really piss me off! For sixteen years I've tried to run my life, and now I'm beaten and whipped and through. You're going to have to take it from here because I can't cut it anymore. Now get me the hell out of this place. Amen.'

"To many folks that prayer would be a sacrilege, unworthy even to be called a prayer. But all I know is that, in that very moment, I knew a sense of calm and peace and felt the absolute certainty that the power of alcohol over me was lifted. Fifteen years later, my prayers continue—only now they are prayers of gratitude, praise, and intercession for others who still suffer. When friends sometimes try to explain away the psychological causes of my recovery, I smile to myself. Like the man in the hymn, all I can say is, 'Once I was blind, but now I see. Once I was drunk, but now I am sober.'

"Ordinary miracles of enlarged understanding, more noble living, sober living—these have happened to me. I didn't read them in a book. I experienced them in my heart. And I didn't do it—a power greater than myself did. I choose to call that power God. No laser treatment or mud placed and then washed from my eyes could be more miraculous."

Chapter 5

MIRACLES
OF LOVE

L ike healing, love is almost by definition a miracle. It comes on us unaware, surprising, mysterious, transforming. Among its many blessings is in fact its power to heal, to make whole. It gives meaning, purpose, and inspiration. It is at the heart of all great religions. It teaches and elevates us by its very presence.

Of all the spiritual paths to losing the ego, to escaping the bonds of the self, love by its very nature breaks those chains. Without even thinking or making an effort, in love we transcend ourselves as, miraculously, we act in the best interest of someone other than ourself—the one or the ones we love—child, brother, lover, mate, friend.

"There is only one kind of love, and that is love at first sight," said my wise old professor at Columbia, Mark Van Doren. I know many people react with shock and dismay at such a suggestion, raising specters of sexism, lookism—every hellishly incorrect emotion or response in today's lexicon of propriety—yet I've found it to be true. In fact it doesn't have anything to do with a person's being beautiful or handsome by some fashion-magazine standard. Rather it has to do with a "click," a connection. The psychic electricity hits, "across a crowded room," as the song says. We all know what it means. My friend Helen Weaver described it when she told of meeting Jack Kerouac for the first time and "our eyeballs locked." It was understood, without any words, that he would stay with her, and they had their tumultuous romance.

It happened to me most stunningly when I met a woman and asked her at the end of our first lunch—before we had even held hands or touched in any way—if she would consider quitting her job in New York and coming to live with me in Boston because I wanted to be with her the rest of my life. She thanked me politely but said it didn't seem possible, then changed her mind that night, and we took the impossible step that led to seven years of the best life I'd known, until it couldn't stand the transplant to alien Hollywood and split apart.

Until those last few months when we started to crack, I'd never known such harmony with another human being. She was a Republican, I a Democrat; she read science fiction, I read the *New York Times* (she thought it was fiction but less entertaining); she was born abroad, a citizen of another land; I'm from darkest Indiana; she loved snails and raw living things that were regarded as gourmet delicacies, while I was raised on well-done steaks and thought fried clams were the outer limits of sophisticated dining. Pure love. The only thing we agreed on was the daytime drama (soap opera to the uninitiated) *All My Children* and its creator, Agnes Nixon, who became our friend and whom we took as our patron saint (as many others have before and since who have fallen under the spell of her extraordinary love for people, life, stories, faith, the spirit).

Despite my nice professor's *mot*, there of course are many different kinds of love. Out of love, my own parents sacrificed to give me the best college education, the best of everything they could offer, and in my rebellion and confusion, it was not until later in life that I was able to return or express a part of that. I don't have children of my own, but I know countless people who automatically place the interests of their children above their own needs, hopes, wishes, plans. "Without thinking," a man said, "I'd hurl myself in front of a bus to save any one of my children, and I wouldn't do that for anyone else on earth, even my wife."

I've been blessed by the love of friends. Without their comradeship I would not have got to where I am or have lived to the age I am. I can't imagine what life would be like without the richness and delight they have brought and continue to bring me or without the deep satisfaction that comes when I'm able to return their friendship and love.

There's the kind of love the poet Richard Wilbur describes in his great poem "Love Calls Us to the Things of This World," and that Rupert Brooke cataloged so eloquently in his poem "The Great Lover," speaking of the blessing of hot water, the daily life delights all around us, like "the little dulling edge of foam / that browns and dwindles as the wave goes home." Most of the time we live by rote, but every now and then we wake up to the miracles at hand, ones that our deadened senses can conjure up like genies when clear and given the opportunity, the time to notice. Then a feeling of love for it all—for *life*—surges within us.

Love of country isn't so commonplace now as it was when I was growing up in Indiana during World War II, and patriotism was a noble emotion. It wasn't just jingoistic flag-waving, either, the war that threatened your country, your home, made you see it fresh, appreciate it anew. That love, recollected years later, inspired me to write a novel called *Under the Apple Tree*, in which I described the feelings that stirred in me and most everyone I knew then, feelings I gave to the main character of the story, a ten-year-old boy named Artie:

> In the crisp clear days of October, America was beautiful, just like in the song. Artie had never been "from sea to shining sea" nor had he seen "the purple mountain's majesty" but he knew they were out there, believed in them, and saw every day with his own eyes the beauty of the gentle hills, the creeks and cornfields, the solid old white frame houses and the ancient oaks of Town. He believed, in fact, that God had "shed his grace" on this land, that this grace was tangible, visible, in the arch of rainbows over wet fields, the slant of shed sunlight on the sides of old barns. His pride in his country was sustained by the signs of nature and the symbols of men, not only the bright stars and stripes that flew from public buildings and hung from private porches but the comforting, everyday emblems of home: Bob's eats, Joe's Premium, Mail Pouch Tobacco. This was what his brother Roy and all the other boys were fighting to save, preserve, and protect, along with the people who were lucky enough to live in and of it, and all this was sacred, worthy of sacrifice, for without it, life would be hollow and dumb.

The love of place, of the ground we grew up on, the scenes we call home, is powerful and sacred.

We all love a love story—it renews our sense of the miraculous. In a real life scene more unexpected than any he would allow in one of his scripts, a famous writer and movie director gets a feeling that something wonderful is about to happen; the next person who walks in the room is the woman he'll marry. A woman visualizes the man she wants to share her life with as she drives to a conference, and she finds him there, just as she pictured him, down to the last detail. A divorced mother spurns the "practical" man she's supposed to marry and chooses a roaming young man with a temporary job. An injured long-distance runner is healed by a yoga teacher and realizes she is literally "the woman of his dreams."

"I THOUGHT I'D BE ALONE"

Michael Crichton

One of the most successful authors in American history, Michael Crichton had three of his novels on the *New York Times* paperback bestseller list at the same time, two of them also hit movies, *Jurassic Park* and *Rising Sun*. A new bestselling novel was soon to follow—*Disclosure*—with a movie soon after, and the hit TV series "E.R."

"I never thought I'd be able to be married and have a family—the notion that a woman was out there who could put up with me and that we'd live together and have a child together seemed impossible.

"For most of my life I'd felt alone. I was beginning to think it was always going to be that way.

"I was casting a movie in '84, and we needed some people for minor roles. One woman was wrong for the part but was obviously a nice person, and you don't want to just say, 'OK, that's all.' So I was talking with her to be polite when suddenly I got tremendously excited. I had this feeling that something wonderful was going to happen to me. When I finished talking with this woman, I went out to bring in the next person. She was my future wife.

"She came into the room and I was struck dumb. I'd just told everyone that these casting sessions were not about my social life; that no matter what they'd heard about me, the only thing I was looking for in these casting sessions was the right person for the role in the movie. When Ann Marie—my future wife—left the room, everyone looked at me, and I said, 'Excuse me!' and ran out of the room after her.

"When I caught up with her, I asked her if she was single, just to make sure. Then started the most horrendously difficult four years of either of our lives. We scheduled the wedding, canceled it, then got married. It didn't suddenly become easy. It's still difficult, but it's worth it.

"This is the longest relationship I've ever had in my life. My daughter is now five years old. This to me is much more of a miracle than having three books on the best-seller list at the same time. Nothing really matters except family. If there is any one thing in my life that I feel blessed with, it's this.

"All you have to do is have anything go wrong, or even the threat of anything going wrong, with the people you love, and you see what really matters. All your ideas about the importance of career are bullshit compared to this."

"GOD, GIVE HIM A PONYTAIL!"

Jennifer Fox

Jennifer Fox teaches yoga at the health spa Rancho La Puerta, Mexico, and gives workshops in yoga and nonimpact aerobics with her partner, Paul Gould.

"For the last six years of my marriage I was trying to decide whether to leave or stay. I was living and teaching yoga in Mill Valley, California, and I decided to take a five-week sabbatical and go down to Mexico to teach at the health spa Rancho La Puerta, figuring in that time I could make up my mind one way or another.

"After I made that arrangement I heard about an intensive yoga workshop in Portland. I really wanted to attend, but most of it was going to take place at the same time I was supposed to go to Mexico. I saw that I could go to the Portland workshop the first two days and then go to Mexico, but it seemed silly to drive all the way up to Portland from San Francisco and then all the way back down again to Mexico. I couldn't get it out of my mind, though, so I decided to do it.

"After I made that decision and got in my car to drive to Portland, I suddenly felt free, and I knew immediately that I needed to end my marriage. As I drove north I started singing and talking to myself, feeling relieved that I'd finally made a decision.

"My husband was a businessman and I said, 'God, next time, please give me a man who's in my own field of work.' Then before I knew it, I was saying, 'And make him tall.' I had to laugh at myself, talking as if I could order up a new mate like that, but it was fun, and so I added, 'And give him a ponytail!'

"At the Portland workshop I met Paul, whom I'd known before, but he'd been married too. He'd just left his wife, and I was leaving my husband. Not only that, he was tall—and he even had a ponytail!

"That was five years ago, and we've been together ever since."

INTO THE WILD BLUE YONDER
Charlotte W. Mannion

Charlotte Mannion tells me that last year she and her husband renewed their marriage vows in a ceremony at their church in Coral Gables, Florida. The theme of the ceremony was "It's a Miracle," because, Charlotte explains, "It's so wonderful, and the way it happened was not just coincidental."

"Two years after my separation from my husband, George, my brother's best friend, Joe, asked me to marry him. He knew the children loved their 'Uncle Joe' and that I was fond of him. He professed his love and told me he would take care of me and the girls. I knew he was a forty-year-old bachelor who still lived with his mother and two sisters and had never dated. I gave it some thought; at the time passion was not my main concern. In 1954, being married seemed my only choice, and Joe seemed a comfortable prospect.

"We arranged that the girls and I would establish residence in Miami. The requests I made of Joe were for him to get a driver's license, find a place for his new family to live, and prepare my home for sale. The day after my final divorce decree, he would come down to Miami, where the girls and I would be living, then we'd return to New York as husband and wife with three children.

"I trusted my intended husband, Joe. He was exacting about details and meticulous about his person. I had some misgivings about his emphasis on this, but I assumed that in time, after marriage, he would be less rigid.

"The day after the girls and I arrived in Miami, my girls wanted to go to the library. I suggested they go across the street to the San Marino Hotel and ask someone for directions. They did and rushed back to tell me that 'Johnny' would go with them that afternoon; he would come by to get them. I thought they had made friends with a high school boy. I was glad. I hoped it would be a chance for my oldest girl to make some friends before starting junior high in the fall.

"When this young man named Johnny appeared, and I told him I'd expected a high school boy, he smiled, and in an Irish brogue he said, 'Ah, that I once was.'

"He had just graduated from the University of Miami, and he'd taken over the valet parking concession at the San Marino Hotel. He'd majored in English and loved language. I invited him for lunch—tuna fish sandwiches—and he took us all to the library.

"I needed a friend, and John became my most fascinating friend. I enjoyed his Irish wit and black humor. Between June and October we spent almost every day together. He escorted us to the zoo, the planetarium, the Keys. All the trips included the kids.

"'It's good to see a group than can manage nicely, thank you, even without a father,' he told me one day. 'My old man died when I was nine months old. The old lady could hardly hold the family together. I'm the youngest—the older brothers made things difficult. Anyway, keep up the good work, kid—you've got a great bunch of kids, a nice family.'

"John was spontaneous. On his day off he'd come over and say to the kids, 'Anyone want to go fishing down in Key Largo better be ready by two o'clock! Any takers?' After a scream of approval, we'd scurry to get going. We'd dash out to my Ford and head south on Highway One, singing, 'Off we go into the wild blue yonder . . . '

"John told me that after the valet job ended he'd be moving on. He didn't know where. He said he didn't want to get seriously involved with anyone at this time. He knew I was getting married in October.

"I couldn't resist the temptation to have this exciting man make love to me. I was the instigator, provoker, stimulator, and never felt guilty. I felt like a woman. I thought about the days growing short until October, but it didn't worry me. I knew the score.

"On October 16 I appeared before a magistrate and in less than ten minutes was no longer a married woman. For a few hours I could be with John as a single woman. I knew I loved him as I'd loved no other.

"The next day I watched my intended husband, Joe, unpack in his hotel room. He laid out his five different color toothbrushes on the dresser. He stepped back and stared at them for a moment, then took the yellow toothbrush and exchanged it with the red.

"'Whoops,' he said, 'I almost mixed up my lunch brush with my late-night brush!'

"I clenched my teeth and told him that tomorrow he could drive us to the lawyer's office where we were getting married. He said he couldn't, he didn't have the license; he had taken one lesson and knew he'd never be able to drive. He also confessed that he had failed to get my old house ready for sale, nor had he found us a place to live.

"I didn't sleep well that night. Around five-thirty in the morning I trudged up the flight of stairs and knocked on Joe's door. I sat at the foot of the bed and told him I was not going back to New York with him. We both realized that twenty years of friendship didn't prepare us for marriage. Joe left the next morning to return to his mother and two sisters.

"When the girls woke up, I told them we were not going back to New York. They asked about Uncle Joe, and then they asked about John. I told them anyone who wanted to come with me to tell John the good news had better be ready in five minutes.

"The three children and I married John. I became his devoted wife, and the girls his loving daughters. He became a wonderful husband and father, and four years later we added a son to our family.

"It's forty years later now, and we continue to live this miracle."

"THE WOMAN IN THE DREAM"

Thom Birch

Thom Birch is a former professional distance runner who is now a yoga teacher. With his wife, yoga teacher Beryl Bender, he is a director of the Wellness Department of the New York Road Runners Club.

"Ever since I was a boy, I had had a recurring dream in which a woman came out of the mist toward me and then disappeared. I had the dream about every five years. I saw the woman's face, I looked into her eyes, but when I went toward her, she disappeared in the mist again. Then in a time of great depression, I found that woman—not in a dream but in real life.

"I was in San Francisco to help set up an international women's road race, and I ran into Beryl Bender. She was a spokesperson for Avon, who sponsored some of the women's road races, and I'd met her in Texas at one of the races, but we didn't do more than say hello. When I met her at this event in San Francisco, I was really in despair. I was sitting in the lobby of my hotel with my head in my hands when Beryl saw me and said, 'What's the matter? You don't look so good.' I told her I didn't feel very good either, and she said, 'Come on, let's go have a vegetable juice.' I'd never had a vegetable juice before, and while we were drinking it I told Beryl why I was so depressed.

"I was a long-distance runner. After I won a major 10K race in Texas, I was ranked fifty-ninth in the world, and a businessman came up to me and said he'd like to be my sponsor. He gave me twenty thousand dollars, and I became part owner of a store that sold running shoes. That gave me time to keep running and training. I'd run in the morning, then go work in the store, then go for a run in the afternoon, letting my partner take over the store, then I'd return and work some more, then run again after work. I was running a hundred miles a week.

"A year after I won that race and got a sponsor I injured my Achilles tendon and was in severe pain. I went to one of the leading orthopedic surgeons in the country, and he said he could operate, but even if the operation was successful, I'd never run again. I accepted this as the result of running a hundred miles a week for so long. I was shattered. I had worked long and hard to get where I was. I had achieved my dream of being a world-ranked runner, and in a year the dream was over. The doctor said I'd always walk with a limp, and I could never run again.

"Beryl listened to this and said, 'Yes you can. I'm a yoga teacher. I can work with you and strengthen you so you can run again.'

"I said maybe she didn't understand how serious this was. In the operation they took the sheath off the calf, sewed the tendon back up, and put the sheath back.

"She still said she could help me run again.

"I said, 'Are you telling me that after a surgery costing tens of thousands of dollars with the best orthopedic doctor in the country, after I'm told I can never run again, you say I can be fixed by doing some yoga?' She said, 'Yes, that's right,' very casually, as if it were no big deal.

"Well, I went to a yoga session with her, and she was working with my ankle, holding it in her hands. She turned it in some way—she did something to it—and the pain was gone. I was healed. I looked at her, and when I looked into her eyes, I realized she was the woman in the dream. She looked just like her, but it didn't really click until I looked right into her eyes. Within the week I had asked her to marry me.

"After that session with Beryl I walked without a limp, and I could run again."

Beryl herself was surprised at the suddenness of the healing: "Usually it takes progressive work, over a period of time. I really don't know what I did."

Tom and Beryl were married in 1983. He studied yoga with her, became a yoga teacher himself, and they are now partners in their own studio and teach classes in New York City and East Hampton, Long Island, and serve as fitness advisers for the New York Road Runners Club. Beryl is the author of *The Power Yoga Workout.*

When relationships end, we fear that love will never come again. Fate or circumstance has doomed us to a solitary life, we believe, and we must simply accept the bleak prospect that love, for us, is past. If we love someone and that ends, it's impossible to think we'll ever know such feelings again. Amazingly, the impossible happens, often when it's least expected. A Harvard professor can't imagine being married again after a painful marital breakup—until he meets a Wellesley professor. After too many "dates from hell," a businessman swears off meeting new women—until a support group friend says she's just found his soul mate. After two years of waiting for his wife to decide if she still loves him, a therapist asks for a divorce, goes to cry in his beer with a friend, and is fixed up with a woman he doesn't want to meet—until he looks in her eyes.

"GODZILLA MEETS KING KONG"

Harvey Cox

Harvey Cox is a world-renowned theologian and professor of religion at Harvard University. His first book, *The Secular City,* became an international bestseller. He has published ten other books since then, most recently *Fire from Heaven: The Rise of Pentacostal Spirituality and the Reshaping of Religion in the Twenty-first Century.* He lives in Cambridge with his second wife, Nina Tumarkin, a professor of Russian history at Wellesley College, and their son, Nicholas Tumarkin Cox.

"When my first marriage was ending eight years ago, I was in the absolute depths of despair. I couldn't imagine ever being married again—much less having a child. I already had three grown children. That part of life was over for me—or so I thought.

"And just at that point Nina came along. We were introduced by friends who thought we were like Godzilla and King Kong. They debated for a year whether to introduce us, thinking we were so much like each other it would be awful. I'm a professor in the Divinity School at Harvard; she's a professor of Russian history at Wellesley. I've written books, she's written books. Neither of us is a shrinking violet. Well, our friends finally said, 'Let's introduce Godzilla to King Kong and see what happens' [posters of the movie monsters hang in their front hallway]. After the first two or three times we met, we knew what we both wanted. We decided to get married.

"That's a miracle. Nina had been divorced about five years before; she was thirty-nine, never had children, never wanted to—but she said, 'With you, I think I would.' I thought, 'Do I want to go through this again?' Did I want to start over with diapers, children's birthday parties? I told Nina, 'I think I'd like to do it again, with you, on one condition—that I don't have to go to any kiddies' birthday parties.'

"Another potential obstacle was that Nina is a Jew and I'm a Christian theologian and a Baptist minister. We're both very serious about our own religious traditions, and we continue practicing, which involves fully respecting and accepting the other person's form of spirituality.

"The child of a Jewish woman is Jewish. We talked to a couple of rabbis, and I said I was willing to have my child be Jewish, but I wanted to help raise him Jewish. We show Nicholas that we participate in each other's religion. He knows we appreciate both traditions and enter into them. Nina and I are writing a book together: We're talking about not only how a religiously mixed marriage works but also what reservations and doubts we have and where our areas of discomfort are.

"Having Nina come into my life and having a little boy in my sixties makes me feel like Abraham. This was totally, totally unexpected—and unmerited."

LOVE AFTER DATES FROM HELL
David Alexander

David Alexander was membership services director of a trade association (the American Die Casting Institute) in Chicago until he met his present wife, Rev. Joan Gattuso, and moved to Cleveland. He now works as executive director of the Unity Church of Greater Cleveland, where his wife is the minister.

"After my second divorce, friends fixed me up with blind dates, but in less than a year I decided to stop dating. Every one was a date from hell. It became a struggle, and I thought 'I don't need this. I'm not going to do this anymore.'

"I was in a support group that had become like a family—people of all ages, backgrounds. We'd hang out together on holidays; we weren't lonely. I figured, 'I'm happy the way I am.'

"I'd done a lot of work on myself, and when I went to a psychologist after my second divorce, after two sessions she said, 'What are you doing here?'

"I was OK. I'd been through a civilized divorce—my former wife and I were simply going in different directions. I'd done a lot of spiritual work, and I wasn't interested in any relationship that was not ideal. I was in a state of openness, but I wasn't looking for anyone.

"I'd been on a retreat in California, and when I got home I had a message from Sandy, a friend from my support group, saying, 'David, you gotta call me. I found your soul mate.' I wondered what was going on and called her back. She said she'd been in Cleveland and met this wonderful woman that she knew was my soul mate. She'd never fixed anyone up before in her life, but she had this deep feeling about it.

"I asked how they'd met. Sandy had been in Cleveland to set up a Diet Center, and this woman who she thought was my soul mate had come in to get in the program to lose weight. It was while Sandy was measuring the woman's thighs that she said, 'Do you mind if I ask you a personal question?' The woman said, 'How much more personal can you get? You're measuring my thighs!' So Sandy asked if she was single, and the woman said yes, and Sandy said she had just the man for her.

"I called up this woman in Cleveland and got her answering machine. I left a message, and said I'd call back. I called later that night. When we finally connected, we talked for two hours. It was like an instant connection. I had never quite experienced anything like it on any level. It felt perfect. We spoke on the phone over the course of two weeks, and then I flew to Cleveland for a blind date. I already knew I'd marry her. I had no idea what she looked like. When I asked Sandy to describe her, all she said was, 'She's a Scorpio like you, and she looks like a real person.'

"Since we'd had all those long telephone conversations before we'd even met, the whole relationship was based on feelings—our bodies didn't get in the way. We were together every weekend till we married, eight months later. We've been together eight years since then. I left my job and moved to Cleveland before I even had a job, knowing I'd find the right one. I do administrative work at her church, plan the programs, put out the newsletter. I do all the things she doesn't like to do.

"From the time I was about nine years old I knew that the kind of relationship Joan and I have was out there somewhere. It took me two marriages and many women to discover it. But I knew there existed a type of relationship that was natural, that was no struggle. Joan had always had that same feeling. When we found each other and started living it, she wrote a book about her journey to get to this and it's been signed up by Harper San Francisco. When we got married, my friend Sandy said, 'You mean I was meant to find *your* soul mate?' She'd looked at Joan, this woman she'd never met before, and thought of *me*. It's a miracle."

"I SAW A SHY CREATURE IN A DRAB BROWN DRESS"

Nelson Wright

Nelson Wright is the pseudonym of a social service administrator. Both he and his wife are therapists, and since one of them works in the school of psychotherapeutic thought that tries to preserve the anonymity of the therapist as part of the therapeutic technique, they wish to remain anonymous.

"My friend Julian agreed to meet me and let me cry in my beer, something I had never done before. My wife had refused to stay at home that evening with me, and after two years of waiting for her to restore me to the primary position in her life, I said I wanted to be divorced. She still said she was going out, so I said I wanted to start a new home with someone else.

"When I met my friend Julian and started drinking beer, I told him my story. We then talked of other things. Suddenly at almost midnight he said, 'I have just the woman for you!' I said I was ready to take a rest, but he insisted on calling her up and getting her to come and join us. I said I did not see how she could be the one for me if she would come out now, at this time of night, but he said, 'You'll see.'

"She now tells me of his calling her. He was an insomniac and sometimes called her when he could not sleep. He had never asked her to meet him as he now did, and she tried to put him off, reminding him that she had to go to work in the morning. He insisted, and finally he told her, 'If you come, your life will change forever.' She said to herself that he really sounded desperate, so she put on her ugliest dress, left her lenses (which she needs) at home, and went to join him.

"'There she is!' Julian said as she walked in the door. My heart sank as I saw a shy creature in a drab brown dress, looking around hesitantly. I felt faced with disaster. However, when my friend brought her to the table, I shook her hand and looked into her beautiful blue eyes. Overwhelmed by her tender face, I fell in love on the spot.

"We have been married twenty-nine years now, and the years simply keep getting better. I feel more in love than I ever did before. It is indeed a miracle."

Perhaps the most inspiring kind of love is the love that survives and grows in the most painful and difficult of circumstances. These are instances of human beings transcending their own ego for the person they love, sacrificing their own welfare and comfort for the good of another, really living out the spiritual teachings to love your neighbor as yourself.

We have a lot to learn about the miracle of love from a man who has AIDS. He has reclaimed his religious heritage and explored the deepest questions of existence; he has loved his lover and mate who died of AIDS and loves again his present partner without fear. As his body goes through horrendous breakdowns, he finds strength in his newly forged faith in God.

At the end of *Angels in America: Part I, The Millenium* (Tony Kushner's prize-winning drama about AIDS and this society), an angel descends in a scene of stunning power and glory and says, "The messenger arrives. The great work begins." More and more, as I listen and look in today's world, I see AIDS and its victims as messengers of the miracle of the spirit, its triumph over the body, the faith it brings in the face of death.

There are other moving stories of love overcoming fear and selfishness. A member of my church in Boston lovingly cares for his wife after she sustains brain damage and loses her power of speech; he arranges a new marriage ceremony when she can't remember the original one. A prisoner is kept alive by the care and love of his fellow inmates. A writer's love of his mentally ill brother sustains him through multiple therapies, drugs, and hospitals. A Vietnam veteran finds a fulfilling life with the woman who still loves and marries him after he comes home from war having lost both legs, both arms, and an eye.

These are men and women whose love in the face of adversity creates miracles.

"I CHERISHED EVERY CELL IN HIS BODY"

Rob Hershman

You have read Rob Hershman's story of the importance of a spiritual life in dealing with AIDS (chapter 3). In the past two years, this award-winning TV producer has become a student of the Hebrew language and the Torah. He gives here his own translation of a prayer from the Hebrew and what it means in his life now.

❧

"The *Asher Yatzar* is a very specific prayer of thanks for the body in all its earthy ingenuity. Traditionally it is said at home, often after using the bathroom in the morning."

Blessed are you Adonai, Our God, Sovereign of the Universe who formed the human being with wisdom and created within us orifices, hollows, tubes, and passages.

It is clearly known, before your glorious throne, that if one of these is ruptured or if one of these is clogged, it would be impossible to live, and to stand before you. Blessed are you, Adonai, healer of all flesh whose works are wondrous.

"I come to this prayer from a very personal and often painful perspective. As a person with AIDS I know what happens when the very basic functions of the body go wrong. I have watched more than one friend literally starve to death when their alimentary systems were clogged. I've looked on helplessly as others, including my late lover, Ron James, had their lives literally drain out of them with massive and uncontrolled diarrhea. There have been times when it has seemed utterly impossible, even a kind of blasphemy, to praise God for creating a body so treacherous, so helpless, so open to pain.

"Sometimes in the face of all this loss, I have gone dead inside. At other times I've been so alive to the power of love and examples of courage that God has seemed right there, close enough to share my grief. But for the most part, day after day, I struggle to understand God's will, knowing that I cannot know, but also that within this struggle is much of the meaning in my life.

"I remember very clearly being with Ron in the hospital during his last days. I remember watching over him and feeling that I loved him so much that I cherished every cell in his body. And then I realized that many of those cells were infected and that they were even then actively doing their work of eating away his life. Did I love those infected cells too?

"My rabbi, Marshall Meyer, helped me with this question—though it wasn't until after his own death that I truly understood him.

"We are not called upon to love everything, he taught me. In fact we must use all our resources to fight destructive forces. What we are called upon to do is to acknowledge God's blessings and to seek wholeness.

"Embedded within the Asher Yatzar, as within so much of our tradition, is precisely the path to this wholeness. In gratefully acknowledging the complex wonder of the body, we are also, in this prayer, acknowledging that our bodies do not come with guarantees. God made us *b'hochma*, with wisdom. Part of that wisdom is our ability—sometimes—to repair the body when it goes wrong but also the acceptance that there comes a time when no repair is possible.

"We speak in this prayer about God as the healer of all flesh and the maker of miracles. Sometimes we must acknowledge that one of God's miracles, one of the ways he heals us, is to grant a successful death. God touches us in the place of our deepest pain and we find release. The healing that ultimately matters is the healing of the soul. . . .

"I have said Asher Yatzar with my dear friend Richard Shapiro, who died of AIDS last month. I say this prayer now with my beloved partner,

Gary Barton, who faces with me the bleak uncertainty of AIDS even as we share the wonder of our love."

"A GIFT FROM GOD"

Jim McNeely

Shortly after I joined King's Chapel, I saw a man at an evening Bible study who looked as if he were in shock. He had every right to be. He had just returned from a vacation in Italy, where two boys on a motorcycle had ridden past his wife and grabbed her purse and yanked it; but the strap didn't break, and Jim's wife was thrown to the pavement. She suffered a severe head injury that left her in a coma. We all prayed for a miracle. We didn't get the kind we expected. This is Jim's story.

❧

"I courted my second wife for eight years. Loving had never been easy for me and a divorce had made it tougher. I was unable (or afraid) to tell my lover that I loved her. Fortunately, she had a sense of humor. She laughed and said I could tell her or not, as I saw fit. She knew I loved her.

"We finally eloped. Our marriage was worth the wait. We had a wonderful time together for a year and a half. Then, during a vacation in Sicily, my wife was mugged and her head severely injured.

"She was operated on in Palermo and flown to Germany. She developed pneumonia, and her kidneys failed. After eleven weeks she reached Boston, still in a coma.

"In desperation I promised God that I would accept—with gratitude—whatever of my wife he would return so long as she could understand when I told her I loved her.

"My wife recovered physically, but for a year her tracheotomy prevented her from speaking. When it was removed, her speech was unintelligible. She had severe global aphasia. She understood little of what I said. She could hardly read and write. She understood that I loved her, but our journey had barely begun.

"Nine months later I brought her home. Speech therapists came every day. She relearned to shop and to cook simple meals and to do the laundry. Her old employer gave her part-time work. We took in overnight guests to give her more work and to give me more company. We went to church. I prayed that her speech would improve.

"After a while, I discovered that she did not remember our wedding. The head injury had erased the years immediately before and after the accident. She would look at our wedding pictures and shake her head in disbelief. She had not taken my name, which reinforced her doubts about her status. We had eloped, so I decided to have a second wedding attended by children, family, and friends. The invitations read, 'Things are lovelier the second time around.' The ceremony was followed by communion, then dinner and dancing. She took my name.

"I worked out of our house. My wife made lunch every day and brought tea to my staff every afternoon. I took over her former role as chef at the dinner parties we both liked to give. We went to the theater, though she must have understood few words. We went dancing. We returned to Europe several times. I bought her childhood summer home and became an avid gardener.

"Although I used to fantasize that one day she would be able to talk again, her speech did not improve. In her frustration, she sometimes lashed out at me, pinching and scratching and drawing blood. A few years ago, I joined a support group for spouses of the head-injured. I went places without her more frequently.

"After ten years, I had to make a change that I hoped would benefit both of us. A nearby residence for the handicapped offered to take her. The day before she was to move, she suffered a stroke. For the last year, she has been in a nursing home.

"In spite of all the pain we have suffered, I still see my wife as a gift from God. Without her patience, I would never have known love. Without her injury, I would never have known life."

I watched Jim, a handsome and talented architect on Beacon Hill, as he lovingly cared for his wife, bringing her to church every Sunday and to retreats, to dinners and social occasions, with the respect and consideration due any well-loved mate. He not only never complained or asked for sympathy about a situation that many if not most men would have found too great a burden, but rather, he bore himself with dignity, graciousness, and love. That, to me, was indeed a miracle.

THE LOVE OF FELLOW PRISONERS

Billy J. Griffin

Billy Griffin helps in counseling fellow prisoners at Sing Sing. He says "I want to give back something so I can feel redeemed."

"Last January I was gravely ill. My face grew to twice its size, and I had a fever over 104 for more than a week. I couldn't breathe without difficulty, and when I did, it was accompanied by a rattling sound coming from deep inside my chest. I lost ten pounds in less than three days. The medical staff of the prison was reluctant to give me anything but aspirin, and said I had the flu. But I knew better.

"I bounced between consciousness and deep sleep. The guys on my housing unit became my nurses and doctors. They fed me, bathed me, cleaned my cube, and made home-style medications. They even took turns checking on me throughout the days and nights, often asking if I were still alive. Looking back now, I'm sure I wore the death mask that went along with the stench of death even I could smell.

"One night I woke with a dream. Someone was sawing my neck with a penknife. The knife was dull, and it was taking forever. I could not feel the pain, but I felt the strains of tissue being severed. I knew that if I didn't wake up before my assailant finished, I would die in my sleep. I had to do something, but I found I had no control. I couldn't move. But I was breathing with that rattling sound, so I concentrated on that.

"With every breath I tried to make a sound. And the sounds grew louder. Soon I was moaning until it was a scream. Everyone but the most hardened sleeper woke and ran to my bed. They called to me, and in an instant the dream popped and I was wide awake. Once everyone was satisfied that I was OK, I realized I felt better. The fear was gone.

"The next few days the guys teased me about waking them up in the middle of the night. Then the medical staff finally got around to having a doctor look at me. After a thorough examination I was sent for X rays. I was immediately put on medication. Even before the X ray results were back, they knew I'd contracted TB. I had survived a major case of TB without medical attention. It was the love of fellow prisoners, guards, and that spiritual spark of inner awareness that woke me within the dream and brought me back from death's door."

"AT LEAST THEY DON'T USE STRAITJACKETS ANYMORE"

Jay Neugeboren

The author of *The Stolen Jew: Before My Life Began,* and other novels and stories, Jay Neugeboren is now working on a book about his brother, Robert. He has raised three children as a single parent and is writer in residence at the University of Massachusetts in Amherst.

"My brother Robert has spent most of his life, since the age of nineteen, in mental hospitals and psychiatric wards in and around New York City. Until the time of his first breakdown in 1962, Robert had been a delightful, popular, and gifted boy and young man—talented at dancing, acting, and singing, invariably winning the lead in the school and camp plays and skits. He was a good if erratic student in high school, won a New York State Regents Scholarship to college, and successfully completed his freshman year at City College. Until his breakdown he showed no signs (except for those that, looking back, any of us might find in ourselves) that such a breakdown was at all likely, much less inevitable.

"Robert's diagnosis has changed frequently in the past thirty years, depending largely on which drugs have been successful in keeping him calm, stable, or compliant. He was schizophrenic when enormous doses of Thorazine and Stelazine calmed him; he was manic-depressive (bipolar) when lithium worked; he was manic-depressive-with-psychotic-symptoms or hypomanic when Tegretol or Depakote (anticonvulsants) or some new antipsychotic or antidepressant promised to make him cooperative; and he was schizophrenic (again) when various doctors promised cures through insulin coma therapy or megadose vitamin therapy or gas therapy.

"During these years, Robert also participated in a long menu of therapies: group therapy, family therapy, multigroup family therapy, Marxist therapy, Gestalt therapy, psychoanalytically oriented psychotherapy, goal-oriented therapy, art therapy, milieu therapy, et al. Most often, though—the more chronic his condition, the truer this became—he received no therapy at all. It is as if the very history of the way in which our century has dealt with those it calls mentally ill has, for more than thirty years now, been passing through my brother's mind and body.

"Though I could talk about what I thought had caused Robert's condition, long term and short term, the more important question, it seemed to me, wasn't what had caused his latest breakdown or any of the others but what, given his life, had enabled him to survive, and to do more than survive—to leave the wards and live in a halfway house, to visit me and my family, mostly without incident, to go with me on trips to places like Atlantic City. Most important, what enabled him to retain his generosity, his warmth, his humor, and his sense of self? This, it seemed to me, was the true miracle and mystery.

"At least, I say to Robert, they don't use straitjackets anymore. When I say this, we both laugh and talk about the time he asked a friend visiting him at Creedmoore if she could take his dirty clothes home for him and get them washed. The friend took Robert's laundry bag to a Chinese laundry and started removing the clothes, only to find that mixed in with the dirty socks and underwear was Robert's straitjacket.

"'In the old days it was straitjackets and wet sheets and electricity,' Robert says, 'and now, I guess, it's isolation and injections.'

"I asked Robert why he thought it was that he had survived when so many others he knew, from Creedmoore and Mid-Hudson and South Beach and Hillside, never got out, or killed themselves, or deteriorated to the point of no return. Had it ever occurred to him to wonder why, despite all he had been through and all the drugs and therapies that had been poured into him, he had not gone under? Why was he able, three decades after his first breakdown (when he tried to kill our father; when he hallucinated extravagantly; when he believed he was being taken, by ambulance, to my funeral; when he tried to chew his tongue out of his mouth; when he was straitjacketed and shot up with large doses of Thorazine; when he had catatonic seizures), to make a life for himself that was so much better than often seemed likely?

"'Well, I had wonderful parents!' he exclaimed. He laughed, then was silent for a while. When he spoke again, his voice was warm, thoughtful. 'I just wanted to survive and persist,' he said. 'That's all. And—I don't know—but it's like Faulkner said in the speech he made, for the Nobel, remember? I wanted to *endure* somehow. I never really wanted to stay on the wards, but I'd get there, and the minute they locked the door on me, I would think, Oh my God! I've got to get out of here! But then I'd throw fits and stuff.'

"'And also,' he added smiling, 'because my brother didn't want to keep visiting me in hospitals.'"

"I LIFTED UP MY ARM AND NOTHING WAS THERE"

Lloyd Kantor

Lloyd Kantor is a Vietnam veteran and political activist who is "determined to stop all foreign wars." He opposed the Gulf War and the sending of U.S. troops to Somalia and Haiti. He and his wife have been living in Tucson, Arizona, since 1980.

"In Vietnam I walked into a booby trap, a mine. There was an explosion, and I was yelling for help. I lifted up my arm and nothing was there. I lost both arms above the elbow and both legs above the knee and one eye. I heard other explosions, as other booby traps went off. One of my buddies was killed and another wounded. I was able to talk, so I knew I was alive. They got me into a helicopter, and when I got to the hospital, they didn't say much. They didn't say I'd live. I was in the hospital in Japan for two weeks, and then they flew me to the States, and to Walter Reed Hospital.

"I was optimistic. I was twenty-three. My mother came to see me in the hospital and gave me a piece of advice. She told me I should tell Loretta, my girlfriend from college, that she was free to marry someone else. That hadn't occurred to me. I thought we'd just go on together. When I saw Loretta, I said she was free to go off with someone else. She said that hadn't even occurred to her. So I'm luckier than most people. We both wanted to get married to each other, and we did.

"It's a miracle that she was who she was. She made everything possible over the years. It flowed. One thing flowed to another.

"When I got out of Walter Reed, we moved to Mount Vernon, New York, where I was from, and we got a great apartment near the Veterans Administration Hospital.

"In spite of what people said, we were determined to make it work. A lot of people were against it. My wife's family didn't speak to her. A lot of people were mean, cruel. But we were determined. We traveled. We went to Europe. We went to Paris on our honeymoon. I was carried here, dragged there, slung over people's shoulders, but it was worth it. Another time we went to Rome. Later on we went to Tahiti.

"We did what we wanted. We're able to live on the veteran's disability benefits. A lot of people in my situation would have to spend most of that money on nurses, special help, and treatment, but my wife did all those things; she did everything, so we were able to do what we wanted to do. Some people seemed angry that we didn't have regular jobs. My wife gave up a job, a career, to do all this.

"'Why don't you work?' some people asked me and my wife. They asked me, 'What do you do?' I'd say, 'I'm retired.' That was really true, because I'd joined the army, and when I was discharged I was retired.

"Actually we did, and continue to do, volunteer work. We worked to get things done in Mount Vernon. We got ramps put in city hall, we got an elevator in the library, a memorial with the names of local men killed in Vietnam. We worked in politics. Politicians wanted my endorsement.

"I was blessed with a capacity to have a wide range of interests. Luckily one of them isn't playing football! I like books, radios, politics (I was a political science major in college). I didn't have to stop or give up my interests. I have a crystal set I was using just now. My wife was in the college orchestra—she plays the violin, the guitar. We go to concerts.

"I pity someone with no interests. People ask us, 'What do you do all day?' I find it offensive. The people who ask that can't understand that we're not just as boring as they are. They never heard of books or making intelligent conversation!

"All in all, things have worked out well. I have to believe it has to do with God. I haven't given up on that—that we're not all alone. But my wife and I are not formally religious.

"A lot of things have made my life great. It wasn't an accident. Being here, all that's happened—this is my destiny."

"HE GAVE ME STRENGTH"

Loretta Kantor

Loretta Kantor has been active in community politics and with her husband, Lloyd, has worked to oppose foreign wars. She is writing a book about her husband called *Private War, Personal Victory.*

"I was initially attracted to Lloyd when I met him in college because he was happy with life. He had that kind of outlook, he was upbeat. I wasn't used to it! He had such a vibrancy and enthusiasm. He gave me strength. When he came back from Vietnam, with no arms and legs, we got an on-slaught of opinion. We decided, 'Screw everybody!'

"Our life is nonstop busy—hectic. We see people all the time. We have two dogs and a cat, and we had a horse, who just died, but he was thirty years old.

"Lloyd's upbeat attitude is totally unchanged. He's got an internal strength. *He's* the miracle."

Chapter 6

MIRACLES
OF CREATION

Of all human endeavors, creative work seems by its very nature the
most miraculous. After writing five novels, ten nonfiction books,
a television series, several movie scripts, hundreds of magazine
articles, stories, and reviews, and "teaching" writing at some of the best
places, including the Iowa Writers Workshop and the Bread Loaf Writers
Conference, it seems obvious to me that writing ability is given rather
than learned. Discipline is learned, technique may be learned, but stories,
thoughts, ideas "come to us." And through us. We are simply the instruments, the transcribers, the channels through which the ideas and stories
move into the world.

One of the most common questions writers are asked is, Where do
you get your ideas? With other writers, I laugh at the question, the naïveté
of the questioner, but maybe we laugh out of nervousness, because the
fact is we don't know. If we are honest, we have to confess we didn't make
them up out of the blue, we didn't learn some technical procedure for
bringing them forth.

When I lived in Boston, someone asked me, "Where do you get your
ideas?" I said, "Walking down Charles Street." I wasn't kidding. That's the
main drag of the Beacon Hill neighborhood, and it was there one day
while I was walking along, just past Gary Drugs and before coming to the
Book Store at the corner of Chestnut, that a picture came into my mind
of a boy sitting on a roof with a pair of binoculars, scanning the sky for
enemy airplanes. The boy was me when I was ten and eleven years old

and was a Cub Scout "plane spotter" during World War II. I had learned the outlines of the dread machines of the Luftwaffe, the Messerschmidt, the Stuka—even the names sounded evil. The fact that I lived in Indianapolis did not deter me or my friends from scanning the skies for enemy aircraft. We thought Indianapolis was a prime target of the Nazis—wasn't it the very heart of the country? If you could knock out Indianapolis, wouldn't you have dealt a near fatal blow to democracy?

That image of the boy on the roof in Indianapolis with his binoculars stuck with me and served as the germ of the story for a novel titled *Under the Apple Tree* about a boy growing up in that era whose older brother goes to war. I had no older brother, but the kid in the story did. How did I know? I *saw* him.

This kind of "vision" or visible presence or appearance of a character or image is hardly unusual for authors. It is described beautifully by the poet Marilyn Nelson Waniek in an essay in the magazine *Image:* "It has often happened that poems have suddenly appeared whole for me before I've started to write them. These 'appearances' have usually been visual: a network of images which I then simply describe . . . or dreams in which my ancestors told me the story of their lives, or words or rhymes. The muse-experience has always been for me an experience of the numinous, the mysterious."

Lest anyone think writing a novel, a story, or a poem is easy, however, that all you have to do is sit back and wait for a miracle, Ms. Waniek realistically explains that "we must work to prepare ourselves for the muse by reading and writing in a strict and serious regimen, and even after a moment of inspiration there usually remains draft after draft to be done before a piece is finished. But being silent, being at prayer, invoking the muse, is like fighting your way to the bottom of a room filled with water."

After I had those first images of the boy on the roof and his older brother given to me, there followed days, weeks, and months of pedestrian plodding as I wrote, rewrote, waited, crossed out, began again, squeezed out several sentences, then a paragraph, then whole pages that were usable, and toward the end as always it began to take off and soar, to move like automatic writing that I was simply transcribing—but that I had prepared for, invoked, cleared the way for by the discipline of daily attack on the typewriter.

These typical creative patterns are perhaps helpful in studying any kind of "miracle"—as the Hindu nun Sister Chandru says, "You don't just wait."

Each creative experience is different, and some work seems more freely "given," or, as the great German poet Rainer Maria Rilke said, "dictated." In a letter to a friend he explained that "in the way they arose and imposed themselves on me, the *Sonnets to Orpheus* are perhaps the most mysterious, most enigmatic dictation I have ever endured and achieved; the whole first part was written in a single breathless obedience, between the 2nd and 5th of February 1922, without one word being in doubt or having to be changed."

Acknowledging the miraculous nature of such an experience, Rilke said, "How can one help growing in reverence and endless gratitude, through such experiences."

Some authors are clearer than others as vessels, as conduits of the message they are given to pass on. In *The Secular Journal of Thomas Merton* the Trappist monk and author wrote, "When William Blake told somebody his poems were dictated to him by the angels, he did not mean that all other poetry was merely written by men, and was therefore inferior to his own. On the contrary, he meant that all good poetry was dictated by the angels, and that he himself could not claim any particular praise for the poems he had written because they were not exclusively his own."

The way such gifts, visions—miracles—of creativity come to and through painters and musicians as well as writers is shared here by creative workers who regard their experience as miraculous. The creators I spoke with all expressed this feeling of being an instrument, of the work "coming through" them. A novelist tells how the new idea for a novel "erupted" in him. A sculptor speaks of how you need the skills of your art, but "you come to a point where something else takes over, where something is coming out of you that is not you." You, the artist, are simply the channel through which the art comes.

A writer tells of her knowledge that the difficult work she is doing "is coming through me," that she didn't choose her painful subject matter but realizes she is "in service" to a force greater than herself. A musician describes how a Native American flute "directed him" in the composition of a musical piece, and a famous singer-songwriter tells about the words and music to the best song she's ever written pouring out in only two sessions. Like the writer's idea for a new novel, the song seems to have "erupted" in her.

These are the testimonies of those whose privilege it is to be the transmitters of the words, pictures, and sounds that inspire, inform, and heal us.

"THIS ART ERUPTED!"

Hugh Nissenson

A novelist and author of *The Tree of Life* and *The Elephant and My Jewish Problem*, Hugh Nissenson is currently working on his next novel, *Song of the Earth*. After meeting and talking with him at a book publication party, I was so moved by his understanding of and interest in the spiritual dimension of life, and how it manifests in Judaism, that I asked him to speak at a conference I was cochairing at Auburn Theological Seminary. His talk and dialogue with participants was one of the highlights of the event. He lives with his wife on the Upper West Side of New York City, where I met him for afternoon tea.

"I'm in the middle of an immense enterprise—a novel—and I've allowed my imagination to take me where it will. I've surrendered to it. One thing haunts me: I'm afraid to talk about this for fear I'll put a hex on it. I worked till one-thirty last night and woke at six because I solved a problem and wanted to keep going. When it's happening this way, you are for a moment taking part in the life of the universe.

"The novel takes place in the twenty-first century, and its about an artist. I've always wanted to write an original novel about an artist. The problem with novels about artists is that the work of the artist is never dramatized: You never hear music in *Dr. Faustus,* or read Orlando's poetry, or see Lilly Briscomb's painting. You believe in Dedalus as the artist in *Portrait of the Artist as a Young Man* because he's an artist to be—Joyce is ten years away from creating *Ulysses.* You take it on Joyce's word that Dedalus becomes an artist.

"I decided to take a shot at writing a novel about a visual artist. I've been drawing all my life, but up to that time the only things I'd ever done to be viewed by the public were five illustrations for my novel *The Tree of Life.* I said to myself, 'I've gotta try.' It's a terrific prospect. I decided to paint the artist's paintings and put them in the book so the reader could see them. My character's name is Baker, so I decided I'd do thirteen paintings—a Baker's dozen.

"It took me three years to do these things. I was flabbergasted that I could do it. I drew as a kid, but I never went to art school. I taught myself to draw from the comics; but now I had to do it to carry the story of the novel.

"This art *erupted* in me. It took me a year of desperate struggle to get to it, and for the last two years I've been seized by this experience. Whence it comes and how the problems I present to myself are resolved I have no idea. I'm in a constant state of heightened anxiety: I live in perpetual fear the damn thing will close, the conduit close. The pain of making the journey inward is always excruciatingly difficult—confrontation with the self—which means for me confrontation with God. It's trying to make sense of what seems a meaningless slaughterhouse.

"I feel privileged to have lived long enough and been lucky enough to allow this to happen. The older I get, the more interesting life gets, and the more mysterious and filled with wonder. This is related to the sense that every day is miraculous and to the mystery that life comes out of death and decay. I believe all creation comes out of an awareness of death. One of the characters in my novel writes in a poem, 'Death, you are my indispensable enemy.' It's true, you know."

"THIS IS THE BEST DAY I'VE EVER HAD!"

Ann Honig Nadel

Ann Honig Nadel is a sculptor who lives in Mill Valley, California. Her exhibition "Scrolls," eighteen freestanding eight-foot-high columnar forms inspired by the Torah scroll, opened at the Jewish Museum of San Francisco in 1994. She has also had solo exhibitions at Bluxome Gallery, San Francisco; Irene Drori Gallery, Los Angeles; Earl McGrath Gallery, Los Angeles; the Graduate Theological Union, Berkeley; and Temple Emanu-El, San Francisco.

❧

"In college I majored in philosophy, but I decided to take an art class. I had no previous training in art—I took it cold. The first thing we did was a still-life drawing. There was a bowl of fruit on a table, and they gave us a white sheet of paper and a piece of charcoal and said, 'Draw.' Without the faintest idea of how to do it, I just dove into the paper. An hour or so later I looked at what I had and said, 'This isn't so bad.' I have no idea where it came from.

"Whenever I go to the edge, when I take that risk—like 'diving in'—I get it. You have to be awake to sustain the creative force when it's there. I constantly tap into nature: I look at birds, flowers, water. From my studio window I look at water. I don't try to analyze it, I don't know the scientific principle of gravity, but I can express it in art. Many of my forms come from observing nature.

"I was in a ski boat on Lake Tahoe early one morning, and I looked up at the sky and saw the sun hit the water and a rainbow emerge. It was inspiring. The rainbow encompassed everything there was. I realized I wanted to do a rainbow. All this came to me in about half a second, yet it was so powerful that it lasted two years, while I made the sculpture—a series of bronze circles that represents the interaction between man and his environment. This is Noah's rainbow covenant at the end of the twentieth century, and it brings to mind our commitment to preserve the earth.

"I didn't think I could be an artist, a sculptor. The process becomes a great feeling. You're not just following your bliss; your bliss is right *there,* inside you. It's a narcotic, a turn-on. It's the best-kept secret in the whole world. That's why artists go into their studio and lock the door!

"I think creating art is God's gift—it's not the skills. You have to work to learn the skills first, but then you come to a point where something else takes over, where something is coming out of you that's not you. It comes too often not to see that deep inside, humans are creative.

"That hooked me. When that feeling first came, I thought, 'This is the best day I've ever had!' This thing, this force, it's independent of what man is, it has nothing to do with your background, how much money you have, where you went to school. It's truly democratic. Talent is a great equalizer. It gives you opportunity. It's a very powerful feeling.

"When artists think *they* do it—create their art—I question that. In my heart of hearts, I know 'I' don't do it. This is a miracle. It's the only reason I believe in God.

"When I talk about God, I don't mean something 'out there,' beyond us. I don't think there's an omnipotent God or a vengeful God. I don't think of myself as 'religious' in a formal sense. The only thing in Judaism I accepted is the idea of monotheism—the sense that everything is one, is part of a whole.

"That authentic feeling I get through art, that sense that something is happening through me, is like having a baby. I had both my children naturally—the Lamaze method—and it gave me the sense of being beyond my body, beyond my mind, a feeling of being myself. It's a miraculous experience. There comes a point when you're so close to death that you go into life. It's this way in art when you get out of your body and let it flow.

"I have to do art or I'll die. It is a reason to be. People understand this in others even if they don't have it themselves. They know that it's magic.

"I feel I'm part of the collective mind that goes back to the very beginning. The cave at Lascaux is religious art in this sense. Regardless of religion or background or genetic pool, we can do this because we're human."

"A PLACE FILLED WITH VOICES"

Marcie Hershman

Although Marcie Hershman had written stories, reviews, and essays in *Ms.* magazine, the *Boston Globe,* and other publications, none of the three novels she had written had been published when she went to Germany in 1987. It was there she got the idea for *Tales of the Master Race,* her highly acclaimed "first novel" (first to be published, that is) and continued the same themes in her powerful next novel, *Safe in America.*

"I was born in 1951 in a pleasant suburb outside Cleveland; my immediate family was intact and secure. The idea of trying to imagine my way into, say, Szacsur, Hungary, where my grandmother's family had been rounded up by the Nazis, seemed to me born of the worst sort of hubris. The slaughter that we have since neatly organized under the single label *Holocaust* could only be further profaned by being made into that polished thing called art.

"But silence isn't a way of maintaining a comfortable distance. Even when its intention is to honor, it doesn't absolve us of struggling to work out other, productive ways to respond. I learned that the day my brother telephoned on his way to Munich.

"I had never wanted to visit Germany. But Robert wasn't going as a tourist. He was going to film a segment for CBS's *West Fifty-Seventh* about the White Rose.

"The White Rose was a group of a dozen Munich university and high school students that distributed pamphlets against the Nazi regime. Caught, five of them—four students and their professor—were tried as traitors and beheaded. The other young members, who would survive the war, were imprisoned.

"Rob gave me this summary, then popped out with, 'Do you want to meet me in Munich in two weeks?'

"I hesitated, frightened. When I stayed silent, he said, 'Listen, these people are some of the good ones. And they have part of the story.' It was a story that, although I believed it ultimately impenetrable, I wanted to know more about.

"Munich is a city preserved, and what buildings had been destroyed in the Second World War were often rebuilt to exact duplication. The streets of the old city center were splashed with sun that last week in June. Yet my mind kept turning back forty and fifty years, to a darker time.

"It wasn't so much what I saw in Munich as what I heard. As in Jerusalem, the past wouldn't rest. Munich is a place filled with voices—echoing between the curve-walled streets and the massive stone plazas. The sharp report of guns, the shouts of fear, the stealthy beat of footsteps, the massed cries of triumph, the single entreaty—these don't quite ever dissolve. The silence was full of voices still calling out for attention, just as the buildings—new and strong—duplicated a landscape long ago reduced to rubble.

"The people I met in those streets looked pleasant and ordinary. They moved around Munich the way I did Boston: going from grocer's to cleaner's, pausing to chat or to offer directions.

"When I returned to Boston, I thought I should write something based on the White Rose. Yet try as I might, month after month, whatever I wrote seemed forced. If I wanted to try to speak about 'the mystery in the center' in the Holocaust, then I couldn't just listen to this one extreme of the scale of human action, as hopeful and full of drama as it was.

"I began to sit quietly. I needed to recall that as I walked the reconstructed München streets I could hear myself thinking: That man I'm passing would have been in his twenties back then; was he in the army? This woman in Passau watching the TV crew, had she seen her neighbors taken away?

"I was being drawn to the voices of 'ordinary' German—Aryan—experience. Perhaps it was that my own life was grounded in the 'ordinary' day to day. In Germany I had already started to hear what the silence of the average citizen had to say—finally, sadly, impossibly—about the crucial years 1933–45.

"I imagined a town, midway between Munich and Passau. In the basement of its police station was one of the Nazis' eleven guillotines—all used solely on Aryans; out on the brick streets was a threat of the silence this brought. Still, 'Kreiswald' (the town I imagined for the novel) seemed gay, strung with flags and full of activity. I halted at Forty-two Ludwigstrasse. This was the flat of the police file clerk and his wife.

"'*Bitte?*' I said when the door opened. The young couple, startled, stepped aside. I admitted I had some questions.

"For three years, my questions didn't stop. No matter where I was in 'Kreiswald'—inside this house or that, out in the fields or along a parade route—someone always showed up, bringing neighbors.

"Inevitably, persistently, my work gathered shape. The town's voices, full of secrets, seemed so loud.

"When I went to Germany it felt like I was opening a big door, and I walked through it. On the other side was a world I couldn't ignore—it was in the past, yet very much alive. I couldn't forget I'd walked through that door.

"In the Bible the miracles aren't confined to blessings of joy. Some are about evil and how to confront it rather than turn away from it. That's what writing this novel was like. Even though I had to work hard and struggle with the writing, I feel it was 'given.' It transcended my own life. I didn't know where it was coming from.

"When I finished my next novel, *Safe in America,* about people like those in my family who came to America and confronted new kinds of challenges and losses, I realized while I was on the way to the airport to pick up Mom and Dad that the book would come out on the fiftieth anniversary of the end of the Second World War. Fifty years ago people were learning about their relatives who had been in the death camps, learning of those who died and the few who survived—like the people in my book.

"I don't know what I'm in service to, but I know this work is 'coming through me,' and I thought: 'Why *me?* I was born in Shaker Heights!'"

FINDING THE VOICE OF THE FLUTE

David Amram

David Amram is a composer and performer of astounding range who plays the French horn, piano, guitar, flutes, whistles, and drums and has written music for every kind of circumstance, from a concert of the Philadelphia Orchestra to the soundtrack of the Beat generation cult movie *Pull My Daisy,* starring Jack Kerouac, Allen Ginsberg, and Amram himself. He has

played with jazz greats such as Dizzy Gillespie, Sonny Rolli
Mingus and was the first composer-in-residence with the N
harmonic. Little wonder the *Boston Globe* calls him the Renaiss
American music. To have the pleasure of knowing this man is
why the author Nat Hentoff describes him as "a ubiquitous de
good cheer."

"I was asked by the solo oboist of the Philadelphia Orchestra, John deLancie, to write a piece of music during the Bicentennial for Eugene Ormandy to present. He said, 'I'd like to have it be for oboe and a mezzo soprano voice, I think they'd make a beautiful sound together. Try to see if you can come up with something.'

"I said I'd like to do it, and he called back and said the Rittenhouse Square Women's Council would commission the piece, and Ormandy agreed to do it for '77. He said, 'Do anything you want,' but he had to know soon what it would be. I was thrilled—I was born in Philadelphia, I'd heard that orchestra as a child. I knew the oboist the piece would be dedicated to—Marcel Cabitau—who was a friend of my father's in the twenties. It was a dream come true, but with all the other writing, conducting, and jazz I was playing at the time, I didn't know how I'd have time to do it.

"I'd been playing for six years then with American Indian musicians at benefits, and the idea came that maybe I could write a piece based on the traditional Native American music I'd learned. I'd played backup for Floyd 'Red Crow' Westerman (since *Dances with Wolves* he's now an actor, but he was known as a great folksinger and speaker for Native American rights).

"The orchestra needed to know what the piece was about in two weeks to be able to schedule it for the next year, and I thought I'd like to do something with Native American poetry and prayers, but I had no idea how to get at it or get it down on paper and to the orchestra in that time. Gus Greymountain came to town and invited me to a party. I told him what I needed and he said, 'That's why I'm here.' He had an oral history of Native American struggle, including a Navajo prayer. I took 'Song of the Sky Loon' from that material, and when Floyd Westerman came to again and he had more for me, I said it must be ESP, and he said, 'No, it's the moccasin grapevine.'

"By the end of the week I had enough to give something to the orchestra—the idea for the composition. Then I had to write it. I went to the Music Inn on West Fourth Street in Greenwich Village. Floyd said the owner had something for me—it was a Sioux flute made by Richard Foolbull, an old-timer. He was the last of the Sioux flutemakers. That flute helped me write the piece. I'd take the flute and play it, and it was almost like it directed me where to go. I wrote a piece called 'Trail of Beauty,' and Ormandy conducted it in '77.

"The inspiration came through that flute. I've had an instrument give me an idea before, for writing a certain part of a piece—a passage or a phrase, like a 'hot lick' in jazz—but with this flute it was different. It was as if I could hear it as a voice. Later a Native American told me they felt every instrument had a voice—the player had to find the voice of the instrument. If you can't find it, you should give it away to someone else."

"WRITING THAT SONG WAS EMPOWERING"

Judy Collins

I was inspired by Judy Collins's voice and songs when I first heard her back in the 1960s. When I had the good fortune to meet her in the 1990s, I found her to be as genuine, insightful, beautiful, and life affirming as her music. Of the many people I know who are overwhelmed with work, demands, and obligations, she is surely the most generous in sharing her time and ideas.

"I was preparing music and getting the band ready for a big concert in Colorado at the Opera House in Aspen in '89. I'm really related to the state—we moved there when I was ten, my mother still lives there. I've skied there in winters, gone there in summers for many years. My father's ashes are scattered at Fern Lake Lodge there, a lodge I ran in '59.

"The whole state has a real ring for me. When I'm there, it's like a meditation. In fact I just spent last week in Estes Park—it's the most nurturing place I know.

"A month before that concert in '89 I began noodling on the piano and a song came. I wrote this song in four hours one night and two hours the next night, and it's the best song I've ever written—'The Blizzard.' Writing that song was very empowering. It really energized all my feelings, the intensity of my feelings about the place in my life Colorado occupies.

"I sang it in Aspen, and it's become the centerpiece of my current concert. I love the story of transformation in the song. The woman in the song goes with a stranger, tells him her life story, and spends the night. We don't know if their relationship is ever consummated. She shares her grief, and the next morning when she wakes up, she's transformed.

"Things happen like that overnight. You wake up and see the sun shining, and you are in fact a different person. I had that experience again last week when I woke up and looked at Long's Peak. It's like a daily reprieve. Now we can be refreshed. It really is miraculous."

These are the words to "Colorado (The Blizzard)":

Colorado, Colorado
When the world leaves you shivering
And the blizzard blows,
When the snow flies and the night falls
There's a light in the window and a place called home
At the end of the storm.

One night on the mountain I was headed for Estes
When the roads turned to ice and it started to snow,
Put on the chains in a whirl of white powder,
Half way up to Berthed near a diner I know
And the light burned inside,
Shining down through the snowfall
God it was cold and the temperature droppin',
Went in for coffee and shivered as I drank it,
Warmin' my hands in the steam as it rose.

Sitting there at the counter was a dark headed stranger,
me and the owner and him keepin warm,

Nodded hello and I said it's a cold one
Looks like there might be a blizzard tonight—
And "yes," said the owner, "there's a big storm on the mountain,
Good thing we're open, we could be here for hours
There's nothing for miles and it's too late to get to Denver,
Better not try for the summit tonight."

And the snow fell, and the night passed
And I talked to the strangers while the blizzard blew.

Me and the stranger, you know I don't talk to strangers,
I'm a private sort of person but a blizzard is a blizzard,
And somehow I found myself saying you'd left me,
Tellin' him everything I wanted to say to you.
You know how it is when you can talk to a stranger,
Someone you're quite sure you'll never see again—
Soon we were laughin', and talkin', and drinkin'
He said, "You must know you're too good for him."

And the snow fell and the night passed
And I talked to the stranger while the blizzard blew.

The stranger said "love, it can cry you a river—
Me, I'm a loner cause I can't take the heartache
and sometimes I'm a fighter when I get too much whiskey—
Here have a little whiskey, pretend you don't give a damn—
My cabin's up here on the side of the mountain
You can go up there and sleep through the blizzard."
I put on my parka, said goodbye to the owner
Followed the stranger through the snow up the mountainside.

Woke in the morning to the sun on the snow,
My car was buried in six feet of snow drifts,
They dug me out, just the owner and the stranger,
Sent me on my way when the snowplow had been by
And the roads were all clear and the sun on the mountains
Sparkled like diamonds on the peak to peak highway—
Then I knew that I would get over you,
Knew you could leave me but you'd never break me.

Colorado, Colorado
When the world leaves you shivering

And the blizzard blows,
When the snow flies and the night falls
there's a light in the window and a place called home
At the end of the storm.

Creativity does not begin and end with works of art. The creative force, the creative spirit, has no boundaries; it operates in all areas of life. Too often we confine the possibilities of our creativity to the page, the canvas, the musical instrument, believing that circumstance or fate creates our daily lives, abdicating our experience to forces over which we have no control. One way miracles occur is when we realize we have some say in the matter, that the same creative power that enables us to sing, tell a story, paint a picture, is also there to be used for creating our work and play, our professional and personal lives.

The spirit of that approach—that opportunity for creation—was captured by Bach in the title of one of his compositions: "Christians, Inscribe the day!" Those who aren't Christian can substitute any identifying name or category they wish (Muslims, Americans, New Yorkers, Californians, women) and catch the spirit of the exhortation. Don't just lie there and let the day roll over. Make your own mark on the day—*inscribe* the day!

These stories illustrate how people use their creative powers to affect their own lives and circumstances. An exhausted novelist on a book tour discovers how to draw mental and physical refreshment from his natural surroundings. A Russian painter who is captured by the German army in World War II uses his art to engineer his survival and eventual escape. Through faith and prayer a Muslim student helps bring rain to an area plagued by drought. None of these things was supposed to happen, the odds were against such occurrences; but in different ways, people created them. Miracles.

"THE TREE SMILED AT ME"

Bill Kotzwinkle

Bill Kotzwinkle is author of the novelization of the movie *E.T.* as well as a
list of original novels, including *Dr. Rat, The Fan Man,* and most recently
The Game of Thirty, a mystery. A student of the Kabbala and the *I Ching,*
and a practitioner of Tai Chi, Kotzwinkle lives on the coast of Maine with
his wife, the novelist Elizabeth Gundy. Kotzwinkle is one of the few writers I
know who uses his creative powers in his daily life as well as in his books, as
he relates here.

❧

"I was on a book publicity tour for my new novel *The Game of Thirty,* and
by the time I got to Los Angeles I was really feeling unfocused, mentally
frayed and jumbled. I went outside at the Bel Aire Hotel and got into the
yoga position called the tree posture to try to get myself rooted. As I stood
there on one leg with the foot of my other leg propped against the standing leg, and my hands in the air over my head, I wondered if this really
worked—does it really ground you, make you feel rooted when you seem
to be flying apart?

"Just at that moment, I looked at this huge tree that must be five hundred years old, with a trunk like iron, and the tree smiled at me and said,
'Brother, take a look at me!' I realized the paltriness of my human effort; I
was relativized in an instant, and it gave me a burst of creative energy.

"At the restaurant in the Stanford Court Hotel in San Francisco,
plants cover an entire wall. While I was sitting there being interviewed
again for the hundredth or so time on the tour, I was pulling energy out
of the plants—they get their energy directly from sunlight. All this mental
stuff was exhausting, so I became part of the awareness of the plants in
order to let my human awareness have a rest.

"In every city there's something to draw on to renew yourself. In
Chicago I went to this huge park, a gigantic green land. This great tree
lent its presence to me. It's a miracle that I've trained myself how to see it.
It's a doorway, a narrow focus out of our positions. I can always regroup
by doing that tree posture. Being in the posture, I wasn't alone, I was part

of a community of trees. Anyone can use these techniques—you can always find trees. Even if you can't, you can do the tree posture.

"Before I became aware of the trees outside the Bel Aire Hotel, I was puffed up like an author on tour, and I was thinking how 'my hot jazz' is here to stay. Then I realized that the trees I walked by had been there long before me and would be there long after my hot jazz was gone. So who's kidding who?

"I better understood human ego, and I applied this to insects, dragonflies, snails, their wholly other perception. I tried to be inside their perception to break down the rigidity of my own position. That's a miracle."

"FOR MY PICTURES I GOT BREAD AND ONIONS"

Alexander Lioutikoff ("Sachal")

I saw the recent paintings of "Sachal," born Alexander Lioutikoff, at an exhibit of Russian-born painters called "Splinters of a Collapsed Colossus" at the Opt Gallery in San Francisco. His work has also been displayed in galleries in New York, London, Madrid, and Málaga. Born in 1924, Sachal volunteered for the Red Army when he was seventeen and was captured by the Germans in a battle somewhere between the towns of Novo Rossiysk and Krasnodad. He was taken as a prisoner of war to a camp where with other prisoners he was assigned to hard labor. Trained as a painter at school in Moscow, he used his art to enable him to stay alive and then to escape from the prison camp and fight in the French Resistance. This is the story of how his art saved his life.

"I was a soldier in the Red Army fighting in the Caucasus when I was captured by the Germans in November of 1942. First we were taken to a transition camp in Frankfurt, and then I was sent to work in an iron ore mine in the Saar. I never knew how long it would be—in '42 no one knew how long the world would last, the way the Germans were marching in and conquering. Maybe five years? I was nineteen years old. My motto was 'Do as little work as possible and get as much food as possible.' I wasn't refusing work, but I was doing it inefficiently—with a smile. I was so bad at working in the mine that they sent me to work in the blacksmith shop. That was my break.

"The blacksmith asked me, 'What do you know how to do?' and I told him, 'I'm an artist; I draw and paint pictures.' He asked if I could make a picture of him from a photograph, and I said yes, of course. From the time I was twelve I'd drawn portraits of party leaders and Russian writers, poets—Stalin, Lenin, Pushkin. The blacksmith brought in a small picture of himself—a snapshot—and gave me pencils, crayons, and paper. I made this big, fine picture of him.

"He liked it, he was very pleased, and he asked me, 'What do you want, money?' I said, 'No, bread.' All we got to eat in the camp was one rutabaga a day—there weren't even potatoes—and a small piece of bread with margarine. They gave you ersatz coffee in the morning and a block of bread like a brick that you had to divide up among four people. It was supposed to last through the day, but we ate it all then, knowing if we left anything, someone would steal it.

"You can't imagine how hungry we were. We'd already been hungry in the Red Army. In the Caucasus, in the mountains, there was no food supply. We'd eat wild fruits and berries. At night they'd bring us a lump of sugar and a lump of bread.

"So I got more bread from the blacksmith. The word got around among the other Germans that I was a painter, and I'd done this picture of the blacksmith, so others brought in snapshots for me to make big pictures from, and I did. They brought me bread, and I asked them for onions, too. My gums were bleeding, and my teeth were coming loose, so I asked for onions. For my pictures I got bread and onions. I was lucky.

"I befriended a part-time blacksmith from Lorraine. He spoke dual languages, German and French; he wasn't a Nazi. I bragged that I could make him a sculpture, a bas relief, from marble, and he got me the tools and brought in a slab of marble. I'd studied sculpture in Moscow and I knew how to do this. I made him a bas relief of himself with this marble.

It made a big commotion—the foreman congratulated me. The Germans loved art, and this earned me their respect. I was still there as a slave, but now I was an artist slave.

"With the extra food I got stronger. I decided to escape. It was a small camp, maybe thirty or forty people, so security wasn't that tight. There were a lot of escapes, but everyone was caught by the border patrol, then they were beaten badly and brought back. This Lorraine blacksmith was also part of the border patrol. Because I'd become friendly with him, when I decided to escape from the camp, I asked him how I could find the border. He stood by the window. I remember it was drizzling outside; it was March. He pointed and said, 'That way, no. This way you have a chance.' I asked how I'd know the border. He said, 'When the forest finishes, there'll be a road and some bushes, and when you cross the road, you're over the border.'

"At five-thirty A.M. we went from the camp to the mines and the blacksmith shop. It was still dark, so you could fall out of line and roll into a ditch. Everyone was half asleep, apathetic. A friend and I did this. We got through the border and walked for a month, going from town to town, trying to head for the Pyrénées and Spain, then Gibraltar and Africa. That was our plan, but we got arrested by the gendarmes in Dijon and put into a French jail. I told the case officer the truth and begged him not to send me back to the Germans.

"In Dijon there were four buildings in the jail, three controlled by the Germans, and one was just French. He said not to worry and put me in the French jail. I made drawings there, too, for the prisoners, and I was paid in food. The prisoners got packages of food from their families. I was paid in fruitcake. I ate like a king.

"When I got out of that jail, I was let go on vagrancy charges and told to go to the police station and get an ID card. I never went to the police station. I joined the French Resistance.

"After the war I went to art school in Paris, then I came to America in '55. When I got a passport, I went to live in Spain for sixteen years and worked and painted. I came back to the United States and painted billboards to make money. I was called the Michelangelo of Highway 101. Six years ago I was able to quit and devote myself full-time to my own painting.

"I want to express what God built into me at the creation. I'm trying to center myself and express life—what's living inside me. I use images to get the feeling out. I want to know what the source of life is, not its problems. We create the problems, but we don't create life—that's given to us.

"Growing up in the Soviet Union—I was born seven years after the Revolution—I knew nothing of religion, of God. When I went to Paris after the war and met White Russian émigrés, they talked of God, religion, the Spirit. They gave me books—Ramakrishna, the Vedas, the Upanishads. In Soviet Russia all that was hidden from us. All I knew of religion was what I saw in paintings, religious paintings. This reading, and talking about spiritual things, opened me up.

"I went through all those horrors—the hardships of the Soviet Union, my mother battling the food shortages to keep me alive when I was a child, then the war, the prison camp, getting shot in the Resistance.

"There must be a reason why we live. We realize who we are through art, music, writing—to each is given his mission on this mysterious earth. This earth is a heaven in the whole universe—yes, this earth."

"WE BELIEVED IT
WAS GOING TO HAPPEN"
Khalid Siddiqi

Dr. Khalid Siddiqi is director of the Islamic Education and Information Center in San Jose, California. I had heard about him as an active and highly regarded participant in interfaith communication and alliances in the San Francisco Bay Area. I went to see him for background on the Islamic view of miracles and learned that Muslims have different words for what we call miracles, with different meanings. Only a miracle of Mohammed or other prophets is called *ayah;* but an extraordinary or supernatural event that is in line with the message of God can occur for a righteous person living anytime, in any society, anyplace, and that is called a *karamah.* I asked Dr. Siddiqi if he had ever witnessed a *karamah,* and he told me about taking part in creating such an event in nature.

"I am from southern India, and I went to study at Ashraful Madaaris, an Islamic institute for young people in a town called Hardoi in the north of India. It's a religious school, where you memorize the Koran and learn about Islam. I was a student, thirteen years old, when it was announced that people from the institute would perform a prayer for rain. There was a drought that had lasted a long time, and people were suffering. Representatives of various religious groups had come and tried to make it rain, through different rituals, but none had succeeded. The weather reports forecast no possibility of rain.

"The principal of our school told us that prayers for rain would be performed, and passages in the Koran to create such an occurrence would be read in a field before an audience. He announced that it would be effective only if for three days before the event all of us in the school would 'collect ourselves'—there could be no taking of other peoples' supplies, no backbiting—in other words, no sin. And we would have to pray. All of us took this seriously, believing that if we did, the rain would come.

"A large crowd gathered in an open field—including a lot of nonbelievers—to see what would happen. It was a hot, sunny day, and no clouds were in the sky. People from our school faculty read passages of the Koran and performed the prayers. Before they could finish, the people performing the prayers were all wet. It was raining! But they couldn't stop reading the sacred passages until the finish, so they stood out in the rain and continued to read until the end. The drought was over.

"Of course, we as students had done our part, so we weren't surprised. We *believed* it was going to happen.

"I've seen people cured from sickness, and I've seen the release of an evil spirit from a person when a righteous person was reading passages from the Koran to exorcise such a spirit.

"And I saw that drought ended by powerful prayers that brought rain."

Chapter 7

MIRACLES
OF ENCOUNTER

I sing the body electric instead of the stranded mind. . . .
For I've changed. One can change, I've learned that.

Walt Whitman

I've learned that too, and I've learned that the most significant changes
in my life, the empowering, enlarging, uplifting kinds of changes—
the ones that seem like miracles—have come about through encounters with other people. I don't just mean other people like myself. As
essential as close friends are to all of us, the truly liberating encounters
come when we open ourselves to people who are not so much like we are,
who come from different backgrounds or professions or fields of work,
who have different interests and styles and habits and worldviews, different incomes and colors and traditions.

I lived in a comfortable little niche I had made for myself in Boston,
composed mainly of other writers who shared many of the same opinions
and politics and who had similar tastes in music, literature, movies, bars,
and drinks. I didn't move out of that cocoon until I returned to church,
where I found myself in a new community, with a broad mix of people.
Because it was a Unitarian church with a complex historical background
("King's Chapel is Anglican in worship, Unitarian in theology, and Congregational in governance," the Sunday program said), there was even a
variety of religious belief, from Christian to humanist.

Becoming part of this community opened me up, led to greater openings, more daring exploration, a larger and deeper sense of connection with the world and with the spirit. I came to see that spirituality flourishes best, not in isolated communion with God on a lonely mountaintop, but in human community. On retreats and in prayer groups I experienced a new kind of sharing of spirit with people I hadn't known before and would probably have never met if I'd stuck in my familiar old circles, and I discovered a depth and fulfillment that was also new.

Countless Americans have found community in one of the varieties of twelve-step groups, which have helped bring about a new spiritual awareness—as well as sanity and freedom—to this society.

I met new groups and kinds of people in Tai Chi and yoga classes and in human potential seminars and courses as I stepped out of my old self-imposed enclosures. For a long time, however, I avoided any "men's groups." I didn't want to sit around with a bunch of guys beating tom-toms. I didn't want to learn how to cry. I was already good at that. I jeered and sneered at the possibility of finding anything worthwhile in an all-male process.

In 1992 I got a call from Rev. Bill Weber, whom I knew from the 1950s, when he was a minister of the East Harlem Protestant Parish and I was writing my book on that neighborhood, *Island in the City*. Bill was now running a program in religious education that the New York Theological Seminary sponsored for inmates at Sing Sing Prison in Ossining, New York. He had heard about my spiritual autobiography workshop and invited me to lead it for his class at Sing Sing.

As I sat at a table with sixteen prisoners, discussing life experiences, I felt tuned in to a new dimension of my own understanding. I was happy to accept an invitation to return, not only for the chance of serving a program I admired, but also sensing that this was part of my own spiritual path, my own growth and unfolding. I assumed it was because of the chance to move out again, into a realm that was unfamiliar to me with people of even more diverse backgrounds, cultures, and experience—and part of the feeling did come from that. But there was something else as well. One day as I sat exchanging views with these sixteen inmates, to whom I felt strongly bonded, it suddenly it struck me: This is my men's group!

Thoughts about the subject of community and its value to the spirit had been floating around in my mind when I came across an interview that told me what I was trying to see and understand. The interview was by one fine novelist with another fine novelist: Larry Woiwode, author of *Indian Affairs* and *Behind the Bedroom Door,* questioned his fellow North Dakota writer Louise Erdrich, whose novels include *The Beet Queen, Tracks,* and *Love Medicine,* for *Image: A Journal of Religion and the Arts.* Ms. Erdrich said, "I think we often don't meet each other because everyone lives in a contained world and tries to keep themselves safe. If you step across lines, you can meet anyone. What it takes is for each of us to go out and be part of one another's lives. It's a risk."

It's a risk to leave our safe little shells; yet the reward can be, well, miraculous. Life changing. Ms. Erdrich, whose intellectual courage and insight draw on her Native American heritage, points out that there is an even larger community to make connection with—the natural world beyond the human:

> *What makes sense to me is that there is a spiritual life in the landscape, and there's an emotional life around you that includes other forms of life. You may be projecting some of your self into it, but what's wrong with that? That's a Western idea: that you're you and it's it. I think we're connected and, however that's expressed, that's part of Native belief; that we are influenced and influence everything around us, down to the last stone.*

Life is encounters. When we're open, they come to us as we need them—or before we know we need them. People appear—seem almost at times to materialize—at the right time and place, with the right gift. A classic instance of such an occasion is told by the poet Elizabeth Bishop, who wrote this account of what she called "A Little Miracle" in her journal during a dreary winter in New York City in the midst of the Great Depression (January 10, 1935):

> *This morning I discovered I had forgotten to get any bread and I had only one dry crust for breakfast. I was resigning myself to orange juice and coffee and no more when the door-bell rang. I pushed the button, and up the stairs trailed a weary-looking woman, shouting ahead of*

herself: "I don't want to sell you anything—I want to give you some-
thing!" I welcomed her at that, and was presented with a small box con-
taining three slices of "Wonder Bread," all fresh, a rye, a white, and
whole wheat, also a miniature loaf of bread besides. . . . I breakfasted on
manna.

Later, this experience, transformed by other experiences, inspired the poem "Miracle for Breakfast."

These "miracles of encounter"—a phrase I was given by Father Gerry O'Rourke—are about transformations, of the self and others. Sometimes people are looking for such experience, are consciously seeking a new opening, a new path in their life, though they may not know exactly how or where to find it. One of the great spiritual themes is the search, told in stories from the quest for the Holy Grail to Somerset Maugham's novel *The Razor's Edge,* made into movies in the 1940s starring Tyrone Power and again in the 1980s with Bill Murray as the young man who leaves his home and travels through the world, studying, questioning, and seeking new experience in his quest for meaning.

Like Maugham's hero, who came home disillusioned by war after seeing combat while serving in the ambulance corps in World War I, a young man returned from service in the ambulance corps in World War II and started his own search for meaning. The right guide, he says, "dropped in my lap." A young man trying to find a way to use his skills in a meaningful career hears a talk by an executive whose values he admires and follows his guidance to create a fortune. Three different women encounter a teacher, a course of study, and a doctor who changes their lives.

Who knows who our own messengers will be and to whom we in turn may bring a life-transforming message? These stories remind us always to pay attention, to scorn no one.

Henri Nouwen, a Dutch theologian, priest, and author who lives at a L'Arche community called Daybreak, in Toronto, caring for disabled people, told how one member of the community continually asked him, "What are you doing here?" while another always smiles and says, "Welcome!"

"Do I regard these people as 'crazy,' as mentally deranged?" Father Nouwen asked an audience. He paused, then said with fervent emphasis: "Or do I see them as angels of God bringing me important messages—

making me continue to think about what I am doing here, reminding me that I'm welcome on the earth, in this life."

THE RIGHT GUIDE
Norm Eddy

I first got to know Rev. Norman Eddy in 1956, as I wrote my first book, *Island in the City: The World of Spanish Harlem*. Norm had come home from serving as an ambulance driver in World War II with solemn questions about his old values. He had had a transcendent experience one night in Africa, in which he saw the folly of humans and knew there was a power greater than that in the universe, a source he wanted to find and live by. But he didn't know how to begin.

Here he describes how he received much-needed direction from a wise guide, a writer named Signe Toksvig.

❦

"My encounter with Signe Toksvig—well, I'd never come across anybody else in the '40s who had her breadth of knowledge of world religions. That I should meet her two or three weeks out of the service was the miracle—having a guide dropped in my lap.

"Signe was married to Francis Hackett, and both were writers who met when they worked at the *New Republic*. They were neighbors of my grandfather Howard Hart on Martha's Vineyard.

"Signe was an immigrant who had come to America when she was twelve years old from Denmark. She went to work in a shirt factory as a child laborer in Troy, New York. She was discovered as a talented young writer at a YMCA and given money for a college scholarship. She wrote a book about this, called *Port of Refuge*.

"When I went to see her, she took me into her dining room, and she had laid out on the dining room table the books that were the spiritual classics of the world—the Bible, the Upanishads, the Baghavad Gita, Meister Eckhart, *The Cloud of Unknowing*—and many, many more. 'This will give you a start,' she said.

"I buried myself in those books, and then I began traveling, working on a farm in the Midwest, hitchhiking, staying in monasteries, and finally going to New York and enrolling in Union Theological Seminary."

Norm became one of a "group ministry" of young veterans of World War II who founded the East Harlem Protestant Parish, a series of storefront churches, and moved with their families to the neighborhood, raising their children there, becoming part of the life. Norm had started the first neighborhood committee to help narcotics addicts when I met him.

We've been friends ever since, and I have watched Norm move on through the years to other areas of need, always working with prayer, bringing others into the realm of prayer, walking through life in a way that his African American and Hispanic American friends and neighbors might rightly call "living large." He still lives and work in East Harlem, carrying on his creative, inspiring mission into politics, housing, recovery—whatever needs to be addressed and dealt with—through what he calls "acts of prayer."

"HE SAW SOMETHING IN MY EYES"

Jim Rosenfield

President of his own retail real estate brokerage and development company, Jim Rosenfield is also a "Big Brother" to a boy in the inner city. He graduated from the University of California at Berkeley, worked as an intern in Senator Edward Kennedy's office, writing speeches and papers on foreign policy, and won a Coro Fellowship in government. After his fellowship he moved back to Los Angeles, where he grew up, and went to work for former Senator John Tunney of California in his boutique business, the Cloverleaf Group.

"The part of the work I loved when I worked for John Tunney's business was leasing and setting up shopping centers. I asked myself, 'What are my passions?' They're business, politics, and the arts, and shopping centers incorporated all three. It's basically a business, but there's also the politics of getting the necessary permissions from the local community and working with local governments, and then there's the challenge of doing them in an artistically pleasing way. Yet I felt constricted in that field because those aspects of the business that I enjoyed weren't the principal interest of the firm I was working for.

"I saw an announcement of a one-day seminar at UCLA called 'The Shopping Center Game,' and I decided to go see what I could learn. There were about fifteen hundred people in the course, and I sat in the back row and never said a word. I didn't talk to anyone in the seminar.

"At the podium was a man named Steve Soberoff, who was conducting the course. He was showing pictures of shopping centers and explaining why some were good and some were bad, and in the midst of this he showed some pictures of his children, his family. The way he spoke about his life made me feel he wasn't just a successful businessman, he was a good person, a good human being, with good values. I thought if I stayed in that business I'd like to know him.

"I decided to try to talk to him, and a few days after the seminar I called him up out of the blue, introduced myself, and said I'd like to meet with him. He said, 'How about two o'clock?' I was shocked—'You mean two o'clock *today?*' I asked. He said yes, and I went to his office.

"We sat and talked for three hours in a garden behind his office, telling each other stories of our life. At the end he said, 'Your ideas about the shopping center business are good. Why don't you do them yourself?'

"I said, 'I'm twenty-four years old; I really don't know what I'm doing.'

"'What about doing it with me, letting me advise you?' he asked.

"I told him I didn't have any money to start my own business.

"'How much do you need to operate your own business for a year?' he asked me.

I said I didn't know, and he asked what I was getting paid then. I told him, and he nearly doubled that and said, 'You'll need this much more for a secretary and this much more for overhead.' He figured I needed a hundred thousand dollars to do this for a year, and he said he'd loan me the money. He said, 'Let's give it a year and see if you can make money.'

"I wasn't sure. It seemed too good to be true. But after thinking about it *a few more seconds* I said yes! My hesitation came from the fact that he had more trust in me than I did in myself or than I had in him. I didn't know anything about him except for the seminar and our talk.

"We met every Monday morning for a year, and I learned the business under his stewardship. But as the year's end approached, I felt that his patience was running short with me. I was nervous, I hadn't made a cent. I hated the thought of starting up my own business and then having to close it, so I thought I'd better do something desperate.

"I found a shopping center with a large building that was vacant in Fresno, and I told Steve Soberoff I was going to Chicago to try to get to see the top executives at Sears Roebuck and persuade them to put a store there. Steve said he'd pack my bags for me. I told him not to get his hopes up, I didn't think a miracle was going to happen. It was a desperation move, but I flew to Chicago and talked my way in to see the director of operations for Sears Roebuck. I said I just wanted to shake his hand. When I told him what I really wanted—to get Sears to open a store in this vacant building in Fresno—he told me he already had a store in Fresno, why did he need another one? I said, 'With all due respect, sir, Fresno is the fastest-growing area in California, and you need a second store there.' He told me I shouldn't even be in his office and politely threw me out by sending me to the director of real estate, whom he called up and told, 'If you were doing your job, this kid wouldn't be in my office.' So when I met *him* he was furious and he bawled me out.

"I went back thinking it was hopeless, but a few weeks later the real estate director called me and said they wanted to come out and look at the site. I sent them plane tickets to come to L.A. I was down to my last dollars and uncomfortably in debt. I had to take the last money out of my savings account to buy the plane tickets, but I knew I had the ball rolling now, and I couldn't let it stop.

"When they came out, they didn't like the loading dock at the site. I told them to give me their favorite plans for a state-of-the-art loading dock, and I'd build one for them that was even better—the best. I made the deal, we leased the store to Sears. This enabled us to buy the shopping center, which we later sold, making several million dollars' profit.

"I made more money in that one deal than I ever thought I'd make in my entire life, much less at that age, that quick. I was twenty-five years old. I knew it was my big chance, and I did a lot of extras with that shopping center—I made it the best I could make it. All the developers said, 'Well, that's great but it'll never happen again, you'll never make something like that happen again, kid.' But six weeks later we did the same thing with other centers.

"That was ten years ago, and I know now that Steve Soberoff, and Rich Green, whom he also got to invest in me, were the two best people I could have learned the business from. To this day we're friends and business partners.

"Steve did an amazing thing, all on his instincts. Later I asked him why he did it, and he said, 'I saw something in your eyes.' My own dream is that sometime I'll see something in someone else's eyes, a young person wanting to go into the business, and I'll know how to respond. Oh, yes— and now I teach at that workshop where I first heard Steve Soberoff talk, 'The Shopping Center Game.'"

"I LEARNED TO REACH OUT FOR WHAT CAN HEAL ME"

Judith Dimmett

Judith Dimmett and I served as cochairs of the Adult Religious Education Committee at King's Chapel for three years, planning retreats, programs, and workshops. One night we went to a Bible study workshop led by Walter Wink, expecting a scholarly fellow with a dry, academic delivery. I pictured a small man with thick glasses—and we encountered a big, glowing "good old boy" from Texas, who opened us up to the real use of Bible stories, making them come alive. Judith is now director of a women's residence in Boston and is a professional mediator.

"On a Friday night in the early spring of 1981 I met at the parish house of King's Chapel with our minister, Rev. Carl Scovel, and other parishioners to begin something that sounded terrible to me—Bible study. I was there only because I was so impressed with the minister.

"Carl began talking about a method he had learned for looking at these stories from a man named Walter Wink. The method allows participants to get into each story as it may have happened in its own time, to peel away any interpretations acquired through centuries of theological discourse, and to relate the story to your own life, in your own time. Now!

"To help people experience this, Wink has exercises that give you a chance to put yourself in the place of the characters in the story. We used the method to look at four of the healing stories in the New Testament. From the story of the paralytic at the pool, I learned not to wait for a miracle to heal me but to pick up my burden and carry on. From the story of the four friends who got Jesus' attention by lowering their sick friend through the roof of their neighbors' house, I learned both to look for friends for help in time of trouble and to be as bold a friend to my friends in need. From the story of Blind Bartamaeus, I learned to speak up about what is bothering me and to keep shouting until I am heard. From the story of the woman who touched the hem of Jesus' garment, I learned to be an agent in my own transformation, to reach out myself for what can heal me.

"In an ideal world, all these lessons would have been perfectly incorporated into my life. Guess what? They're not. I am not completely healed. But I have come a long way from those days, and I have more tools to deal with difficulties than before. I got to take a workshop with Walter Wink himself and became one of the leaders of his method of Bible study in our church, on retreats, and at assemblies of our denomination, so I could pass on this gift to others. Walter Wink helped me to a greater understanding of my faith, and my life."

"ALL I HAD TO DO WAS CHANGE MY MIND"

Angela Maffeo

"I was divorced in '82 and went through the usual throes. I walked around very confused. I'd been the one who wanted the divorce, so I thought it would be OK, but it hit me hard. I had a difficult time.

"In '87 I heard someone on the radio talk about '*A Course in Miracles.*' I ordered the books, but found them very intimidating. There are 365 lessons, and you're supposed to do one every day. Then I saw in the catalog of Interface [an adult education facility in Cambridge, Massachusetts] an 'Introduction to the Course in Miracles,' and I signed up for it. Some of us who took that introductory workshop at Interface continued to meet once a week on Thursday mornings at a restaurant in Boston called Blazing Salads. We've been meeting for six years now.

"The course gave me a way of integrating other work I'd done, from meditation to some of the Werner Erhard methods. This really made it all cohere. I saw that a miracle is a change in perception.

"Here's one change I experienced: I was a self-educated adult who regretted not having gone to college. I carried around this belief that I missed my opportunity. I was complaining about this to someone a few years after I started doing the Course in Miracles, and he said, 'All you have to do is change your mind.' He said instead of deciding that I'd missed college and it was all over, I simply had to decide to go to college right now. I'd heard this before, but this time I heard it in a new way. I saw that it was true. All I had to do was change my mind. So I did.

"'Undo the past in the present and it releases the future'—that's an important teaching of the Course. I was able to drop a lot of stuff that weighed me down. It released an opening. I worked at MIT and took courses at Harvard. I graduated from Harvard last June with a B.A. in psychology."

"HE SUGGESTED I TRY PROZAC"

Judy G.

Judy G. is a housewife, mother, and horsewoman who lives in northern California.

"When I was sure no one else could possibly understand the kinds of feelings and pain I was experiencing, Dr. Tom MacDonald of Kaiser Hospital put it all into words far more eloquently than I ever could. He perfectly mirrored me back to myself and let me feel like all that pain was legitimate but unnecessary. The world would not change because of my pain. For some reason, years of counseling had never touched me in this way—at a time when I needed it most desperately. It was a gift, a moment of grace that turned my whole life around; a true communication with a kindred spirit. I went to him for healing and that was what I got.

"He discovered an underlying thyroid condition that was undoubtedly contributing to many of my problems. Surprisingly, he at first thought my thyroid was OK but went ahead and did some tests at my request. (He was listening; he didn't automatically overrule me.) Also he suggested I try Prozac, which I did and went on to feel better than I'd felt as far back as I could remember.

"I truly feel, though, that he personally was more responsible for my recovery than any drugs were. I felt sort of 'saved' leaving there after my first visit to him, and I don't think I'm embellishing the memory."

Sometimes people who encounter a person or place or idea that changes their life are not looking for anything at all. That's part of the mystery of miracles—they can come into someone's life without invitation, maybe even without a person's desiring the kind of change that is brought about. There are paths we have never heard about that may be waiting for us.

A woman's death brings a young hospital orderly to a study of Buddhism, which becomes his own "way" and leads to his career as a writer. An Irish priest comes to America and meets a cousin who enrolls him in a personal growth program that changes his life, leading to a deeper experience of prayer and reconciliation with his own church. A Harvard psychiatrist meets an artist who does research on UFO abductions and begins a new kind of practice and a new kind of spiritual growth. A woman in a boring job meets a drunk whose advice leads her to a new and fulfilling career.

Before these encounters, none of these people anticipated following the paths that opened to them.

Keep your eyes, ears, and mind open. The next person you meet may bring a miracle.

WHAT'S MISSING?

Rick Fields

Rick Fields, the Buddhist writer and editor whom I quoted in chapter 2, is also the author of *The Code of the Warrior: In History, Mythology, and Everyday Life.*

"I was an orderly in a hospital in Detroit. A woman asked for a bedpan. I lifted her up and put the pan under her. I closed the curtains around her bed and left to take care of other duties. When I came back and opened the curtains, she was dead. She died while relieving herself. I had such a strong experience of 'something has been there that is no longer there.' It was—and now was not—in the time it took to draw the curtain around. Where had it gone, and where had it been? Just to say 'dead' didn't explain that. There was a sense that something was missing.

"I'd been reading the *I Ching,* and I went to the Detroit Public Library and got a book on Buddhist meditation. One meditation was on the body. It went into lurid detail about decomposition, which was meant to be freeing. This made sense to me. At that point I began to pay attention to the Buddhist point of view. That became my koan: '*Where has it gone, where has it been?*'

"I think we are already all Buddhas. The training we need is to recognize that. People stumble over how to achieve enlightenment. It gets to be a huge project. But the project is to see that there's nothing to accomplish spiritually. So people of no spirituality are farther along."

MIRACLES DON'T STOP

Gerry O'Rourke

Father Gerald O'Rourke was born in Ireland, where his brother is a priest and two of his sisters are nuns. He lives in San Francisco, where he pastors the Catholic church in Haight-Ashbury and is ecumenical director of the

Catholic Diocese of San Francisco and a member of the board of the Mastery Foundation.

"One of the most meaningful kinds of miracles to me are miracles of encounter. Who you meet and when—the moment you meet them. When I came to the United States, I looked up my cousins in New York, and I met Helen Gilhooley. If I'd never come to the States, I'd never have met her. She had just run into a woman who had recently done the est training and told her to do it. Though Helen didn't usually trust this person's judgment, she could tell that something had happened, something had changed her, so she recommended it to me, even though she hadn't done it herself yet.

"I did it, and it opened up a whole new avenue of my life and work.

"I used to think miracles were isolated, not available to most of us— they're of the saints, particularly dead saints. So this encounter opened me up to a new possibility of miracles. Through that work, now carried on by Landmark Education, I regained my own faith; and after having left the church, I returned to it again, I returned to the priesthood, with renewed commitment.

"Another significant encounter occurred when I met Father Basil Pennington, the Trappist monk and author of *Centering Prayer*. At the time I was just coasting along in my prayer life, and suddenly I ran into this guy who re-created from our own tradition a powerful kind of prayer, centering prayer. In my tradition, contemplative prayer had been for the spiritually elite—people like Saint Teresa of Avila or Saint John of the Cross. Basil opened up prayer of contemplation not just to me but to people all over the world. A real miracle was my giving up my resistance for a moment to let that in.

"Meeting Basil also opened up a whole new avenue in relationships—with God, with people. Both of us did est, and we both wanted to bring some of that power, that 'technology of transformation,' into ministry. I joined him and other priests, rabbis, and ministers to found the Mastery Foundation, which uses the transformational work we learned in those programs of Landmark Education, combined with Basil's teaching of centering prayer, to put on workshops all over the world on 'Making a Difference in Ministry.'

"Encounters happen all over the place. Another important one for me was my opening to the Russian Orthodox Patriarchal church. Ten years ago I didn't have it on my to-do list; I'd never thought of it. Through an encounter that turned around. Some people in the Bay Area wanted to make a contribution to people in Moscow and felt it should be an ecumenical contribution. When they looked for someone to forward that, I was the one. It was a miracle that I said yes instead of 'I'm too busy.' I went to Russia, and we created a significant relationship for people there and here, which led to food and medicine being sent to Moscow. It came from the ecumenical base in the Bay Area: Six thousand families contributed boxes of food, which reached people in Moscow.

"That was a miraculous healing between the Orthodox church and us, the Catholics. I'm accepted now as a brother by Orthodox clergy at a time when they have grave suspicions about us.

"No one is excluded from miracles—we can only exclude ourselves. Miracles are usually for ordinary people—they were the ones in the life of Christ who saw his miracles. At our peril we sneer miracles out of existence."

CLOSE ENCOUNTERS OF THE THIRD KIND

John Mack

John Mack, M.D., is a professor at Harvard Medical School's Cambridge Hospital and the author of *A Prince of Our Disorder*, a biography of T. E. Lawrence (Lawrence of Arabia) that won the Pulitzer Prize in 1977. His latest book is *The Abduction: Human Encounters with Aliens.* Dr. Mack has been interviewing and counseling men and women who believe they have been abducted by aliens. As the *New York Times Book Review* explained in discussing his new book,

> *Nothing in Dr. Mack's conventional psychiatric training had prepared him to hear such stories from people introduced to him by an experienced UFO researcher, Budd Hopkins. These articulate and sensitive men and women were not, it seemed to Dr. Mack, psychotic, delusional,*

or self-promoting. They were troubled, but their experience with UFO abductions seemed to be the source, not the symptom, of their troubles. As Dr. Mack listened, he began to believe that their experiences were in some sense quite "real" and that "the abduction phenomenon has important philosophical, spiritual, and social implications for all of us."

"The big stir began when I said these people had an authentic experience that I can't explain psychiatrically, and it sounds like whatever it is, it's very important. That's all I did—that simple act. It led to a huge book contract, controversy, a vicious attack in *Newsweek,* plus invitations from Oprah, Donahue, *48 Hours, People* magazine, you name it.

"I was most interested in this. It's very jarring in terms of my identity to be accused of some things I can't relate to—being described as a gullible old professor, or a 'high priest' of UFO abductees. It tells me a lot about how entrenched interests work.

"There are two kinds of entrenched interests: financial interest, like those who have a vested interest in the arms race; and a vested interest in terms of a worldview that supports a whole economic system. I guess what I'm doing threatens that worldview. I say we're not the only intelligence in the universe, we're not in control, and if there is a higher power, it doesn't look like us. I seem to tread on everyone's toes.

"A lot of miracles are in my view quite real. Hindu savants like Sai Baba can create ashes out of nothing; they do psychic surgery in Brazil. These people have a spiritual energy that can actually bring about change.

"This UFO experience is very transformational—there's a lot of spiritual growth. I did a session with a woman today who believes she is the mother of hybrid babies; she doesn't know if she can ever see them again. It's horrible. She and others like her are convinced these beings are using their bodies to create these creatures.

"It's an extremely powerful growth experience. A strong bond is established with the abductees through the eyes of the creatures, and the abductees have an expanding sense of a larger reality. They feel it's a miracle. That's part of the problem: They're experiencing things or places that 'can't be'; they are as skeptical as we are.

"These beings pass people through closed windows. Our physics doesn't allow that. They float to the sky and see houses receding below. There are many miracles in this.

"When I first heard a story like this, my reaction was to think that the man who told me about it must be crazy. He's a crazy artist with a crazy story. So I should be more tolerant of people who say that about me! But my critics are not willing to expose themselves to material that would show them a different point of view.

"There's fundamentally a spiritual hunger, and people assume aliens are good beings who do good things. But it's not necessarily so. Spirituality is a much more hard-headed notion. It means something that bursts the boundaries of the psyche. If someone hits you with a baseball bat and you have a vision of the universe, that doesn't mean it's a good thing.

"The UFO material is spiritual not because aliens are uplifting but because it opens an expanded connectedness and an expanded sense of possibility in the cosmos. It breaks us open to a wider notion of our place in the scheme of things."

"HE WAS DRUNK AND MOROSE WHEN I MET HIM"

Nancy Granese

When Nancy Granese graduated from the University of Wisconsin at Milwaukee she thought about being a social worker or joining the Peace Corps or VISTA, but she needed to earn enough money to pay off her college loans and moved to Washington in July to be a management intern with the United States Postal Service. A chance encounter of an unlikely sort changed her life, turning her toward a new and more satisfying career.

"He was probably an alcoholic. He was certainly drunk and morose when I met him.

"It was a weekday afternoon in January 1969. Hubert Humphrey, having been anointed by LBJ, had lost the presidential election to Republican Richard Nixon, and people like this guy were in every bar in Washington. They had had eight years of unimaginable power and good times interrupted and finally ended by assassins' bullets. The unthinkable had happened to them—Jack and Bobby were both gone and most of them were older than Teddy.

"I don't even remember his name; I met him only that once. He was handsome in the outdoorsy way that all the Kennedys and their entourage were. He could have been anywhere between thirty and fifty. I was twenty-one.

"Our meeting was accidental. An acquaintance at the sprawling bureaucracy that graciously employed me invited me for a drink after work. At four-fifteen he was standing at my door, urging me to go—like all political appointees, he was on his way out, so his drinking started early.

"When we arrived at the bar, a voice beckoned us deep into the dim smoky recesses of the room.

"There he was, tie askew, slumped on a red leather banquette under the blue mirrors that gave the dive its name. We were introduced, and he launched into a subdued but vicious tirade against everyone and everything not related to Jack or Bobby. For him, Teddy was a snot-nosed twit unfit to bear the Kennedy name. 'Nothing will come of him,' he predicted.

"Then he turned on me: 'What the hell are you wasting your time in the post office for? Pretty girl like you, you should be on the Hill. Get into politics—you'd be a natural.'

"And so I did.

"I devoted my lunch hours to searching for a job on Capitol Hill. It took about six weeks, and I found a job as a legislative secretary (I was a girl, after all, and girls were secretaries) for a senator. Over the next five years I worked in political campaigns—gubernatorial, congressional, and presidential—and on the personal staff of members of the House and Senate.

"Later I got into the private sector of politics by working in a corporation's government relations office and have been a lobbyist ever since. I am now with a law firm (four hundred lawyers) where I represent clients on the Hill and before the executive branch.

"My whole career in government has been exciting and fulfilling—far more so than if I'd have stayed at the post office! And yet it's something

I'd never have considered—it wasn't even 'on the screen'—until my brief encounter with that man at the bar."

There are times when we fight against being led down the path that produces a transformational miracle in our life. The last place a hard-drinking, chain-smoking French teacher wants to go is a vegetarian yoga retreat house where no liquor is served; she gives in and finds a new career and way of life. There are also times when the least expected result opens us up, when good comes out of a tragic event. The Attica Prison riots that resulted in the deaths of guards and prisoners alike led one inmate to conceive a way of transforming the experience of people behind bars and gave him a new sense of his own humanity.

"A SENSE OF HAVING ARRIVED"

Danielle Levi Alvarez

Danielle Levi Alvarez is a yoga teacher in Cambridge. After I'd taken her class a dozen or so times, I was curious to know how she happened to take up yoga and to become a teacher of the Kripalu style. My impression was that Danielle, a bright French woman with a slim, well-toned body she could move into any *asana* imaginable with great beauty and ease, was one of those people who must have been born doing all the healthy things. I imagined she came into the world doing yoga, sipping herb tea, and eating tofu with bean sprouts.

I was mistaken.

"I was disillusioned, bored, teaching French at Boston College, smoking two packs of cigarettes a day, drinking too much. I wanted to die. I didn't attempt suicide, but I thought about it. I was staying alive till my kids got out of college, then I thought no one would need me and I could kill myself. My kids were my only reason for living—there was no joy in my work, my marriage. My husband is a doctor, a medical researcher—he had his science, his medicine. I was teaching French because I didn't know what else to do; I had the right degree.

"A French woman friend of mine named Liliane Verdier, who lived in Hingham, Massachusetts, and taught French at Milton Academy, had been to the Kripalu Center in Lenox, Massachusetts, and she wanted me to go there. She wanted to give me a week there as a gift. She said it was a great place, with wonderful food. It's out in the woods; you can go there and really relax. But she said it didn't serve wine. *What?*

"'No, and there's no coffee,' she said. 'And no smoking.'

"I thought it was out of the question. If I can't drink, I can't smoke, what can I do? What's left?

"My friend told me to sign up for the week but that if I couldn't stand it, I could leave after one day. I was scared—I feared I might become con- taminated by health. But I went, and I didn't leave after one day.

"Not much happened the first few days. I found the place very unattrac- tive. I thought the buildings were ugly, I couldn't stand the pictures of their guru all over the place, and I hated the 'disciples' on the staff for looking so happy. I wasn't impressed by the yoga either. It wasn't very precise, and everyone kept smiling at me, till I wanted to slap their faces. 'Why are you smiling at me,' I thought, 'when you don't even know me?' The whole thing was too lovey-dovey. The nicer they were, the more I felt rebellious. All the smiling faces reinforced my despair at first. I felt something was wrong with *me*. 'If I can't be happy here,' I thought, 'I can't be happy anywhere.'

"I began to politicize my despair—I told the smiling staff people to look at the unhappiness in the world. 'Your happiness won't change that,' I told them. 'The world is a terrible place.' I told them they were apoliti- cal, they were living in an ivory tower, sticking their heads in the sand.

"I talked to one of the women on staff this way. I was very angry and aggressive toward her. She smiled and said, 'I'm very impressed with your anger—it shows how much you care!' That completely disarmed me. She said, 'Anger is energy waiting to be transformed.' That shook me. Instead of being bitter at my bitterness, she actually loved me for it!

"At the same time, on the physical plane, in the morning there wasn't any coffee to drink, but I discovered if I did yoga in the morning I got so much energy I didn't *need* coffee. I was pleased with myself that I didn't run for the first bus home. What was 'solid' in my angry attitude became less solid. These were the first cracks in my armor.

"On the last day of my week there I was feeling well, feeling nice, but nothing major had happened. I wasn't expecting anything when I went to the afternoon yoga class that day. I don't even remember much of the yoga we did, but afterward there was a long meditation. The teacher said something about going inside ourselves and extending love to ourselves. My body was relaxing piece by piece, and there was something about holding my own self in my mind's eye and extending love to that person that affected me deeply.

"I felt a physical sensation in my chest, as if my heart were a nut that had just been cracked open by a nutcracker. There was a pain in my chest and a clear feeling of my heart being freed from a shell. I started crying, very softly. It seemed like time dilated—just a few minutes seemed like eternity. The moment was filled with space and time, and time stopped—there was no more time. When I heard the bell at the end of the meditation, I was somewhere else. It was very odd. It took me a while to get back to the room, to realize I was still on the floor. When I came back up, I felt different than I'd ever felt before. First I felt gratitude for my teacher; then I felt devotion and happiness, and a sense of having arrived—not being a seeker anymore. I was home. I didn't need to go anywhere. I just wanted to stay at Kripalu.

"The teacher—a man called Sudhir—knew something had happened. I was very sober, self-effacing—in deep shock. I told him I didn't want to go home. I was in a panic that I had to leave. Just when I'd found home I had to leave!

"'Look, you can come back,' he said. 'I have a tape, a guided meditation. You can take that home and continue to meditate, and then you can come back anytime if you want.' He didn't try to explain what happened; it was just a recognition of it.

"I took the tape and went home. My family knew I had been to some odd place—they all hid, wanting to see what I'd look like. They didn't know what I'd be like. My son was the first to peek out from hiding. He called to my husband, 'Randy, she looks really good.'

"Everything felt strange, and new—as if I were seeing my kids and husband for the first time. Everything felt fragile. I had a responsibility not to break anything—everything looked precious, delicate. Within a week or so I realized I couldn't live in an ashram, that was not my place. I had to bring it here to Boston by being a yoga teacher. It was completely clear to me that this was what I was going to be doing with my life. I went back for their three-week yoga teacher's training course, and that was it. Oh—and I never drank coffee or smoked again. That was twelve years ago.

"My husband and I went to a 'Deepening Your Love' workshop at Kripalu, and he joined me on that path of transformation in his own way and at his own pace.

"I've been teaching yoga in Cambridge ever since then in church basements and in my home. One of my students brought me a book by the Vietnamese Buddhist monk Thich Nhat Hanh, and I learned he was coming to the Omega Institute in Rhinebeck, New York, in 1991. I signed up for the workshop, got to know Thich Nhat Hanh, and he asked me to translate one of his books into French. I went to work with him at his home in France, to translate his book *Inter-Being: The Fourteen Precepts of the Order of Inter-Being*.

"Dr. Jon Kabat-Zinn gave a retreat a few years ago at the Cambridge Medical Center, and I attended. I'd read his book, *Full Catastrophe Living*, and I knew I wanted to expand my own work into that of health-care professional—I wanted to bring yoga to the sick. After the retreat I asked Kabat-Zinn if I could be an intern in his program at the University of Massachusetts Medical Center in Worcester. He offered me a job, and last year I went to Worcester three days a week and taught yoga and meditation to inner-city people, mostly Hispanic and African American women, as part of the Inner City Stress Reduction Program." [Danielle, and the program, were written up in an article in the *New York Times Magazine*.]

"LIFE EMERGED LIKE A PHOENIX"
Cardell Shaird

After the Attica Prison riots, one of the prisoners, Cardell Shaird, had the idea for a program that is now given to prisoners by the New York Theological Seminary in religious education. After leaving prison, he earned a bachelor of arts degree.

"Oppression has an odor. It stinks. It stings the olfactory senses with such pungency that the brain ceases its action for need of fresh air. Such was the aroma of 1971—September 1971—the thirteenth to be precise. Obstetricians say that the smells of birth differ little from those permeating the air in an abbatoir.

"In that yard, in that place of slaughter, where death walked arrogantly among the unarmed and filled the air with the smells of ruptured bowels, splattered brains, and feces leaking from blasted intestines, life emerged like a phoenix, bringing something new and strong into existence. Attica, where so many died, also became mother to many children that day.

"College education, the think tank, the creative energies of newborn convict geniuses, transformed the outhouse vapors of Attica's killing ground into the vitalizing aromas of hope. And oppression will never be the same!

"Attica was the event in my life that made me a true human being."

Miracles can occur even in the midst of bureacracy, despite narrow interests, backbiting parties, and partisans, when the right politician encounters the right citizen who sparks his or her own idealism and determination. Politics and politicians have been so bludgeoned in recent times that it seems a miracle that anyone still chooses to be a public servant and accept the personal and public attacks heaped on them by what has become a bloodthirsty, scandal-mongering media.

There are still caring, intelligent, courageous politicians who make good things happen against all the odds, including the pulverizing forces of cynicism, negativism, and distortion of the truth. In these two stories of politicians who produced results that changed the lives of countless people for the better, each one was influenced by encounters with citizens who became inspirations for action.

"SHE HAD A DREAM OF BEING A DOCTOR"
Michael Dukakis

Michael Dukakis served as governor of Massachusetts, and was the Democratic Party candidate for president of the United States in 1988. He now teaches at Northeastern University in Boston and at Florida Atlantic University in Boca Raton.

"When I was reelected to the governorship in 1982, people were as angry about welfare as they are today; and nobody seemed to be doing anything about it. We decided to try something different. We asked welfare recipients what they thought would work for them. They told us three things. First, they wanted to be trained for real jobs with a future. Second, they pointed out that it would be difficult to go into a training program unless they could leave their children with somebody or at someplace in which they had confidence. Third, they suggested to us that losing Medicaid coverage for their children as soon as they got a job was not the greatest incentive to get off welfare.

"And so we launched our program with three basic elements: real training for real jobs; child care; and guaranteed medical benefits after you got a job unless your employer provided health insurance as part of the job.

"The results were more than we could possibly have imagined. Over half the mothers on welfare voluntarily signed up for the program. We had a waiting list of twenty thousand. And thousands of women with children on welfare are now working and earning and supporting themselves and their families and will never return to public assistance.

"One of those women is Ruby Sampson. Ruby was divorced with three children and had been on welfare for fourteen years. She decided to give the program a try even though she had never gone beyond the seventh grade in school as one of thirteen children of a Georgia sharecropper. She had had a dream of being a doctor since she was very little, and so she chose the training program for surgical technicians. Today she is one of the finest surgical technicians in the world. She is so good that some of the surgeons at the Brigham and Women's Hospital insist on having her in their operations. She is making a handsome salary and is a proud and confident citizen and mother.

"A miracle? Maybe. I'd like to think it is plain common sense that treats people as human beings and recognizes that there is potential in every one of us, no matter how down we may be."

THE CIA SAID IT WOULDN'T HAPPEN

Senator Richard G. Lugar

What I most admired about my high school friend and classmate Dick Lugar was his fearlessness. He was a natural scholar, but not a natural athlete, yet he hurled himself into the line on the reserve football team as if he were Bronco Nagurski (a legendary fullback of ancient times) and ran the mile on the track team, always finishing, if never first. I also admired his fearlessness in saying his prayers aloud at night when he and I roomed together at a high school journalism conference (I know of no other teenage boy who'd have been so brave).

I've admired his career, which took off with a Rhodes Scholarship, led to his serving as an innovative and community-healing mayor of Indianapolis, and from there to the U.S. Senate, where he especially distinguished himself as chairman of the Senate Foreign Relations Committee. When I asked if he had a "political miracle," he told me about his role in the Philippine elections that ousted Ferdinand Marcos and ushered in an era of democracy with Corazon Aquino. In playing the crucial role that he did, he had to face many encounters far more threatening than a high school football team could offer, yet he plunged ahead as fearlessly as he did back at Shortridge, this time facing down physical danger, an entrenched and powerful dictator, and, perhaps most difficult of all, the president of the United States, who was also the leader of his own party and its most popular hero.

"My experience as President Reagan's observer of the Philippine elections in February of '86 came closest to anything in my career I'd call a miracle. The fact that Corazon Aquino became the candidate opposing Marcos was itself a kind of miracle. Only by an extraordinary coalition of all Marcos's opponents—which meant veteran politicians withholding their own egos—was her candidacy possible. And then she was a terrible candidate and made some bad miscues, but as the widow of the slain leader Benigno ("Ninoy") Aquino, she was seen as the only unifying factor.

"Before I left for the Philippines, the CIA told me that private polls showed Aquino should win—but at the same time that I should realize it wouldn't happen, the election wouldn't turn out that way.

"Our observers were scattered around the countryside, and we were walking through dangerous places. A hundred people were killed during the elections, as Marcos's followers tried to perpetuate his regime. The lives of the American delegates were never safe—we were seen as instruments of change.

"The government party performed a blitzkrieg on Aquino and her UNIDO Party in Manila, holding down the vote through registration hassles and blatant intimidation, with goon-style violence carried out in front of world television cameras. Hundreds of thousands of people were disenfranchised and ballot boxes stolen.

"At first even our government in Washington was counseling Aquino to 'be a good sport' and let Marcos win. I came to the White House after the elections to say they'd been fraudulent, that the Marcos government was guilty of fraud and abuse. [Describing that meeting in its issue of February 24, 1986, *Time* magazine reported that "the normally terse senator spoke movingly of brave souls like an ordinary Filipino housewife, who confronted armed thugs in order to defend her ballot. He urged the White House not to resign itself to a Marcos victory too quickly." But to no avail.] Reagan was not convinced. He went on television that night and said there was fraud on both sides, which blew the whole thing wide open.

"In an interview the next day I indicated that the president was misinformed. It wasn't until four days later, at his ranch, that Reagan came to a different conclusion.

[Lugar's leadership in Congress led to the end of military and economic assistance to Marcos and a Senate resolution that the Philippine elections were marked by such widespread fraud they could not be taken as the will of the people. With the United States withdrawing its support, Marcos finally left the country, and Aquino became president.]

"Somehow what had been a dictatorship was changed to a democracy that took root and actually stuck. It was *not* inevitable. Aquino's regime survived five attempted coups. Now the Philippine democracy has inspired other underdeveloped nations and given hope to Koreans and countries in Latin America. It's one of the extraordinary events in the history of democracy."

Chapter 8

MIRACLES
OF PRESENCE

*We must assume our existence as broadly as we in any way can;
everything, even the unheard-of, must be possible in it. This is at
bottom the only courage that is demanded of us: to have
courage for the most strange, the most inexplicable.*

Rainier Maria Rilke

On an ordinary school night when I was nine years old, I went to bed, turned out the light, said the Lord's Prayer as I always did, and prepared to go to sleep. I lay there only a few moments, not long enough to go to sleep (I was clearly and vividly awake during this whole experience) when I had the sensation that my whole body was filled with light. It was a white light of such brightness and intensity that it seemed almost silver. It was neither hot nor cold, neither burning nor soothing. It was simply there, filling every part of my body from head to foot. I didn't hear any voice or sound, but with the light came the understanding that it was Christ. The light was the presence of Christ and I was not simply in his presence; his presence was in me. The experience lasted for several minutes, long enough for me to be fully aware of what was happening, to know it was real and not an illusion or trick of the imagination.

The experience was not frightening but reassuring, like a blessing, a gift, and a confirmation all at once. I didn't tell anyone about it for some years, and I didn't need to ask anyone about it, since I knew what it was. I went on about my life, and I think the only thing different about me was that I decided for a while that I wanted to be a minister instead of a football coach.

Later, as a teenager, I worried about the "light" experience, wondering if it meant I was crazy or deranged. When I got to college and became a devout atheist, I was reassured on several levels by reading William James's *Varieties of Religious Experience*. James wrote of many people throughout history having had the experience of "the light." He used the psychological term *photism* for it and declared it fully "normal."

I was relieved to know I was sane, then, and that I could categorize the experience in a psychological rather than a religious way, which satisfied my new atheist orientation. Later, when I returned to church and faith, I saw the light in a new way (or rather the old way) as an affirmation, an experience of grace. I know how deep and significant—how miraculous—such an experience of the presence of the sacred is, whatever its form or context.

I have also heard stories of the presence of loved ones who aren't physically there. Their presence is nevertheless deeply and surely felt, in dreams and in "waking" life. To the person having this experience, it *is* real—perhaps more real than many "normal" experiences.

The year after my own mother died, I once heard her cry. I have talked to people about this, and I've been told that this was a "memory" of her crying, that it wasn't really "her voice," or her presence. But I know differently. It happened at a time when I had just hung up the phone from making a decision that would lead to great stress and disappointment for me, though I thought at the time it was the right thing to do. Looking back more than a decade later, I still believe it was my mother crying, that somehow she (in whatever form she then existed or exists) sensed what would come of this decision, knew it would bring me heartbreak and trouble, and cried, and I could hear that unmistakable cry that I knew so well.

Perhaps I am open to such beliefs because of my own experience, because of my dear Aunt Ollah, who told me she was in touch with her own son after he died and who saw and foretold things in the future of my family. Though Aunt Ollah was sometimes (not always) able to conjure up presences, I think that was a psychic or spiritual gift that few people have. In fact I think when we try to force such things, we can get into trouble.

My conscious attempt to find such presence backfired. I went to the island of Iona in the Hebrides because I'd heard it was a place of great spiritual power, that a saint called Columba had gone ashore there centuries ago and used it as a base for spreading the message of Christianity. From the first, my trip there seemed plagued. My luggage was sent to the wrong airport (in the wrong country) and didn't arrive until my last day on the island. It rained and was demoralizingly bleak most of the time.

In the middle of the night, I got a kind of presence, but not the one I wanted. I woke to see in my mind's eye a black wall with the words "There Is No God" painted in white. An eerie silence and coldness accompanied this, and I couldn't sleep soundly the rest of the time there. I was told that others had also had "dark" experiences on Iona, and they, as I did, left the island early.

Like many writers, I have felt a presence of writers of the past when I was immersed in reading their work, or when in my own work I sensed their encouragement, their inspiration. Henry James is a writer who seems to have such an effect on people, as I feel he has on me, not in terms of writing style or politics or even "religion" in the narrow sense of the term, but in the spirit, in the sense of the sacredness of life that runs like a bright thread through the rich tapestry of all his work. He exerts, I think, a spiritual power.

In one of my visits to Aunt Ollah's house when I was in high school she described a man who was standing beside me in spirit, who was going to help me, and when in college I saw for the first time a portrait of Henry James, I said to myself, "That's him!" I "recognized" him as the presence Aunt Ollah had described. Later, at a critical juncture, I read a journal entry he made after suffering a shocking failure with his first play on the London stage, and the words and sentiment seemed addressed to me and gave me the will to go on with writing a book I was near giving up on (the book became my greatest success). Martha Collins, a fine poet and old friend of mine who directs the writing program at the University of

Massachusetts, told me that when she was writing her doctoral thesis on James she felt his presence on more than one occasion.

The novelist Louise Erdrich tells of such an experience while she and her husband, Michael Dorris, were writing *The Crown of Columbus:* "I hated the man [Columbus] and what he did in sending back the first slaves to Europe. And yet he had a fascinating questing spirit and a brilliant mind that showed through so much of his journal. I could feel his presence sometimes. It sounds absurd, but I wanted so much to meet this man."

The presence of God, spirits, saints, and loved ones who have passed on to another realm is not confined to any one religion, belief, school of thought, culture, or part of the world. It is part of the human experience. We saw earlier how such presences were accepted and recorded by the great historians of ancient and biblical times, but in our modern "enlightened" era, the conventional wisdom is that such phenomena are part of a pre-scientific past, before people knew how the world really worked and reduced it to the dimensions of humanism. No self-respecting historian nowadays would dare include the actions of God, saints, spirits, or non-human presences in accounts of contemporary life. She would not get published, much less get tenure.

Yet here are perfectly intelligent, educated people, many of them highly successful in their field, telling of their personal experience of such phenomena, in a variety of places and circumstances, all of them in our own time. Now.

From earliest times, one of the principal reasons given for God's intervention in the lives of humans was to save them—from physical harm, mental and emotional distress, and their own demonic ("self-destructive") ways. It still happens. A Hindu nun from India tells of driving across a bridge in Texas when her car is stopped at the last moment from skidding off, and she learns a lesson about not taking God for granted. A rabbi feels the presence of God lifting him out of despair. A prisoner feels God enter his cell and free him of his life-destroying habits.

"WE STOPPED ON THE EDGE"

Sister Chandru

Sister Chandru was born and grew up in Bombay, in a family of the Brahmin caste. As a teenager she joined the order of Brahma Kumaris (Daughters of Brahma), was sent by them to work in Africa, Canada, and the United States, and was one the founders of their Meditation Center in San Francisco, where she now lives and serves.

"When I was twelve years old I began to have dreams and visions. I was seeing myself in this role as a sister, a religious person, in other lives, too. I believe in reincarnation. I saw myself in many lives—seven lives before this life.

"Miracles come to me with God in meditation, but the things people relate to are the physical. I've had those happen too. I was driving on the freeway in Texas around four o'clock one morning—we meditate then, because our sisters meditate in India at four in the afternoon, same time as four in the morning here, so we can be in alignment with them. The other sister drove all night and she was meditating. It was between Christmas and New Year's, and it was cold, the road was frozen, and I was a new driver. I didn't know what to do when you skid. We were crossing a bridge and the car started to spin, and I turned the steering wheel the wrong way. We stopped just on the edge of the bridge, right where the car would have fallen off if it had gone any further. We were so happy, we said, 'Oh, God saved us!' At that moment, in our joy, I took my foot off the brake, and we hit the railing. And stopped. I felt the presence of my God. He takes care of you, saves you, but you have to be careful too.

"God is with you if you are with him. But if you take him for granted, you're in trouble—you can't be careless. Miracles don't happen all the time."

SOMETHING REDEMPTIVE

Rabbi Harold Kushner

A graduate of Columbia College, Rabbi Harold Kushner is author of the international best-seller *When Bad Things Happen to Good People.*

"After our son's death I was able to transcend the depression and helplessness and turn it into something redemptive—a book that brought healing to millions around the world. It didn't have to happen that way. It doesn't always happen that people are able to move on from the despair of such an event. I felt the presence of God in my life then, and I felt that was what enabled me to do it—to move on and to write the book."

"REVEAL YOURSELF TO ME"

José Berdicia

José Berdicia is a criminal justice graduate from Marist College in Poughkeepsie, New York. In June 1994 he received a master of professional studies degree from New York Theological Seminary.

"Call it what you might, but when I woke up around three A.M. and felt that my cell was the universe and that God was with me, it had to be a miracle.

"It was in a cell of the Green Haven Correctional Facility. I woke up not just thinking of God, I also felt his presence. No, it wasn't a correctional officer or a fellow inmate. I couldn't see what it was, but it was there. I did not kneel, nor was I frightened. The only words that came out of my mouth were 'If you really exist, reveal yourself to me in ways that can prove your existence.'

"I had always wanted to be different, a trustworthy, God-fearing person. I wanted to quit smoking, quit drugs, and to change my vulgar speaking. I had a real negative attitude. But still, deep inside, I always felt the need to change. And the day came.

"Two weeks later I was a new person—no smoking, no drugs, and fighting my vulgar language. Today I'm a totally different person, and I thank God.

"When my family and friends come to visit me, and they see my new attitude, the first thing they say is 'What a miracle!'"

We've learned that visits to sacred shrines and holy places have become the most popular kind of tourist travel in recent years. Many pilgrims go to such places in hopes of healing or of finding or restoring faith. The result is never guaranteed. Some go for other reasons—curiosity, historical interest, the beauty of the area. And sometimes they find a spiritual experience they didn't expect and weren't even looking for. A magazine editor who grew up Catholic but doesn't go to church anymore travels with her husband to a therapy association meeting in Poland and feels the presence of the Madonna at a village shrine of the Black Virgin. A best-selling author goes hiking on Mount Sinai, feels her connection to her earliest Jewish ancestors, and speaks to God—who answers.

"THERE'S SOMETHING LARGER THAN US"

Anne Simpkinson

I was discussing article ideas with Anne Simpkinson, editor of *Common Boundary,* a magazine exploring the relationship of psychiatry and spirituality, when the subject of miracles came up. Our abstract ideas on the subject soon shifted into personal stories. She had her own experience of sacred presence.

"My husband and I went to Poland, back to the village where my mother was born, Czestochowa. I wanted to go the shrine, it's a Black Virgin, mother and child, an image I grew up with in the Catholic church. The shrine goes way back, painted on wood in the twelfth or thirteenth century, and there are two slash marks on her cheeks. In one of the invasions of Poland, soldiers slashed the Madonna statue and it bled. Usually the Madonna is very beatific, but the history of Poland is so painful, it's as if she's been wounded too. You feel you could give her your pain and she'd understand.

"I was sitting on a small bench praying, and I felt a power—it was like a river of prayer generated by the people there praying. You could feel the prayer rising and moving. I felt carried, sustained.

"When we came out, my husband asked, 'What did you think of the Madonna?' I realized I had wrongly concluded, from something I'd read in a travel guide, that I had just seen an imitation of the famous Black Madonna, not the real one. So I wanted to go back inside.

"Instead of going where the pews were, we went up near the altar. As I stood there waiting for a space, a woman got up and left, and it was as if something picked me up and put me down there on my knees. It was like being in an absolutely clear—a crystal clear—presence. It was impersonal but not threatening. It asked a question like 'What do you want?' I wanted to pray for my mother and for a friend who had breast cancer, and then at the end of the prayer, it was like the audience was over, and I got up and walked out.

"It was a totally unforgettable experience. I believed before that but now I know that there's something larger than us. I want to go back some time. I have not found that kind of experience in the United States. I find that tremendously sad."

LISTENING TO GOD
ON MOUNT SINAI

Sara Davidson

Sara Davidson is a journalist, novelist, screenwriter, and producer who lives with her two children in Los Angeles. She's the author of *Loose Change: Three Women of the Sixties*, as well as the novel *Friends of the Opposite Sex*, a bestselling biography of Rock Hudson, and *Real Property*, a collection of essays. She created the series *Jack and Mike* and *Heart Beat* for ABC television, and is one of the executive producers of the hit CBS dramatic series *Dr. Quinn, Medicine Woman*.

"The first time I went to Mount Sinai, in the Israeli-occupied Sinai Desert, the place spoke to me, in a way I had never experienced. The place felt like what Carlos Castenada calls a power spot. It was an unusual desert of steep red and black mountains, and I felt that the landscape itself—the mountains, the rocks, the sand, the trees—was a presence that was powerful, watchful.

"I stood in the er-Raha Valley, a vast, shimmering diamond of pink sand, where supposedly the children of Israel had gathered to experience the presence of God, and I felt that presence. I felt I could talk to God as simply and directly as I'm talking to you right now.

"In Jewish legend, Sinai is the place where the children of Israel received the Ten Commandments from Moses, and it's believed that the soul of every Jew who has ever lived or will live was present at Sinai. If one Jew meets another and says, 'You seem familiar. Did we meet before?' the other might say, 'We know each other from Sinai.'

"The first time I visited the Sinai, I was on a bus with twenty German tourists. I knew I had to come back and spend more time there—why, I didn't know—so I arranged to stay at an Israeli Field Study Center at the base of Mount Sinai. I went on hikes and jeep tours with groups, but I really wanted to go on a trek with a friend so we could take our time and truly experience the place.

"In the fall of 1979, my friend Kathy in New York asked me if I'd like to go trekking in Nepal. I said no, but I wanted to go on a trek through Sinai and would she do that with me? She said yes, so we flew there, hired a Bedouin guide and Bedouin camel driver and set off.

"A few days later, I was sitting on a high ledge at sunrise and speaking to God about my path in life. I was divorced and wanted desperately to have children, but I hadn't been able to connect with a man who wanted a family. I prayed with all my heart that I might have children. 'Please,' I said, 'don't let me be one of those dead stumps on a family tree, a line that stops in a dry ball while the others continue to fork and branch. I want to be part of the river that flows on.' And I heard an answer, 'You will be.'

"As I sat there, I saw myself as part of a living chain, a chain that reached all the way back to the Jewish nomads who had wandered in the desert and continued ahead through my children and their children.

"Within two months after I got home I met the man whom I'd marry and with whom I'd have two children. My whole life changed direction."

Novelist Louise Erdrich has said, "There's a spiritual life in the land-scape," and from the beginning of time, humans have found signs and wonders of God and the spirit in nature. People with no religious beliefs and those of every variety of religious belief share the common inspiration and healing power of mountains and sea, trees and clouds, flowers and lakes. The tiny spots of nature preserved in big cities—the Boston Public Garden, Central Park in New York—are like powerful magnets drawing people who seek relief from concrete and stone, who need the nourishment and joy that nature gives the soul.

Rainbows seem like one of nature's miracles—reminding us of the miraculous all around us—for they suddenly appear, as if out of nowhere, like a heavenly light show, revealing the splendor of earth. A rainbow served as a sign in the Bible, and we still instinctively regard rainbows that way today. A college student decides to relay a painful truth to her parents, and when she sees a double rainbow, she feels that all will be well. A Buddhist editor and writer feels justified when a triple rainbow appears at his guru's cremation.

GOD'S TOUCH

Karla Fritsch

Karla Fritsch has her own handmade greeting card business and is a singer who performs in cabarets. She most recently appeared in the cabaret room of Don't Tell Mama, a club in the theater district of Manhattan.

"I guess I define 'miracle' as anything *I'm aware of* that is touched by God's hand. God is only part of the 'miracle recipe'—my awareness, my willingness to open my eyes and heart, are the other. I believe God's hand, Great Spirit, whatever one chooses to name it, is always at work, but I don't always notice. I'm not always open to receiving those gifts of the universe.

"There have been some moments when I've been awake to witness what have been simple yet powerful miracles in my life. I went through an extremely difficult period during college. I was battling a major depression, skipping classes, ultimately dropping out of school, but in my shame I couldn't admit that to anyone. I lived a lie. During a confrontation by my best friend, I finally realized I had to confess to my family and friends that I wasn't in school. I was scared to death.

"My salvation came in the form of a summer camp job, a thousand miles from home. I knew I could write letters to everyone and be a safe distance from any angry fireworks. It was still extremely difficult to sit down and write the letters, especially to my mother. I knew I couldn't wait any longer. I found a rare time of quiet in my cabin, and through tears I wrote the letter to my mom.

"When I finished, I was still filled with fear and uncertainty. Then I heard shouting outside and went to investigate. There in the sky over the lake were two complete rainbows. That was the touch of God's hand I needed. It let me know everything would be OK—and it was."

A TEACHER'S TRIPLE RAINBOW

Rick Fields

Rick Fields, editor of the *Yoga Journal,* is author of *When the Swans Came to the Lake,* a landmark book about the transmission of Buddhism from the East to America. He studied with Trungpa Rinpoche, a Tibetan Buddhist who came to the United States and settled in Colorado. Trungpa was a powerful teacher whose drinking and sex with students made him controversial, but he kept the devotion of many serious followers.

"When a lama dies, people talk about miracles or extraordinary events that happen. When Trungpa was cremated in Vermont, I was editor of the *Vedanta Sun*. The cremation became a huge media event, something like a hundred journalists wanted to come. The Associated Press hired an airplane to fly over, but I got them to change the time, so they wouldn't do it at the moment of cremation. I told them, 'Look, we're burying our beloved lama. Please don't fly your plane over at the same time.' A guy from *Time* magazine was very snotty; he said it was like Woodstock, which it wasn't at all. Ari Goldman, who was then religion writer of the *New York Times* came and seemed rather condescending. Right after the cremation he and the *Time* reporter left, and most of the other journalists followed. Right after they left, a triple rainbow appeared in the sky. I wanted to say, 'Hey, get those guys back!' The only reporter still there was from the local newspaper. The Barnet, Vermont, paper was the only one who had the story, with a headline that read, 'Rainbows Appear at Lama's Cremation.'"

Dreams were powerful signs in the Bible, means of important communication and guidance from God to humans. They have been so regarded in many cultures, including the Native American religions. In contemporary Western society, dreams were relegated to the level of superstition and soothsayers, unless psychologically (that is, "scientifically") interpreted. We owe credit to the work of Carl Jung and his contemporary followers for the culture's current inclination to take dreams seriously and to make use of the power and insight they can provide. Because Jungians ascribe significance to dreams, they offer a kind of respectability for intellectuals who want to learn from their dreams.

Most people, however, don't care what the cultural fashion dictates, and they go on having dreams they regard as miraculous, just as people in the Bible did. The administrator of a legal office has a dream in which three spirits like those in Dickens's *Christmas Carol* lead her to answers that solve a friend's problems. A stepmother who has died appears in a woman's dreams, bringing news about the child she is bearing and a new belief in God. Deceased mothers appear in dreams to comfort a prisoner and to help a woman who had lost her faith.

"THE SPIRITS LED ME TO A GRAVEYARD"

Suzette Martinez

Suzette Martinez is executive director of the Association of Defense Counsel of Northern California. She no longer has time to devote to the hypnotherapy work she once practiced, but she continues her spiritual journey, observing seasonal and personal rituals, and continues to find wonder in her life and work.

"Along with a part-time hypnotherapy practice, I was director for a large legal group in San Francisco. A strange mix? A perfect balance, I thought. It certainly brought me into contact with people who did not have a particular spiritual bent but with whom I had the most interesting conversations. These were professionals who respected my work and were therefore open to me and were somewhat fascinated by my holistic/metaphysical bent.

"Margaret was one of those professionals—a hard-driving woman who seemed by turns puzzled and doubtful but entertained by our sporadic conversations.

"After I hadn't seen her for several months, she called me sounding frightened and confused, reporting strange occurrences in her downtown office. She was feeling a 'presence'—things were being moved, the radio was going on with no one touching it. She was freaking out and couldn't think of anyone to turn to, but she knew my 'bent' and thought maybe I could help her.

"I may be holistically inclined, but I don't consider myself a ghost-buster. I was at a loss also. What she reported surprised me, especially in light of how 'corporate' she was. I referred her to June, a well-respected psychic I knew, with the hope June could help her out in an area where I felt completely at a loss.

"June later called to say that Margaret's office had been the site of an apartment building that burned down in the 1930s. To my disbelieving ears, she said family members had died there, and Margaret was responsible for animating that spiritual energy by her anger. Margaret was ready to move out of her office, but she was advised to 'wait and see in three days if something happens to resolve the whole situation.'

"It was over my head. I didn't want to get in the middle, and I decided to leave it alone.

"That night as I was preparing to sleep, I fell into an unfamiliar, trancelike state. It was as if I were dangling between two worlds. One part of me was clear about being in my bedroom, and the other part of me was aware of three spirit presences in the process of communicating with me telepathically.

"As I lucidly entered this dream state, I was being taken on a tour of Margaret's office by three spirits. I did not 'see' them, but their voices and energy had a bell-like clarity. It was like Dickens's tale. They walked with me, exhorting me to 'do something about Margaret!' I was literally being nagged to get her to stop being so angry, to get her to do something about her negativity, because her energy was driving them nuts. I argued against the whole thing. Who was I to interfere? She was a professional acquaintance. I didn't know her well enough to talk to her about anything so personal as her anger. No, I can't do it!

"The spirits led me outside the office to a graveyard, and one of them said, 'We'll show you what will happen if she doesn't deal with her anger.' Suddenly I was standing in front of a Russian icon of the Blessed Virgin and I had the strong feeling it represented Margaret's relationship with her fiancé, Ivan. It symbolized the death of her engagement.

"I resisted. 'C'mon, you guys, don't make me do this! This is getting way too personal. Why do I have to be the one? Why don't you make June tell her?'

"The spirits answered, 'Because she trusts *you*. You must do this!'

"I surrendered. 'OK, fine, but I'm telling you right now, I will not call her. You make her call me if I'm meant to give this message. And another thing—give me absolute proof that I'm meant to talk to her.'

"They replied, 'Ask her about "Donna" in regard to anger and control.'

"'Who's Donna?' I asked. The only reply before I awoke was 'Ask about Donna.'

"The next morning I arrived at my office at nine A.M. Four minutes later Margaret called, crying hysterically. She told me she'd had a fight with Ivan, and he had called off their engagement. He accused her of being too controlling and said he couldn't deal with her anger anymore. She wept about the broken engagement and the weird things going on in her office. She said she didn't even know why she was calling me about it, except maybe somehow I could help her.

"Oh, Lord. Softly, tentatively, I asked, 'Who's Donna?'

"She wailed at me, 'Why? Is she going to die now?'

"'No! I just had a dream. Who's Donna?'

"'She's my mother,' Margaret said. 'Why?'

"'I think we'd better talk.'

"Margaret came to my office, and I learned among other things that the Russian icon I had seen in my trancelike state was exactly the same as one that hung in the bedroom of her ex-fiancé. After talking, we went through a hypnotic session, tracing back a recurring nightmare she'd had for many years of someone coming into her bedroom when she was a baby and hurting her. She had amazing insights that afternoon, and she felt they would lead to a healing with her mother. Pieces of a puzzle were put into place, and it brought her a calmness and peace.

"She later reported that all 'spirit activity' had ceased, and she had become more active in pursuing spirituality in her life. I think this experience opened up her life. She later met and married another man and is now very happy.

"The power of 'spirit intervention' continues to amaze me to this day."

"I BECAME ACUTELY AWARE
OF MY SURROUNDINGS"

Sue Moreno

Sue Moreno is a wife and mother of two children and runs her own medical supply business in Merced, California. She studied the *Course in Miracles* and feels that it "opened a whole other area of my life."

"I was married in 1980 and came to live in California, where my husband lived. Henry and his parents were from Spain, and he was the only child, dearly loved by his parents, especially his mother, Carmen. In 1983 I had my first child, a boy, and six months later I became pregnant again. That same year Carmen developed bone cancer. We hoped she would live to see the birth of her next grandchild, who we thought would be another boy, but the baby was due in April and Carmen died in March.

"Two or three days after the funeral I had a dream about Carmen. She said to me, 'My next grandson is not going to be a grandson, it's going to be a girl.' I said, 'What?' and she said, 'You're going to have a girl.' Carmen and I were sitting on the couch in her living room, and one of her Spanish lady friends came and sat down between us on the couch, but she didn't see that Carmen was there. Carmen was smiling and laughing a little because this lady just kept on talking and she couldn't tell she was between us. Then I woke up.

"I had turned away from religion after growing up in a very strict religious household, and there was even a time in my early twenties when I considered myself an atheist. When I told my husband this dream, we'd had no sonograms, and we decided if the baby was a girl, we'd believe that the 'message' was really from his mother and God. If not, it was just a dream.

"When the doctor said, 'It's a girl!' we couldn't say anything. It was a confirmation to us.

"Immediately after the birth, I became acutely aware of my surroundings. I found the life and the love in everything. I was deeply touched. I knew something most people either don't know or don't express. For the first time in my life, I began to think of myself as a spiritual person. This just came naturally into my head and into my life. That has never changed. Carmen drew my attention, and my own soul's knowing, into the light of truth and love and the oneness of life that comes from acknowledging and knowing there is God."

A MOTHER'S PRESENCE

David Bookhart

David Bookhart is a prisoner at Sing Sing. He earned a degree in the New York Theological Seminary program.

"I believe that my mother and I share a very spiritual connection. Things have happened time and again to prove that we do. I can remember dreaming one night that I was a small child. I had stepped off the curb and into traffic when suddenly a hand pulled me out of the way of an oncoming car. When I awoke, I told my mother about the dream. She said that it was not a dream, it had actually happened. When I was about three years old, I ran out in the street while walking with her. She pulled me out of the way just before I was about to be struck by a car.

"One of the most powerful experiences I had began when I saw my mother alive for the last time at my grandmother's funeral. At the time she looked younger than she had in recent years, and I couldn't believe my eyes.

"When it was time for me to go, she hugged and kissed me as if she would never see me again. And as the guards drove me away, she stood on the sidewalk watching, with a forlorn look in her eyes. It was at that time that I knew I wouldn't see her alive again. On the ride back to the prison, the thought would keep coming up, but then I would push it back down. I even saw myself in chains going to view her body, and it all came to pass.

"A few months later, I dreamed that my mother had come to me to say good-bye. She was dressed in her nightgown, and she looked younger than ever. She had tears in her eyes as she reached out to embrace me. As she held me close, I could feel the warmth of her embrace and the wetness of her tears as she repeated over and over, 'Good-bye, son, good-bye, son.'

"I awoke with a start. My heart was pounding and in my mind I knew she was gone. Later on that day I was summoned to the chaplain's office, but I knew the reason why before he opened his mouth. She had died that night, February 9, 1992. I will always remember that last good-bye. After all, she had come to find me. Just as she did when I found myself lying in a hospital with a gunshot wound in my stomach. She called every hospital in Brooklyn until she found me, simply because she felt my pain and knew that I had been hurt. To this day the miracles in my life continue, and she is right there in the midst of it all."

"WITH ANGELS AND ARCHANGELS"
Mary L. Robertson

Mary Robertson is retired and lives in Boston. She writes, swims, goes to concerts, and takes courses at the Boston Center for Adult Education. It was there I met her when she took my workshop in "Spiritual Autobiography."

"Though he had a long illness and I knew he was getting worse, no one had told me my father was going to die. I was thirteen years old. While he was in the hospital, I joined a church along with other members of my Sunday school class. Our only preparation was memorizing passages of catechism and reciting them in response to questions from a kindly but stern group of older men. I felt hypocritical but numb, unable to summon the spirit to protest. As the months went by, I ceased believing in any kind of God, and for a long time felt appalled by organized religion. Death is the end, I felt certain.

"When I was in my forties, a friend told me about losing his mother. To my surprise, I found myself saying that since birth was such a miracle, perhaps it was the same with death. I had become open to the idea of an afterlife.

"The night after my mother died, I dreamed that we were dancing together in a bright green meadow under a bright blue sky. I awoke, feeling certain that her spirit still existed. I visualized a small stream of sparkling light joining an immense stream of gleaming yellow light. Her spirit had become part of some cosmic energy or force. I did not know if she still had an individual identity. But the day after her burial, when I was swimming in a pool, I thought of words in the *Book of Common Prayer:* She is 'with angels and archangels.' Now, more than five years later, I am still astonished by the conviction this gave me that there is a kind of existence after we die."

Not only people who have died but also people who have come close to death bring hopeful, inspiring messages to us. The "near death" phenomenon has come to be a staple of contemporary experience of the miraculous. The beauty and good feeling of the experience, so often filled with light, seems universal. These reports are upsetting to some skeptics, who can't believe anything but darkness lies beyond us and are evidently disillusioned to hear otherwise. Still, people keep having the experience of moving beyond this current state of existence, being welcomed in the next, and then returning. During coronary surgery an accountant sees her family holding out their arms toward her and smiling. A woman having a blood transfusion feels she is leaving the planet and experiences the presence of God. Both women stress the reality of their experience.

"DURING THE SURGERY I SAW MY FAMILY"

Mary Ann Mennenga

Mary Ann Mennenga was an accountant in Nebraska, and when her family moved to California, she worked there for Bell and Howell for eighteen years. Now a grandmother with four grandchildren, she is retired and lives in Pasadena.

"On June 18, 1981, I was operated on for replacement of a microvalve in a coronary artery. It was serious surgery. During the surgery they had to bring in a high-risk modifier. That's to keep you alive. I didn't know that till afterward, when I saw the paperwork.

"I felt I was close to being gone. During the surgery I saw my family, who had passed away. There was my mom and dad and brothers. They were all in a group, as if I were taking a picture of them. They were holding out their hands toward me and smiling. My youngest brother especially was holding his arms out toward me. It looked like they were giving me a welcome. It was real. It wasn't like a vision. I can still see it today. It really happened.

"At first I told people about it, but I know it sounded strange to most of them. I told my doctor about it, and he said, 'Well, maybe it was the anesthesia.' I had another operation just last month, but nothing like that happened. Still, I stopped talking about my experience. It's hard for people to understand."

"I WENT TO A PLACE OF PERFECT PEACE"

Debby Osborne

Debby Osborne is an ophthalmic technician in Portland, Oregon. She says that when she told her father of this experience, he said that his grandmother had a similar one and had described it to him in some of the same terms.

"I started having stomach pains just before going on a trip to Egypt, and one night it got so bad a friend took me to the doctor. The doctor took an upper GI that showed nothing. He gave me medication, but that night I started throwing up blood, and I couldn't stand up. I was taken into emergency.

"There I began to feel as if I were leaving the planet. It was a feeling of euphoria, and I went to a place of perfect peace and contentment. I had never felt so wonderful in my life. I was in the presence of God. I felt so complete. I said, 'God, here I am. I'm ready to come if you're ready for me, and I'm willing to stay if you want me to stay.' It felt like I was enveloped in a womb. I told my father later it was like 'God's waiting room.'

"I was in emergency unattended for several hours, and then they took me upstairs to intensive care. I was in the hospital for eleven days and had four blood transfusions. They said I'd had an acute gastric hemorrhage.

"I realized after it was over that when I leave this life I'm going to an eternal, wonderful place, though my experience called 'Debby' won't go on. I won't do this life again. Having this body, being 'Debby,' all this is a gift.

"I have a whole different view of life now. I have a willingness to be in my humanity in a way I've never had. I feel strongly about being here now. I didn't appreciate it before.

"My life has changed in a lot of ways since that happened. I'd moved to Portland a few years before and had given up my old work as an ophthalmic technician because I was bored with it. But after I got out of the hospital, I felt I should go back to it, and now I love it, I enjoy what I'm doing. I love working with the patients.

"Ten years ago I got divorced, and after that I closed my heart and my body. I wasn't looking for any more relationships. After this experience, though, a man came into my life. It was wonderful, beautiful, entirely different. I was able to do it completely differently, bring something to it I never had before. I was able to watch myself doing it in a healthier way, a healthy way. It didn't last, but I'm glad it happened. When it ended, I was able to deal with it with greater acceptance."

The presence of the Divine often comes through other human beings. People gather in churches, synagogues, ashrams, mosques, prayer groups, retreats, meditation groups, and twelve-step groups to share and evoke the spiritual element in their lives. Speaking of her own conversion experience, Rabbi Nancy Flam said, "It began in community." When we find a way of service to others we often feel the spirit moving in us, for, in Saint Thérèse's words, "Whose hands are God's hands but our hands?"

Sometimes miracles come to us in the form of connections with people, appearances of people, from our past, or in the form of a teacher. Parishioners at an Episcopal church in Mississippi experience Jesus' presence in a prayer group. A woman on the Staten Island ferry sees her own ancestors who came from Europe. A new mother feels the spirit of her grandmother-in-law who just died emerge in her newborn child. An economics major finds she has psychic gifts and channels a teacher who teaches through her. A rabbi practices "the ministry of presence" and feels herself a conduit for the Divine to heal others.

"AN AMAZING THING HAD HAPPENED"

The Reverend Ed Bacon

The Reverend Ed Bacon, minister of an Episcopal church in Jackson, Mississippi, told me, "We had nineteen prayer groups in Lent, laypeople. I suggested they pray every day. I had four messages in the first week about what happened to people as a result of prayer."

"One woman called and said an amazing thing had happened. The prayer group she was in was a very intellectual group, some of them college professors. They tended to be more skeptical than others. Then at one point in the last meeting they all had a clear sense that Jesus was present. They felt his presence. One of them was a man who's a law professor, and he told me after that experience he slept better than he had in years.

"I told about it in a sermon—not as something weird or bizarre, but as something that's accessible to all of us."

TIME COLLAPSED AND EXPANDED
Pamela Gordon

Pam Gordon is a writer and teacher who grew up in New York City, went to Emerson College in Boston, and now lives in Florida with her husband, Steven Ditmore, and their young daughter, Leah. She has written articles and stories for newspapers and magazines and coauthored the book *Choice Years* with model Judith Paige.

"The summer I was twenty-one I had just graduated from college and was living at home. On a late August night I went into Manhattan with two friends. It must have been cool because I was wearing a dark green cape that I'd bought before going to college and worn faithfully every fall since, but I don't remember the temperature. I just remember the look of the air as we drove over the Brooklyn Bridge: orange and gaseous as only the late summer polluted sky of New York can look. Joni, Ed, and I ran around town and ended up down by Battery Park. I'd grown up in New York, but I'd never ridden the Staten Island Ferry. It was still five cents, a bargain, and the two of them insisted we take a ride.

"Ed and Joni settled on a bench, holding hands and nuzzling, and I wandered out onto the deck, finding a comfortable spot against the railing. New York's harbor churned darkly below, and the orange sky glowed like a muted neon globe over my head. My cape moved in the wind. I knew that my grandparents had sailed into this body of water, two from Russia, two from Hungary, each at different times between 1905 and 1920, under different circumstances, but destined one day to meet. All of them had died by then, but as I looked out at the water I had the strongest sensation of each of them being there with me on deck, and of my complete understanding of everything they had gone through: the disruption of their early lives, the loyalty to those back home, but the break from that home as well, and the building of a new life in New York. The feeling of them being there with me was very solid and real; then something else happened.

"Under the eerie sky and the night wind I felt myself move beyond the immediate moment, beyond the time and place in which I stood. Not only were my grandparents surrounding me but each one of the many people who had traveled these waters over the centuries were there too. Time, it seemed, had both collapsed and expanded. What I'd always experienced as a continuous line, event following event from the beginning until now, was suddenly circular. I knew with a calm certainty that all of history had existed simultaneously; everything that had ever happened, was happening, or would happen flourished at the same moment in a continuous circle. The quality of the night, combined with the ride on the ferry, had allowed me to enter a reality outside my usual recognition, a fuller and larger reality.

"The realization was very strong—more an experience, really, than a realization. It was not in the least unnerving. Instead of confusing or up-setting me, it seemed to affirm something I had always known but had never felt so concretely and had never put into words to myself before. I didn't try to explain it to my friends. I just breathed deeply and looked around and soaked it in until it faded, and I've kept it with me ever since. I'm usually too preoccupied with the hectic business of daily life to appreciate fully or even remember what to me, after that night, is a solid fact. Writing it down brings that knowledge back."

"PART OF A CYCLE"

Marie Hershman

Marie Hershman studied in France from age fourteen to nineteen and earned a degree in French literature from the University of Wisconsin. She now manages a household and raises two small children in Ohio.

"My husband's grandmother Anna Knournas, 'Nonny,' was someone who really took my heart. She was so honest, so blunt—but truthful. I felt close to her. She was a very 'present' person. I admired her a lot. I didn't see her as a 'nice woman' the way my husband and his brothers and sisters did, but I felt she was a warm and true person. Her bluntness didn't offend me, it made me smile.

"She was Jewish, from Hungary, and very different from my own background. My father's family is from England and Scotland, and my mother is French. My father met my mother in World War II and brought her back to America. I was brought up Roman Catholic.

"When I was pregnant with my second child, and we learned it would be a girl, my husband and his family wanted me to name her after Anna, their grandmother. I was against the idea. I'm not Jewish, and it felt strange—like it was a huge load to put on the baby.

"We went to see Nonny when she was passing away, and I was pregnant. When I held Nonny's hand, the baby started kicking like crazy—it felt like a communication. One life was coming into the world and one was leaving. I felt it very deeply, it was very intense. I felt strongly then that I wanted to name the baby after Nonny, and we named her Anna Lee.

"I'm very glad we gave her that name. It's not a burden; it's a nice thing. It's like she's part of a cycle. Though Nonny didn't know her, she's *with* her. I sense it. It's not like she's physically with her, it's her living essence that's with her."

"THE PRESENCE WAS LIKE A HUGE ENERGY FIELD"

Nina Zimbelman

Nina Zimbelman grew up in New Orleans, earned a B.A. at Louisiana State University, and has a master's degree in economics from Oklahoma State. She is now a metaphysical teacher and directs the Gleanings Foundation, a center for vibrational research and education in northwest Portland, Oregon. She leads classes, retreats, and study trips to Egypt and to Machu Picchu in Peru.

"Up until the time I was thirty-five, I was totally materialistic, in 'the real world' of money and machinery. My husband and I had a business selling tractors and motorcycles. I had forty employees under me. I was stressed out and doing cocaine. When you do that, you lose your appetite, and I was losing a lot of weight. One day in 1980 I looked in the mirror and a voice said, 'Choose to live or choose to die.' I called up a friend who lives on a farm in Ohio and asked if I could come there and dry out. I did it cold turkey.

"When I came home I realized I had to have a new life—the old places and the old friends didn't work anymore. I wanted to get healthy, and I started doing the macrobiotics diet. After I started that I heard about a meditation class and I began meditating. One thing led to another, like an unfolding.

"I began to sense that I wanted to get out of business. We were in a world of 'stuff.' I started selling everything off. I'd also begun to have a feeling I knew things on some other level, and I wanted to find out if I had any psychic gifts.

"In December of '83 I had an experience that literally changed the course of my life. A friend invited me to come to a 'metaphysical weekend,' led by a psychic from California, who told me I did have a talent. I did a three-day intensive with the psychic, and on the second day while I was sitting in the room with her a presence entered the room—not just entered the room, filled the room. The presence was pure love. The room became love. It was beyond any experience I'd ever had. I had the feeling I'd been waiting my whole life for this. The word that came to my mind was *finally!* My whole body shook. The presence was like a huge energy field.

"This energy field personified itself as a teacher I affectionately refer to as Baba. I was invited to study in the nonphysical realms, and what followed in the next decade was a true journey through consciousness.

"This presence came back to me, and when it was there, people could walk into a room and feel it. It was palpable. I'd be in an airplane and the person sitting next to me would suddenly start crying, feeling this presence, this love.

"My awareness amplified, it got bigger and bigger. I could see a tumor in somebody's body. I was learning to activate my brain and learn how to do it for others: I could amplify their brain waves to raise them to a higher field. I could do it over the phone. One friend said that after our last telephone conversation she felt high for three weeks.

"I learned that humans can achieve a state of pure love—an ecstatic state or bliss state or what some people call God. What I feel now is that state exists like anything else. I tapped into that state and taught myself how to be whole. That state is available to everyone. We all have the capacity for being in nonphysical realms, if we have a willingness to move beyond the physical. Only three to five percent of my clients don't tap into it when I'm around.

"Yet what I wanted to happen quickly took almost eleven years. This journey has brought me to a level of acceptance that is known as love. I am filled with gratitude for the entire trip. I have found that when you are willing to live from an open heart, endless journeys on all levels of consciousness become open to you. And with an open heart you are free, finally, to enjoy them."

TURNING THE KEY

Mark Matousek

After searching as far as India for faith, the editor and writer Mark Matousek (he's a friend and neighbor of mine) was discouraged. Nothing clicked. He found, however, that the old adage is true: When the student is ready, the teacher arrives. Mark writes a column for *Common Boundary* magazine and is at work on a book about his own spiritual journey, titled *Sex Death Enlightenment*.

"A friend told me, 'There's a woman in Germany who can help you.'

"'Who is she?' I asked.

"'It doesn't matter. Just come.'

"The next week I flew to Frankfurt and drove with my friend to the small village of Thalheim. We stopped on a quiet street in front of an ordinary house. Having no idea what to expect, I followed my friend inside. We walked through a shoe-lined foyer, into an atmosphere of deep silence. I heard a strange ringing in my ears as my friend led me upstairs. Then I saw the woman my friend said could help me.

"She was a small, dark woman seated in an armchair with her eyes closed, holding the head of a kneeling child in her hands. Without thinking, I knew instantly that this person, whoever she was, was of an entirely different caliber than anyone I'd ever seen before. Her silence, stillness, and concentration were what can only be called paranormal. The room was charged with power; I was overwhelmed, just watching her, by a strange inner peace.

"Forty unremarkable-looking people sat waiting their turn in folding chairs. One by one they went to kneel in front of her. She held their head in her hands for a minute or so, then looked them straight in the face. Her expression was fierce, unwavering. Then she lowered her gaze, and they returned to their seat. After the last person had come forward, she left the room without a word.

"The woman's name was Mother Meera. I learned that she was the daughter of an Indian peasant and that she had been recognized since childhood as an *avatar* (one born possessing full God-consciousness) and the rarest form of enlightened being, a mahatama, a saint. Her work, she said simply, was to 'bring down the light.' She embraced all religions equally, had no ashram, no cult, no price, no rules, no tradition, no verbal teaching. Everything was done in silence. Anyone who wanted to come for her blessing was welcome. And that was that.

"In the days that followed, I read the books that had been written about her, filled with accounts of healing, miracles, visions. But I'd read this sort of thing before. I would not have believed a word of it had I not seen Mother Meera with my own eyes. Night after night, I watched her like a hawk, waiting for a slip, an indication that she was a fraud, that this serenity she invoked was born of wishful thinking. There was nothing; she could not be faulted. When she wasn't giving *darshan* (literally 'divine presence') four nights a week, Mother Meera lived the simplest of lives— shopping, painting, gardening—far from the public eye. She gave her time, her house, her personal attention to thousands of people every year (as she had since her teens; when I encountered her she was twenty-six), asking for nothing in return. Her message was practical and crossed all borders: 'Do your work, remember God.' By the end of the week, I was forced to admit that although I didn't want a guru, I had undoubtedly encountered a holy human being. This had been, without question, a sacred experience.

"That was five years ago. I visit Thalheim every now and then when I need to have my faith renewed. The most important lesson of this search has been that hearing about spiritual life and knowing firsthand the rush of the inner journey are two entirely different things. Imagining enlightenment and watching it in action are equally unrelated. As a lifelong skeptic, I demanded visual evidence before faith could begin to take root. Even so, it's impossible to understand how an unlettered woman like Mother Meera could convince me, a skeptic, without a word, that God exists. But that's the mystery. Each heart has a key of its own. It only needs to be turned."

THE MINISTRY OF PRESENCE
Rabbi Nancy Flam

Rabbi Nancy Flam is one of the founders of the Jewish Healing Center in San Francisco. Her work was described in chapter 2 as she conducted a healing service at a temple in the Castro district of the city.

"I remember when I was five years old coming home on a bus from day camp and hearing a song on the radio, the 'Smile on Your Brother' one. The message got to me, the power of love, the unity of humanity. It was very powerful. Music played a big part in my religious experience. I can identify another spiritual moment when I was seven; it was right after the Six Day War, and I heard someone sing 'Jerusalem of Gold.' Something hit my heart.

"My own Jewish upbringing was very thin. I went to Jewish Sunday school at a Reformed synagogue till I was ten or eleven, that was it. When I was a teenager, there was some conflict at home, and like many teenagers,

I felt a lot of internal pain. When I went to college, at Dartmouth, I met a woman who became my best friend, who knew what it was to love fully and to pay attention fully. We had an immediate spiritual connection, though she was not Jewish. There was a spiritual dimension to my suffering that I hadn't been invited to share, and she shared it with me. She 'heard me into being,' as one writer described this kind of process. She acted as my healer, and I learned then what it is to do what we call the ministry of presence.

"At Dartmouth I rediscovered Judaism in a non-Jewish environment. I had a conversion experience from being a secular to a religious person in the summer of '79. I was living in a group house, it was *the* house at Dartmouth that had the intellectuals and people who were politically committed to the left. We all were 'weird,' but not misfits—we just weren't the normal lacrosse-playing Dartmouth stereotype. It was like a converted fraternity house. We had all our meals together. There was a real graciousness and respect for individuality—part of the ministry of presence is seeing that individuality. It was the first place I felt I was 'coming home'—to myself, in a community that recognized me. The generosity of that community was very glorious.

"There was a two-week period when I felt like something in me opened. I began to use the word *God* connected to my own experience, and it was like walking a foot or so above the ground, like on a cushion. I felt transformed, I felt like a religious person, and everything was different from that time on.

"It began in community. The art of the ministry of presence is being able to be with someone and invite their story, to have their story be shared in community. You listen not to fix anything, not to change anything, but through the quality of your listening, your attention and love create a place where two can stand where one has stood before.

"I've experienced God's presence in that connection. The person who's listening, who's being with the other one, the one who needs to be healed, is being a conduit for Divinity to express itself. In that way, our hands are really God's hands. That's why it's important to keep in good shape physically, to exercise and get enough sleep: We have to take care of our bodies because we are the vessels."

Chapter 9

EVERYDAY
MIRACLES

When Einstein said you see either everything as a miracle or nothing as a miracle, he was describing an outlook, an attitude, a way of perceiving things. I didn't realize he was also describing how some people are able, literally, to see the world. Then a friend sent me an excerpt from Walt Whitman's poem "Miracles," and I realized that a vision of life in which everything is a miracle is possible (the "literal truth" may often be found in poetry).

MIRACLES

Why, who makes much of a miracle? As for me, I
know nothing else but miracles. Whether I walk the
streets of Manhattan, or dart my sight over the roofs of
houses toward the sky . . .
To me, every hour of the light and dark is a miracle.
Every cubic inch of space is a miracle . . .
To me the sea is a continual miracle. The fishes that
swim—the rocks—the motion of the waves—the
ships with men in them.
What stranger miracles are there?

My minister, Carl Scovel, spoke in a sermon once of suddenly noticing water—the miracle of water. He had finished shaving and was washing his hands, holding them under the tap, and he looked at this substance we take for granted, this fluid "stuff" we drink, bathe in, dive and swim in, look at, walk beside, sail on, paint, photograph, write about, cook with, catch fish from, skate on when frozen, listen to as it laps the shore.

The morning after Carl's sermon, when I turned on the water tap to shave, I *saw* it, felt it, became aware of it, awake to it, appreciative of it, thankful for it. Who could have thought of such a thing?

Water. So simple. So unutterably complex. So miraculous.

So, when we stop and think about it, is the taste of a pear, the color of a beet, the scent of woodsmoke, the feel of a cat's fur, the sound of wind in maple trees. So, when we wake to it, is our everyday world, a world we can come to live in more fully when we practice what the Vietnamese monk and teacher Thich Nhat Hanh calls "mindfulness," simply by using our senses, focusing on what's here, now; what we're doing, perceiving, now, this moment, in which all past and future, all that *is* (and was and will be) is contained.

Everyone can experience this, yet few accept it, many refuse or don't know they're able or forgot how to do it—to open their eyes and ears and nose and mind to it, to the now, the miracle of the moment.

Father Gerry O'Rourke, a man who looks alive in each moment, advises, "We should give up our idea of scarcity. We ignore miracles with simple blindness. We get rid of our miracles."

Playing my role as reporter I ask him to give me a specific example. Let's pin this down!

Without losing a beat he says, "Think of the inspiration we get from people we consider 'of no consequence'—like doormen we pass by all the time, whom we take for granted, pay little attention to, yet they offer incredible inspiration. Despite what may be the difficult conditions of their lives, you never hear their problems; all you see is this love coming forth from them."

At first I thought, What's he talking about? For one thing, I always thought of doormen as uniformed guards at luxury apartments, but two years ago I moved to a building in Greenwich Village with a desk in the lobby that is manned around the clock by men who greet guests and buzz the residents to get permission before allowing them up. These men don't stand by the door and open it—but they take our packages, messages, deliveries from cleaning to food to flowers, hear our complaints, negotiate noise and hallway problems, always with smiles, interest, concern. I depend on them, rely on them, look forward to their smiles and greetings, tell them about what I'm doing, where I'm going, where I've been—and know little about them beyond their names.

For nearly ten years I've been going to the health spa Rancho La Puerta in Mexico. I always ask for Pedro, my favorite masseur, a gracious man with an aura of goodness as well as strong hands and arms and a mastery of massage. We greet each other as friend, *amigo,* and yet I knew nothing more about him until my friend Bob Smith went to Rancho last year when I was there and after a massage told me, "Hey, that Pedro, what a guy! Did you know he has fourteen children, and two of them are nuns and one is a priest?"

No, I only knew I could depend on him to make me feel good and to be always friendly and welcoming, fully present, fully intent on his work, on *me.* Without my ever thinking about it, I took this man and what he does for granted—like the sunrise, another "ordinary" miracle.

"We have people looking for the wrong kind of miracles," Father Frankie Murray, the curate of Longford, Ireland, tells me. "We see people looking for weeping statues—people see religion and God as something extraordinary, like a rabbit out of a hat, as if God were saying, 'Hurray, it's me!' That misses the 'every morning miracles'—the sunrise and friendship."

All the true spiritual teachers, whatever their faith, bring us to an appreciation of our "daily life" miracles. But recognizing the miracles that are already present takes some work, some concentration. The worst way to look for a miracle is to fail to appreciate the ones we have, then sit back, do everything the way we've always done it, and hope that something fabulous will happen to us in spite of ourselves. Remember the advice of Sister Chandru, the Hindu nun: "You don't *wait* for a miracle; you come to the point gradually, and then it appears, something clicks, and everything changes, so in your life it seems a miracle."

Of course, we forget. We forget to notice, look, appreciate, acknowledge.

I forget.

I write all this and I'll still forget again. But I'll be reminded. At least I've put myself on a path where I get a lot of reminders to wake me up.

One of the best reminders I've had in a long time came a few years ago at a place called Ferry Beach, a Unitarian Conference Center in Maine. The big lodging house there is "rustic," to put it nicely. The rooms remind me of a Salvation Army barracks. But out the window is the ocean. Across the road is a grove of tall trees with a clearing where we gather every morning for an informal homily by one of the ministers or laypeople. With the sun laying gold stripes through the dark green foliage, I listen to Ed Lane, a pastor of the First Parish of Waltham, in Massachusetts, talking about the "everyday" miracles—the ones that, again, I'd forgotten about.

"I don't know anyone who doesn't believe in grace—no one—it's a universal," Reverend Lane tells us. "This universe into which we were born, this planet on which walk, are unearned gifts. That's what grace is. Take gravity—rather, take it away, and this planet and everything on it would fly apart. We would be dead in a matter of moments.

"Grace is unearned. Life itself is a gift of grace. We didn't 'earn' the right to be born. We didn't have to ask to be born. We didn't have to do anything about it. Birth came to us as a gift.

"When we think of grace, we usually think of something out of the ordinary, even what we sometimes call a miracle or supernatural. We think of the biblical stories of healing, of bringing the dead back to life, of turning water into wine. In the process we have forgotten the everyday grace that takes place under our noses all the time.

"If I cut my finger, I can clean it, perhaps put an antiseptic and a Band-Aid on it. If it's badly cut, I go to my doctor and she may close the cut with stitches. But the miracle is in the healing of the wound, the tissue growing back together again. We do not heal the wound, we only create the conditions in which that healing can take place. The healing is a gift of grace.

"The redwood seed is one of the smallest of seeds, yet from it grows a giant tree, which with time and the right conditions is as large as forty feet in diameter—earlier ones as much as a hundred feet across. That's a miracle! But while the redwood awes us in its majesty, the tiniest plant, even the weed that we pull out of our gardens is a miracle—though some of you may object to calling the weeds 'grace.' But stop a moment and think about that.

"If you could really just sit in your rocking chair and have your garden grow, would you like that? Most gardeners I know consider the gift, the grace, of gardening to be in the labor of doing it. As a friend of mine said, 'I certainly don't do it for the money. If I calculate the costs and add payment for my labor at a minimum wage, I figure my tomatoes cost about twenty dollars each!' So even your weeds may be a gift of grace.

"Some of us go through life searching for miracles, wishing that one would come our way. Our difficulty is we don't look in the right place. I mentioned turning water into wine. We look for the supernatural event, the touch of a hand that makes it happen. That's the wrong place. Go to the vineyard and watch the grapevines being set out; wait for the rain to fall and the vine to draw up the water and the nutrients that makes the vine grow and the grapes to form; watch as the grapes are gathered, the juice extracted; smell the fermentation process as the juice turns into wine. There's the miracle of turning water into wine! That's grace!

"If you would appreciate grace, look for it in ordinary places. As Emerson said: 'If the stars should appear one by one in a thousand years, how we would believe and adore, and preserve for many generations the remembrance of the City of God which had been shown! But every night come out these envoys of beauty, and light the universe with their admonishing smile.'

"And it was Whitman who said, 'A mouse is miracle enough to stagger sextillions of infidels.'

"The first time Buckminster Fuller saw the photograph of the earth beamed back from space by the Apollo astronauts, he scribbled this prayer on the back of an envelope:

Dear God of Galaxies,
We give thanks for being,
We give thanks for being here,
We give thanks for being here together;
Rides on earth together,
Brothers and sisters on a bright loveliness in the eternal cold,
Brothers and sisters who now know they are truly brothers and sisters,
Amen and amen!

One of the experiences that is part of life yet never ceases to renew our sense of the miraculous is childbirth. It's almost as if this guaranteed miracle is built in to the human experience to keep reminding us of the miraculous nature of life. We understand it best when we hear it from the parents. Here a mother tells of the birth of twins, and the father then describes his own view of that birth, which for both of them seemed a miracle.

The miracle of birth can be experienced even by those who themselves are unable to bear children. A woman and her husband are able to adopt a baby who's about to be born and feel that this gift is "a double miracle."

THERE'S NO DIVISION OF LOVE
Adelaide Ketchum Perry

Adelaide Ketchum Perry was vice-president in charge of quality control for a software company before she left to devote full time to motherhood. She is also a fine athlete, a marathon runner. I have the honor of being her friend and godfather of her first child, Nicholas, who is now the older brother of twins Mark and Laura.

"Having twins was especially a 'wonder' after having been told I couldn't have any more children. After our first child, three and a half years ago, we tried for a second. Nothing happened, nothing happened, and nothing happened. We went to see the obstetrician, and he sent us to a fertility clinic. The fertility doctor said it was not likely I could have children again. He would give me a fertility drug, whose possible side effects were multiple births, but he said I didn't need to worry about that; I'd be very lucky to get even one child.

"Then boom, two months later I'm pregnant with twins. I guess it was a miracle I got pregnant at all, much less had twins, and I guess the other miracle was that it wasn't more than twins.

"The miracle of the delivery was when it was over. I was afraid something would go wrong. I was worried about delivering early, which often happens with twins. I had to spend last two months in bed. But delivery was totally normal, no C-section, no drugs, which is really unusual. They were born two weeks early, which is really normal.

"Just looking at these two little babies is enough of a wonder. To look at one is a wonder, and to look at two, to watch them grow and turn into individuals, is amazing. They're so different, yet they're the same age, they both come from the same two people, they both came out of me.

"I lie awake at night thinking how much I love my three little children. Maybe the most wondrous thing is that it doesn't divide your love three ways—you just have more love. It's a wonder, a mystery. Where does it come from?"

"HOW MUCH CAN YOU LOOK
AT THE FACE OF GOD?"
Charles Perry

Adelaide's husband, Charles Perry, and I are friends who took part in a prayer group at King's Chapel on Monday nights for four years. Charles is a graduate of Middlebury College and works as a foreign policy analyst for a think tank in Cambridge, Massachusetts. We had dinner at our favorite Vietnamese restaurant and talked about miracles.

"With all the medical and scientific knowledge we have, no one really knows when the birth will happen. The top OB-GYN said to Adelaide, 'We're going to induce you,' and they gave her this IV solution. The first hour nothing happened, the second hour everything was fine, and the doctor said he had three other babies to deliver, she wouldn't be ready till that night. He told me to go get lunch. When I came back an hour later, she was in labor.

"It was so sudden there was no time for any drugs. It was natural birth. It seems it's like a freight train coming down the middle of you—or passing a ten-pound bag of sugar. Adelaide was wailing like a wild cow, a sound of incredible agony, wailing you never heard any other time before. Sounds like that only happen in childbirth.

"Laura came out first; after that Mark got through. Laura just popped out—she was like a dog because they were so small. The animal quality of it is just there, no question about *what* we are—animals. In three seconds they started to 'pink up'—from blue to pink—then they cut the cord, put a little hat on them, wrapped a blanket around them, and they were ready to go. The incredible resilience of humans is clear then.

"The spiritual aspect is when you look at a newborn child. That first moment the child looks into your eyes, and really sees you—maybe it's a day or two later. It's a very deep, very powerful, innocent, all-knowing kind of look—it's very hard to hold that look. It's a feeling like, 'Am I prepared to look into the eyes of God and not blink?'

"When it's first out of the womb, the baby is still in another world. But when our babies finally looked at me, I was overwhelmed with tears. I had a hard time staying with the gaze; it was too much. How much can you look at the face of God? Who is he or she? It brings me back to the flow of life, down to it or up to it—the miracle of life. The miracle of birth brings you back to life."

"THE HAND OF GOD"

Maggie Monroe-Cassel

Maggie Monroe-Cassel is an ordained Baptist minister and pastor of the Judson Fellowship, an American Baptist church, in Sinclairville, New York. I got to know her when she took a workshop I led at Auburn Theological Seminary.

"My husband and I are among those thirty percent or so of couples who do not conceive and never know why. There is no clear reason.

"We were married in 1980 and graduated from seminary together in 1982. That spring we decided to try to start a family. As months rolled into years and tests results proved nothing, the humiliation of the fertility testing wore us thin. The first church where we served as co-pastors was very difficult for us. Describing it as hell on earth is not much of an exaggeration. On top of that we were dealing with the infertility stuff. I cried a lot. Every time a friend got pregnant, I cried. I could spot a pregnant woman a mile away. It was as though I could sense it even if it was not yet obvious!

"In January of 1985 we decided to take advantage of our childlessness and take a trip to Mexico. We needed to get away from it all. We were scheduled to be gone from the beginning of January to February 4. The Wednesday before the Saturday we left, I received a call from a Baptist colleague outside Syracuse. He was calling because his neighbor, a sister in charge of adoptions for Catholic Charities of Onandaga County, was looking desperately for a Baptist family who might adopt a baby yet to be born. A teenage couple wanted to find a Baptist home to adopt their baby, and there were no Baptists on Sister Mary Jane's long list of applicants. My colleague knew we were not able to conceive and thought we might be interested. My first reaction was no! We hadn't even started to think about it for ourselves, though my sister had recently adopted a child. It was all too sudden. But I told him I would ask around. I talked to my husband about it, and he was more open to the possibility; but I persisted and called around to friends and family. In each case they said, 'Why don't you do it?' In each case I responded, 'I'm not ready.'

"By the next morning, John and I were in the same place about this baby. You just don't look a gift horse in the mouth when it wants to plop a newborn baby in your lap! So we frantically tried to reach Sister Mary Jane and prayed she had not found someone else. Little did we know that she was convinced the hand of God was at work with us. We finally got hold of her, learned of the situation of this baby, and said yes. We then left for Mexico. Wow, what a trip it turned out to be!

"Five weeks later, having put our signature on one piece of paper and having yet to pay a small fee (a thousand dollars) for adoption, we walked out of Catholic Charities in Cazenovia, New York, with the most gorgeous, bright-eyed baby in the world.

"Because we knew about her birth before it happened, we were able to name her from the beginning, and we sent her tapes of our voices while she spent the mandatory thirty days in foster care. The day we first held her and spoke to her, she looked up at us as though we had always been together. And I believe that we have been.

"Every birth is a miracle of sorts because it is so beyond human understanding. (Even though we have the knowledge about what happens, I still do not think that we understand.) Chelsea's birth was a double miracle. I believe that she was conceived to be our child. And that the hand of God really was at work in its mysterious way. She looks like us. She thinks and acts like us.

"The fact that Chelsea is part of our lives is the one sure thing that my husband (who questions everything) says keeps him believing in a Divine Being at all. For me, she is the most profound example of a modern miracle. I give thanks to God for working through her birth parents and us to bring us together."

In the years of giving my workshop in spiritual autobiography, I've seen a theme emerge: Everyone has a story of how another person's act of kindness or understanding—whether large or small—makes a tremendous difference in their life. Hearing these stories over and over has made me want to paint a reminder on my wall with this simple message: everything counts. Whatever you say, the way you look or fail to look at another person, the tone of your voice, the noticing of someone else, may take only a moment, may be nothing to you, and yet it may create a miracle in someone else's life.

A Sunday school teacher's visit to a little girl in a hospital begins a healing process that the grown woman will never forget. A young rabbi is summoned late at night and arrives just in time to say a prayer for a dying woman. A young man from the Bronx realizes his dream and serves as an inspiration to his younger brother. A world-famous woman's thoughtfulness lights up the life of an unknown admirer.

"HIS LOVING-KINDNESS
FORCED ME TO LIVE"

Mary L. Robertson

Mary Robertson wrote about the dream of her mother in the chapter "Miracles of Presence." The following experience might be considered a story of presence or healing, but it seems to me to speak powerfully of the "daily life" nature of simple acts we all perform (or forget to perform) that turn out to be, literally, of life and death significance.

"The year I turned eleven I was taken to the emergency room of a downtown hospital. The pain in my right ear was severe; in the 1930s mastoiditis was a life-threatening illness. After several days I was wheeled, screaming, to an operating room. I was given ether, and the operation began. Later I awoke to more pain.

"Though I was given medication, I did not rally. I did not rally despite the doctor's daily attentions, my parents' visits, the excellent care of two private nurses, and the many cards I received. The card I liked to think about was from Mr. Scarlett, my own Sunday school teacher.

"Mr. Scarlett was a tall, rugged bachelor whom my mother referred to as a diamond in the rough. He had moved away from my city neighborhood to a small country community, where he farmed seriously. On his card Mr. Scarlett had written about his spring planting and about the wildflowers in bloom.

"One morning my day nurse told me I had an early visitor, a large man in dungarees who had stopped by on the way to a farmers' market downtown. Mr. Scarlett had created quite a stir, apparently, but was not allowed to visit me at such an unorthodox hour. For the first time I was really aware of the spring. I could see none of it, but I could hear the birds in the early morning. A day or two later I saw the green grass across the street when I was allowed to sit in a chair. Easter was near, I realized.

"That very day Mr. Scarlett, in leather jacket and dungarees, appeared in the doorway with a bunch of violets he had picked from the edges of his field of vegetables. He told me about my Sunday school friends, especially my best friend, Mary. When I got well enough to be discharged from the hospital, Mary told me the Sunday school class had prayed for me two weeks in a row.

"Today, more than fifty years later, I feel certain that the loving-kindness of Mr. Scarlett forced me to live. It was a healing."

"THE GREATEST GIFT"

Jinny Henenberg

Jinny Henenberg works in market research and is a volunteer at a hospice, which she says is "a transforming experience, in which you learn that death is part of life." She has written and published a book called *Be Prepared* on how to keep personal records for the elderly, the ill, and those who wish to do future planning.

"The night my mother was dying of cancer in a hospice I was with her. Family members gathered and began the vigil for what was going to be a long night. We often visited her room and talked to her, said our good-byes, and then would fall silent. My mother was comatose by this time and never regained consciousness.

"As I watched her drift from me, I felt there was something I wanted to do for her, so I asked the staff if they had a rabbi who would come and say a prayer for her final journey. It was late by now, and they cautioned me that my mother was very near death and would not be aware of what was happening, but they said they would try. Shortly thereafter, a young, humble-looking rabbi appeared at my mother's doorway. I asked him if he would say a prayer for her before she left us. He entered her room, put his hands on her head, and began to chant in Hebrew. When he was finished, we all turned to leave the room when she suddenly awakened. With the last of her energy and love, she opened her eyes and looked at me and said, 'Jinny, thank you for bringing God to me.' Then with a final breath, she died.

"The miracle of love and prayer brought her back from where she was for just a moment, but long enough to carry me for a lifetime. It was the greatest gift God could have given me."

REDEEMED IN THE MIDST OF SUFFERING

Julio Medina

Julio Medina received a graduate degree from the New York Theological Seminary.

"My older brother has been one of the great inspirations in my life. When I was nine years old my brother Robert was about fourteen and in his freshman year of high school. He ended up joining the Cardinal Hayes track team and fell in love with the sport. He began to encourage my friends and me to participate and started to organize us. I was quietly impressed with the sport and soon developed into a pretty good runner. Under his direction I placed third in a national event held in Washington, D.C. I went on to become a top high school runner in cross-country.

"Throughout this time my brother would shine shoes and take odd jobs in order to provide trophies for the first-, second-, and third-place finishers in races he would sponsor in the neighborhood. This tactic would encourage inner-city kids to excel, both academically and physically, as well as build esteem in the tough streets of the South Bronx. He became the founder of the Bronx Athletic Club that would eventually become a force in the running world.

"The startling thing about my brother is he never abandoned his childhood dream. From the ghettos of the inner city he has now become the head coach at the State University of New York at Albany. He was recently honored as coach of the year and has been nominated as one of the coaches for the 1996 Olympics being held in Atlanta.

"His perseverance to overcome all obstacles has been a force that continues to provide me with hope in the dark chambers of prison. . . .

"In September 1993 I was transferred to Sing Sing Correctional Facility to begin an intensive year of biblical study. It was something new in my life because much of my life never consisted of anything spiritual. Although I was raised in a Catholic home and attended Catholic schools, anything Christian remained remote. Considering that this program offered a master's degree in professional studies, I said to myself, 'Hey, why not? Besides, it would look pretty good at my parole hearing.' In this frame of mind I began the program offered by New York Theological Seminary.

"After discovering my spiritual gifts, my attitude completely changed. I was interested no longer in the degree but in my spiritual growth. I couldn't believe that God had provided the spiritual insight to return back to my family as a whole. In the gloomy halls of Sing Sing, where men are executed, God transformed my intentions.

"The degree has become of no value if I do not use it to change the conditions of the inner-city community. The miracle is God has redeemed me in the midst of suffering."

A LETTER FROM JACKIE ONASSIS
Lisa Fay

Lisa Fay lives in Boston, where she is a community activist in the housing field and a photographer.

"It was a miracle I met Jackie Onassis. She was the last person I expected to meet, knowing how private and elusive she was. We met at the Kennedy Library in June of 1992 when the Hemingway Award for First Fiction was announced. She snuck past me in the lobby, but I knew it was her: the sunglasses, the kerchief, those long legs.

"The winner of the award read in such a monotone I was bored, but I used this to advantage. I started writing a letter to Jackie, explaining how

I knew many members of the family and recently went to Paris, where I remembered a street there named after her late husband. I invited her to the Very Special Arts exhibition at the Boston Public Library the following month. When I finished the letter, I had it delivered to her, hand over hand, down the row where she was sitting.

"When the talk was over, I introduced myself to her. Friends can no longer chuckle when I say, 'All life is meeting people.' Despite our differences in wealth, our lives and interests were extraordinarily similar. We are both Irish and Catholic, tall, thin, and talented, and had been educated abroad; we are both private, secure in who we are. We love arts and culture, photography, horseback riding, preservation of words and landscapes.

"She went downstairs for the reception, milling through the crowd. When it was time for her to leave, she raced up the stairs, and as she did, I said 'Bye.' Her eyes lit up and she smiled. Then she was gone, but she stays permanently in my memory.

"Nearly three weeks later, I received a letter saying she was sorry she couldn't come to the Very Special Arts exhibition I had invited her to attend. I was shocked because people don't usually respond if they're unable to attend events—they just throw out the invitation. This just showed how thoughtful she was to me.

"I cried when she died. Her death was a big loss to me. Now I can only emulate her dignity and grace, never quite touching it—a tall order on short notice."

Joy comes unexpectedly, breaking through the mundane routines of life in simple ways. Joy itself is a miracle, an upsurge or overflowing of feeling, unaccounted for, lifting our spirits. Joy wakens us to the miracle of life through unexpected changes in the wind and sky, accomplishments that once seemed beyond our grasp, sudden appreciation of the beauty of nature when we see in a way we didn't before. A man piloting a hot-air balloon finds perfect weather conditions and realizes the blessing of life. A woman runs a marathon in her seventies and makes her first appearrance as a dancer on stage in New York in her eighties. A novelist looks at wild primroses and glimpses paradise.

ABOVE THE FIELD

The Reverend Doug Green

Douglas J. Green is minister of the First Congregational Church of Christ in Ithaca, New York, and has served as chair of the New York Special Olympic Summer Games.

"For our opening ceremonies of the New York Special Olympics Summer Games we wanted to have a hot-air balloon rise up from a nearby field and then fly over a stadium filled with seventeen hundred mentally handicapped athletes, their families, and friends. If the weather was good and the wind was right (two big ifs in Ithaca), and if it wasn't too dark, we felt this would be a moving experience for all who were gathered there.

"My wife, Laurie, was chair of our special events, and she contacted Ron Rogers, who pilots hot-air balloons. Ron owns a trucking company in Binghamton, and is a tough, hard-nosed guy who's successful in a tough business. He drives a brand-new Cadillac complete with a cellular phone.

"Though Laurie explained to him that this was a nonprofit, low-budget event, planned and executed by volunteers, he said flatly that he wanted a $150 deposit now, and when he showed up with his crew in Ithaca, he wanted another $200 on the spot, whether he flew or not. If he flew, he'd be paid an additional $200. Laurie, a tough negotiator herself, said Ron was one of the toughest she'd met. He was not at all sympathetic to the cause; this was like any other business deal. It would be the most expensive part of the ceremony, but we decided it was worth it.

"On the day of the event, the conditions needed to fly were perfect—the wind speed and direction, light, weather, everything. The balloon took off and sailed over the reviewing stand, and then it just hung there. In a hot-air balloon, you go where the wind goes; you can go up and down, but you can't just make it stand still. But Ron was just hanging there.

"Ron said that in his thirty years as a pilot, he'd never experienced weather conditions like that—conditions that allowed him to hover in the same spot, right over the reviewing stand. His crew on the field was in radio contact with Ron and asked if he was all right. They wanted to know whether he was caught or something. He told them he was OK and that he didn't know what was going on.

"Ron said as he looked down and saw the faces looking up at him with excitement and pleasure, I thought of my own life, of my two healthy sons, and felt very blessed. I heard an inner voice say, Give it back. You don't need this money.'

"He threw something to the ground, and one of our volunteers ran over and picked it up. There was an envelope with the checks in it that Laurie had given him. He called her the next day and thanked her for what he said was 'a spiritual experience—the experience of a lifetime.'"

"I CARRIED THE SOLOIST OFF THE STAGE"

Helen Stout

I met Helen Stout—who writes and dances under the name "Heleri"—at a workshop in Seattle just before her seventy-ninth birthday. What she wrote about approaching that age with a sense of wonder, excitement, wisdom, and humor ("No, I didn't learn everything I need to know in kindergarten") was an inspiration to me. Her only fear was that "there's not enough time to do it all," but since then—some five or six years later—she has done a lot more, including appearing in her New York dance debut, which she tells about here. She also describes the marathon she ran back when she was seventy-four— and other triumphs. Meet Heleri, a continuing miracle of daily life.

"Something happens that you don't deserve, don't expect—there are other times that go in the opposite direction, with one tragedy following another. You survive (or maybe not), but you learn from them, and in a way they add a richness to the whole experience of living. My husband, John, used to say, 'Those are the things you often remember most vividly, with the most satisfaction: the backpack trip when it rained fourteen consecutive days. Surely it brought your group closer together, it cemented your friendship as no amount of partying ever could.' Something that seems impossible becomes possible.

"I ran a marathon (actually walked) 26.2 miles in Honolulu in 1984. I was seventy-four years old and had been in shorter races for two or three years. It started when John brought home a flyer called 'Run, Walk, or Crawl'—something I could do, he said. I often came home with an award just for getting to the end—generally the last one.

"After ten miles of the marathon I didn't see any way to get back if I quit, so I kept going. The farther I got, the better I felt—but somewhere near the halfway point I stumbled and fell. I got rather dizzy—light-headed. My kidneys weren't functioning, so it seemed I was dehydrated. I just kept plugging away. I must have been on automatic pilot. One step at a time. You hear of 'hitting the wall' at 20 or 21 miles, but I hardly noticed. When we got to the top of a long hill, I tried to jog down, but my knees wouldn't do it.

"I wasn't sure I'd make that last quarter mile, but I did. Seven hours, fifty-six minutes. Someone put a lei over my head. *Then* I collapsed. I had to lie down, or I would have been sick to my stomach—they got a first aid person. My blood pressure was low, and they made me stay still for a few minutes and brought me a soda and a banana. Then I was OK. I walked a mile back to the hotel. I had done something 'impossible,' and I didn't even have a blister! I learned there had been fourteen women in my age group (seventy to seventy-five), and I was number seven. The two winners were Japanese women, much faster—a little over five hours each.

"There are times you can accomplish something beyond will by releasing consciousness, practicing a kind of utter concentration that somehow gets you there. Like a dance I did, written up in this review of a dance performance of Scott Heron in the *Village Voice* (October 19, 1993): 'A green-haired, squat person called Heleri spelled Heron during a costume change by playing a wonderfully sly leprechaun. The 83-year-old English-woman slipped from one perfectly ineffectual stunt to another with sure timing and unbeatable confidence.'

"To start it I barged in and carried the soloist off the stage and dumped him—then did my impossible 'ineffectual' little piece. My 'New York debut' at age eighty-three! If I stopped to think about it, I couldn't do it.

238 *Wakefield*

"Over the last few years I've had a friendship with a young, gay dancer—we have been very close and shown great support, respect, and love for each other. He has a partner, both share the scourge—and at age eighty-four, I too face the end of my life sometime in the not-distant future. I would be very lonely without these men. I admire and love them, and it seems only a miracle could have brought them into my life after my husband died.

"I believe there are miracles that will visit every one of us if we are open enough to see them. For me, it involves the God within, not some Deity in the sky. It is part of nature and within our nature."

"A CARPET IN PARADISE"

Hugh Nissenson

Hugh Nissenson is the writer who spoke so passionately of the novel he is working on, "Song of Earth," in the chapter on creation. His senses are highly receptive to all his experience, as we see when he speaks of the wonders of daily life.

"I was there when my first daughter was born, by natural childbirth. I went into an ecstatic trance for three days—reality was transfigured. I was in a cab and looked up to see the stoplight turn from red to green, and they were the most beautiful colors I had ever seen. It lasted three days and then it went.

"Frequently I experience the intrusion of terror or the fear of death, but I also have transfigured moments. I look at my kids, I look at my wife, whom I've loved for thirty years. She and a friend of hers have just written a wonderful book, and it's getting great reviews and attention and selling, and I feel joy about it. The 'veil' is rent by that.

"The older I get, the more I relish the varieties of the natural world. About ten years ago my wife and I and another couple bought a house in France in the Loire Valley. We went there for a week last spring, when I was sick from exhaustion. It was April, cold and rainy, and my friend Paul and I went out into the garden. The gardener hadn't cut the grass, and there were wild primroses. It was twilight and Paul pointed at this profusion of primroses and said, 'Look—it's a carpet in paradise!' It's true; that's what it is, if you can see it."

Appreciation of life itself, becoming suddenly aware of the miracle of being alive, on this planet, can turn what we call ordinary life into a miracle. We come awake to such a realization when we recognize our connection to a spiritual dimension or perceive the awesome mystery of our journey, its amazing twists and turns, its connections to others, those we meet and those from the past who touch us with their words or art or spirit.

Revelations, moments of turning, large and small, alert us to new possibilities of being in the world. A pro baseball pitcher gets a new sense of values when his son faces a crisis. A minister looks back on his life as it moved from Iowa to East Harlem and realizes he was "led by the spirit." From his prison cell, a man sees each new day as a gift. A housewife in Connecticut makes a list of a hundred miracles in her life. A prisoner in Sing Sing who survived drugs and gunshots believes it's a miracle he's still alive.

Miracles are not limited to any place, person, faith, race, creed, color, size, or fortune.

Miracles abound.

"IT MADE US A FAMILY"

Ron Darling

Ron Darling is a starting pitcher for the Oakland Athletics, and before that he pitched for nearly nine years for the New York Mets. He was named to the National League All-Star team and played in that game in 1985. A year later he won a game in the World Series that helped the Mets defeat the Boston Red Sox. He is a graduate of Yale University.

"When our son Tyler, our first child, was a year old, he had a seizure. He was unconscious for three or four minutes. After that he had trouble learning, and we took him to a doctor who said he was autistic. My wife and I couldn't believe it. We were told he would always have to go to special schools, that he wouldn't be able to live a normal life—that he'd never be able to live on his own. We were in a taxicab in New York coming from the doctor's, and we both got very emotional. I told the cab driver to stop at Fifty-eighth and York, where I saw a bookstore, and I jumped out and got about twelve books on autism. In the next year or so we sent him to special schools, tried special programs, but nothing worked. We were very frustrated.

"My wife and I are not very religious people, but we prayed.

"A year and a half after the seizure, we took him to see a woman on the Upper West Side who worked with autistic children. Her name was Shoshanna Goldman. I'll never forget her. She played with Tyler, and after a while she said, 'He's not autistic at all. He has a developmental problem.' We found out he had a little language impairment, and it caused his frustration, and that led to behavior problems.

"Now he's in the second grade, in one of the top schools in our area. He's doing as well as his peers, and as poorly as his peers, which is great too. He's a normal seven-year-old.

"This experience brought us closer. Before it happened everything was going well, my career was going well, and I'd started to get into that self-centered stuff—the kind of thing that happens when everything is revolving around you. This made us think about what's real and what's not. It made us humble. It made us a family. It's the greatest gift ever."

"LED BY THE SPIRIT"
The Reverend Bill Weber

George W. "Bill" Weber was one of the founding members of the East Harlem Protestant Parish, served as president of the New York Theological Seminary, and now directs the seminary's educational program for inmates at Sing Sing Prison in Ossining, New York. I met Bill back in the 1950s when he was a minister of one of the storefront churches of the East Harlem Protestant Parish and reconnected with him in the 1990s when he asked me to give my workshop for the class he teaches at Sing Sing. I've come to learn from him about prisons, theology, addiction, law, and many more aspects of life on the trips "up the river" we take.

"I guess you could say that how I ended up doing what I've done and what I'm doing is a miracle, but there wasn't any lightning coming out of the sky. I grew up in the Plymouth Congregational Church in Des Moines, Iowa; it was a liberal, 'postscientific' church, where miracles were not taken as 'real.' My mother was typical of the outlook: She'd been brought up Baptist, with a lot of rules, and for her the Congregational church helped her deal with Jesus as a human being—she didn't have to buy the miracles that now seemed outdated. It was a church like Riverside Church in New York, where heroes were people like Lincoln and Schweitzer—people who had the spirit of Jesus *in them*. Those were our heroes when I was growing up.

"Once I got into East Harlem I couldn't discount the fact that when people there talked about miracles, they were describing experiences that were absolutely real, particularly in terms of healing stories. At New York Theological Seminary I've time and again heard stories from people who grew up in those neighborhoods who you had to take seriously. It's always a paradox in Christianity—Jesus is fully God and Jesus is fully man. Or you're justified but still a sinner; or you decided to do something or you were drafted by God.

"I've come to believe it's both. We don't know all the answers, we're not God, so it doesn't have to all hit the right side of the brain or whichever the 'logical' side is. I didn't have that kind of sudden and dramatic miracle like the people from East Harlem describe. I feel more like I've been led by the Spirit to do what I've done. Is that a miracle?

"When I got married in 1942, I promised my wife I'd be a lawyer. But when I really had to decide what I was going to do for a living after the war, I tried to think of someone I knew who had meaning and significance in life. I thought of the pastor of my church, a wonderful man, and the lessons I'd learned in the YMCA, and I knew what I wanted to do.

"I became dean of students at Union Seminary and associate professor of church and community while working part-time in the East Harlem Protestant Parish, this group of storefront churches, with other Union graduates.

"My father wrote me an eight-page letter saying it was all right whatever I wanted to do and where I wanted to live, but he was not going to stand for his grandchildren being raised in East Harlem. As it turned out, East Harlem was probably the healthiest place in America to bring up white, middle-class kids. My colleagues had terrible times with their kids—lots were on drugs, one died of an overdose. Suburbia was hell on kids. My kids, and the kids of the other ministers, all grew up to be remarkably wonderful people.

"I never planned the major turning points in my life. Later I could see God in this. I sure as hell didn't plan to have five kids—I thought two was the right number—much less raise them in East Harlem.

"That's why I say I've been led by the Spirit. In retrospect, yes, I'd say where I've been led is a miracle."

"I PREVAIL"

A Prisoner at Sing Sing (Anonymous)

"It is a miracle to me that I was conceived through the contact of my mother and father. The gift of life for me is a miracle. Every day that I live on this planet is an amazing miracle. As I grow older and see the experiences that I and others go through, it becomes a miracle simply to live every day.

"God has the ultimate power in life, and that power is a miracle. As a human being I believe all things rest with God. No matter how much I would want to change or make things different, there are some things that I cannot do. In my struggles sometimes I wonder how I continue to go on. Nevertheless I continue to prevail, and that in and of itself to me is a miracle."

ONE HUNDRED MIRACLES

Pat Gralton

Pat Gralton lives with her husband on a farm in Connecticut whose one-hundred-year-old house they are renovating. She keeps a journal and designs jewelry. She told me when she got my letter requesting miracle stories, she let it lie around for several weeks, then noticed it in the trash one day, pulled it out, and sat down and wrote this response.

100 Things I Know About Miracles

1. They sneak up on me when I'm not looking.

2. They fall into the same category as guardian angels, stardust, and fairy wings.

3. They occur so regularly that every once in a while something bad has to happen to catch my attention.

4. There is no mistaking a miracle for anything else.

5. I always know when I have experienced a miracle. I don't suspect, think, surmise. I know down to the soles of my feet.

6. It amazes me that I can feel comfortable in a place where stardust and fairy wings exist.

7. Once I experienced one miracle, they started coming faster and faster.

8. Miracles are happening all the time, but when I acknowledge they exist, I'm really saying I believe in God.

9. I had a spiritual awakening as a result of the twelve steps and ACOA.

10. I met a shaman-therapist who helped me heal so many wounds. I was ready; she appeared.

11. Miracles are spontaneous. I can't plan or orchestrate one.

12. Miracles are a gift I have to claim. I'm open for deliveries. Put my name on it. YES.

13. I survived an alcoholic home.

14. The miracle of tomorrow when I can change my mind, start over, or throw it out.

15. The miracle of letting go. When I'm holding on too tight or making a fist, it's hard for a miracle to land in the palm of my hand.

16. The miracle of mentors and wise old folks who are willing to show me the ropes.

17. My garden is a miracle. It teaches me everything about life that I will ever need to know: anticipation, birth, joy, changes in color and texture, different shades of the same color, buds, dead blossoms, killing frost, burial, saying farewell, hope for the spring, renewal.

18. A seed catalog in January is a miracle.

19. A child's hug.

20. All the things that don't go wrong.

21. The *Oprah Winfrey Show* told me about ACOA. That started a chain reaction of recovery.

22. The day my husband didn't drown in Hawaii.

23. The surgery that saved my husband's life.

24. The way I met my husband.

25. The day we renewed our wedding vows.

26. My friends.

27. An engineer listens to God through his dreams (and I get to sleep with him!).

28. My journal.

29. My marriage to Gary.

30. Addictions are just lifted effortlessly—alcohol, excitement, shopping, food, drama.

31. The way my body works.

32. Watching the seasons change.

33. Human endeavors for good.

34. I learn God's plan for me through my pen.

35. It will be a miracle when I finish this list with one hundred statements.

36. I believe in a personal God that feels right for me.

37. I became free of that vengeful, fickle God of my childhood.

38. I'm alive.

39. I am loved.

40. I am able to love.

41. I have all of my teeth.

42. The nonfat, decaf cappucino that really tastes great at Peter B coffee shop in West Hartford.

43. I didn't go crazy.

44. The will to live.

45. Someone remembered my name.

46. I didn't become an alcoholic.

47. Watching Elizabeth grow.

48. My Aunt Annie's sense of humor.

49. I saw my work in print.

50. I'm halfway there!

51. Unfoldings.

52. A pat on the shoulder; a peck on the cheek.

53. Someone says, "I know what you mean, I hear you."

54. Creative expression on any level—a person's soul shining through her work.

55. Tasting love in the food my friends prepare.

56. Flow, bliss, connectedness, attraction.

57. The microsecond before I realized I was experiencing a oneness with God.

58. My husband doesn't think I'm crazy.

59. We are going to remain partners until one of us dies.

60. Robert Bly's reference to a third body that is formed because of our relationships.

61. Because Gary and I chose to marry each other, the universe will never be quite the same.

62. Every night that we return safely to our home.

63. The ability to remember.

64. The ability to forget, forgive, and move on.

65. A sense of awe.

66. Amazing grace.

67. The click when a shift of consciousness falls into place.

68. Roses, peonies, pansies, gardenias, camellias, lilacs, zinnias, orchids, violets, geraniums, kittens, puppies, and fireflies.

69. The Constitution of the United States of America.

70. The hummingbirds and butterflies that fill my garden.

71. When the student is ready, the teacher appears.

72. I want to live.

73. My women's journal group.

74. It wasn't cancer.

75. I happened to be standing behind the shower door when the wall-sized mirror fell and shattered into a million shards.

76. The hummingbirds and butterflies find my garden.

77. I have everything I want.

78. I expect a miracle.

79. Miracles happen all the time, but choosing to accept them multiplies their power.

80. God reveals so much of God's majesty through human creativity.

81. Modern technology and electronics that I don't begin to comprehend.

82. A man has walked on the moon, and they transplant organs.

83. So many things just keep going right.

84. Wishing can make it so.

85. The knowledge, love, and medicines that keep me healthy.

86. I can give up bad habits and develop healthy ones.

87. Possibilities: I can't wait to meet the woman I am willing to become.

88. Once I put the question into words, the answer always comes.

89. Buy a ticket. You can't win if you don't play.

90. See miracles in the simple stuff: The shop down the street always has four flavors of nonfat yogurt.

91. Use my imagination; it's a miracle collector.

92. People say thank you, all day long. You can too.

93. People talk about miracles. Tell your friends. It pays to advertise.

94. Miracle stories come in handy when I'm scared. I collect them.

95. We can all be a channel for a miracle to manifest itself. Look into someone's eyes. Pay attention.

96. We can cooperate with the power that makes a miracle happen; when it's conceived, it's born.

97. You usually don't get what you ask for but what you need.

98. It's a miracle I ever had the courage to let someone read this list!

99. Thank you.

100. I made it to a hundred.

"SOMEONE IN THE MIRACLE BUSINESS"

Luis Serrano

Luis Serrano is a prisoner at Sing Sing. He graduated from the program given there by the New York Theological Seminary.

"The only miracle that I can think of is that I am sitting here in a classroom and not lying in some cemetery. During my years of drug abuse and criminal activities, I overdosed on heroin five or six times. I should have died from any one of those overdoses, but something kept me alive.

"In my life I have been shot at with pistols and rifles, close and long range, and yet I am still here. I even fell off the roof of a whorehouse that I was burglarizing and came off with minor injuries. So I believe I'm either very fortunate, or someone in the miracle business is looking out for me."

YOUR OWN MIRACLE

In one of my talks with Father Gerry O'Rourke, he said, "Your book should challenge everyone who reads it to have her or his miracle story."

He didn't mean only that people should be challenged to see the miracles that already exist and operate in their lives, in large and small ways, day by day and minute by minute—although that's a great way to start. He also meant I should challenge people to open themselves for a new and unexpected miracle to occur in their life, to live in a way that will help create one.

One?

Why not a hundred?

Why stop there?

What's yours?

THE MIRACLE OF
THE MIRACLE BOOK

❧

This book came through me. All books come through the writer—the transcriber—as all art works come through the artist, all music through the musician. William Blake talked of his poems as being "dictated" to him. The creator of a work of literature, music, or art realizes the work does not come "from" but "through" her. You have to work to get yourself to the point of letting it come—you have to be a good conduit to let it flow. But when it flows, you know if you are honest the source was not you. You may not know what or who or where the source was; you may wish to think of it as "source unknown," but you know it was not your own brain, "your" imagination. (Where did you get "*your* imagination"?)

Sure, you have to work hard and sometimes slave over a book, to shape it, or let it out, *get* it out, into the world, but the origin of it was "given." The theologian Elaine Pagels told me in her own struggles to write those marvelously illuminating books of hers (*The Gnostic Gospels, Adam and Eve and the Serpent*) she had the feeling that the work, the book, was already "there," but all these boulders were in the way of it. Writing, for her, seems not so much a matter of "creating" or inventing the book, but of "getting to it," around and over and through those boulders blocking the way.

In that sense it's always been clear to me that whatever I wrote—whether novels, articles, scripts, memoirs—came *through* rather than *out of* me, but none so clearly as *Expect a Miracle*. In a quite literal way I just transcribed it, for much of it was written or told me by other people. I was the framer, the designer, like someone who got some lumber, sawed off four pieces, and nailed them into a rectangle, then put this wonderful art work into it.

This has a familiar resonance, for it's how I explain the process of workshops I lead called "Spiritual Autobiography" in which I explain to participants that I don't really teach them anything, I'm more like a stage manager who puts up a frame or raises a proscenium arch and gives them a place and a way to come forth and tell their own story.

To bang together the frame for these stories I had to go out and learn about the kind of thing I was framing so I could set it off in the right way. This required a lot of reading, researching, traveling, and interviewing around the country and to Ireland and France, but those travels too, and those people I found to help me do the framing, were "given" in a more direct and natural way than in any work I've ever done. There was a sense that all I had to do was keep breathing, relax, and trust, and I'd be taken to where I had to go, and the people I needed to see would appear, materialize, like apparitions, or characters in *Star Trek* who were beamed down to me.

Most of my ideas for books come as pictures that appear in my head while walking down the street or through a "chance" meeting with someone or when a subject or experience catches my interest and attaches itself to me until I pay attention to it and follow. Sometimes other people have given me an idea that sparks in just such a way that I know it's exactly what I want to be doing next. That happened in 1967 when a conversation with Robert Manning over his backyard barbecue grill in Cambridge, Massachusetts, led to him commissioning me (inspired by a spring breeze and several martinis) to travel around the United States and write on the effect of the Vietnam War on this country for a whole issue of the *Atlantic Monthly*, later published as a book, *Supernation at Peace and War*. A man named David Sontag called from Hollywood in 1976 and asked if I'd like to write a television script about a boy growing up in America, and the boy became the TV series *James at Fifteen*. It happened again when Art Cooper, editor of *GQ*, assigned me to write a memoir about my friendship with James Baldwin, and when the essay appeared, the late publisher extraordinaire Sam Lawrence wrote to say it should be part of a book I ought to write, on *New York in the Fifties,* and he provided me a contract to do it.

Out of the blue, the cosmos, these things come, just as other ideas come for novels without an intermediary, dropped into my conscious mind. But you can't make it happen. You can't order it up like a chef's special. You can't depend on other people to do it for you, either; their well-meant suggestions may only make you grimace or yawn. Sometimes you go to your own well of ideas, and the bucket comes up empty. You reach for the next card and draw a blank.

In the summer of 1993 I was drawing a blank. I'd gone to my well and hauled out a dead fish—I had tried to recycle an idea for a novel and was told by people I trust it wasn't even breathing. Ugh. I saw they were right. I threw away the hundred pages I'd worked on all spring, knowing I would have to start from scratch. In the meantime, I was running on empty, in terms of cash as well as ideas. "I need a miracle," I told a friend. Those were my exact words. I didn't even know they were lyrics to a Grateful Dead song.

Three days later I got a call from Harper San Francisco, a publisher I'd never done business with before. It seems their executive editor, a man I didn't know named John Loudon, had an idea for a book, and my name had come up at their editorial meeting; he and the other editors thought I'd be a good person to write the book.

"What's it about?" I asked.

"Miracles," I was told.

I restrained myself from saying this phone call was the first miracle.

When I asked what kind of miracles they had in mind, I was told "contemporary miracles—extraordinary things that happen in ordinary people's lives." I immediately thought of the stories I'd heard from people in workshops I've given, from people I've met all over the world. I'm inspired by the stories people write and read, stories out of their own experience, their "ordinary" lives that shine and explode and surprise with extraordinary events, insights, transformations.

I've already started, I thought.

I wrote letters to all of the people who have taken my workshops, asking for help in this undertaking—asking for miracles. Stories came in from people all over the country. Those were the basis for the book's categories; those were the heart of the book that made it come to life. But it also needed to grow, take shape and form, flesh out.

I went to see theologian Harvey Cox, whom I'd met as a fellow retreatant at the Benedictine monastery Glastonbury Abbey in Hull, Massachusetts, back in 1984 and later written about in the *New York Times Magazine*. As he is the most articulate theologian I can imagine, I went to ask him for background and guidance on miracles, and when he'd given me a marvelous overview, I asked, "Have you had any miracles in your own life?" Without a moment's hesitation he smiled and said yes, proceeding to tell me the story that is now part of "Miracles of Love" in this book.

That same day in Boston I went to have coffee with Ivan Gold, a writer friend from Columbia College days, and when I told him I was working on a book about miracles, he smiled and said, "That's not my field." I nodded and was about to go on to another subject when I stopped and said, "Well, I want to have a chapter on miracles of recovery. What about your own experience in that?" Ivan began talking about his recovery from alcohol with such insight that I grabbed my pen and began writing, transcribing what I feel is one of the most insightful perceptions on the subject I know.

After that I asked everyone I saw if they had a miracle. I told them the dictionary definitions and then simply said to describe anything in their life they considered a miracle in their own terms and understanding. Most did.

I was on my way to give workshops in Belfast and Dublin when I decided I needed to go to Lourdes, the most famous of all miracle sites, to experience such a place of pilgrimage for this book. I needed some way to pay for the journey to France and tried to think of a magazine I could interest in Lourdes when John Sedgwick, a writer friend from Boston, told me he was just named as a national editor of *Self* magazine and asked if I had any article ideas. Lourdes is the last thing I thought would be of interest to a magazine for young women, but John said they'd been talking about the mind-body connection and this might intrigue them. Editor Nancy Smith commissioned me to do the piece.

I wrote another old Columbia friend, the novelist Sam Astrachan, to ask if I could stay at his house in the south of France. He and his wife, the

French sculptor Claude Jenneau, drove me to Lourdes, a seven-hour trip, and we stopped at the hotel where Claude stayed as a girl when her family went on pilgrimage. Sam spoke my journalistic needs to Lourdes officials in French and found Christine Bray, a young woman on the editorial staff of *Lourdes* magazine who spoke English. She quickly and graciously opened all doors for me.

In Ireland I went to the town of Roscommon to enjoy dinner with people I'd met years before at a workshop on ministry in Dublin. Father John Cullen, Father Frankie Murray, Father John O'Rourke, and Sister Katherine O'Rourke took me to meet Marion Carroll, the Irish woman who was healed at Knock, the Irish pilgrimage site. Marion's remarkable story was all the more meaningful to me because she was introduced by these clerics who had known her for years, before her miraculous healing.

The story of this book is a crowding of miracles; the book flowed. I kept remembering the thought of my old mentor and friend C. Wright Mills, the sociologist, who said, "When you're really into a book, living it, everything you see and do is related to it." I was standing in line for a wedding brunch when a woman told me of her mother's near-death experience and arranged for me to interview her. Out of the blue I got a mailing from the Jewish Healing Center and so attended a service, where I met Rabbi Nancy Flam, one of the most powerful conveyors of the spirit I've encountered in any faith.

In mentioning physical or spiritual disciplines and teachers I have found beneficial, from yoga to meditation, seminars with est and Landmark Education, or in my church or my faith as a Christian, I am simply giving testimony to my own experience rather than urging others to follow it. I do not intend to proselytize for any methodology, program, practices, or beliefs, nor do I necessarily endorse the beliefs or practices of the many other people of all faiths, backgrounds, and persuasions who share their experiences in this book. I give respect to their personal experience, as I wish them to respect mine. The manner of one person's miracle may be another person's mirage, and each must listen to his or her own true call.

What fascinates and inspires me is the variety and depth, the surprising and resourceful nature of human experience and its unexpected encounters with something "more," beyond, above, inside and out, finding meaning, strength, beauty, understanding, illumination. I admire the seekers, the ones who, whatever their path, are looking, searching, sharing, celebrating; who are, as the Navajos put it, "on the gleaming way." And I love the mystery, the fact that any of us, at any time, may be, as C. S. Lewis said, "surprised by joy."

If someone had told me twenty years ago I'd write a book about miracles, I'd have said "Get lost." Now here it is. Another miracle.

Acknowledgments

When I came back from Europe to finish writing this book, I went to the home of my friend Mimi Mindel in San Francisco, was provided with a room overlooking San Francisco Bay, bought a seventy-five-dollar no-speeds bicycle, which I rode to the Golden Gate Bridge every day, and enjoyed the company of a fabulous family: Mimi's dad, Sonny Marx, the patriarch, whom I want to be like at age eighty-five; brother Mel and wife, Carol (Ducky), son Michael and new bride, Joni, daughter Laura and husband, Steve Reinertsen, and son, Tony. Every one of them helped in some way with the book: Mel introducing me to his friend John Brodie, the former 49er quarterback who contributed a miracle, Michael putting me in touch with the PR man of the Grateful Dead, who tried to help, though it turned out they're keeping their miracles to themselves these days; Tony taking us to our first Grateful Dead concert and explaining the esoterica of their fandom, nutritionist Laura finding the no-speeds bike for me, and on and on, with leads, ideas, dinners, and kindnesses. And the company of Buster, the talking cat.

And Mimi's second family, her friends Annie Honig Nadel, who contributed a miracle of creativity; Suey Honig Weinstein, who hosted us at Napa; and Elaine Freedman, who has reached down deep, along with Bob Smith, who each day lives the miracle of being alive and who put me in touch with Lloyd and Loretta Kantor, whose story is one of the greatest miracles of the book. Dave Perron of the Oakland A's set up my interview with pitcher Ron Darling. And Mimi herself, whose miracle is a gift of love and friendship, embodied by the most extended loving family I know.

Many successful people whose abilities and hard work have given them celebrity status are understandably reluctant to respond to requests to take time out when none is available, so I'm especially grateful for the generosity of spirit of those who did: Judy Collins, Michael Crichton, John Brodie, Kathy Baker, Ron Darling, Rabbi Harold Kushner, Michael Dukakis, and Richard Lugar.

I not only met people with miracles of all kinds but came to appreciate the miracles of my own life, including my own family of friends, who bolster my only living relatives, Clayton Ridge, Jr., and his daughter, Paula Ridge Hall, and "adopted" blood brothers and sisters such as Ted the Horse Steeg, Jane Wylie Genth, Theresa Mackin, Shaun and Dorothy O'Connell, Marcie Hershman, April Smith, Sara Davidson, Pam Gordon, Charles and Adelaide Perry, Bob and Theresa Manning, Ivan and Vera Gold, Michael and Lisa Pressman; and new relatives such as Barbara Graham, Hugh Delahanty, Mary Lou Coudal, Chris Jones; and friends who are spiritual guides and coaches—Norm Eddy, Pamela Barz, Joseph Brenner, Sarah Wolfe, Anne Overton, Fran Travisano, Henri Nouwen, Elizabeth Retivov, John King, Nancy Cantor, David Zucker, and many others, including people now gone whose presence I still feel, such as Amy Frantz and Ollah Toph, May Swenson and C. Wright Mills.

My church family at King's Chapel in Boston remains crucial, from my minister, Carl Scovel, to my fellow worshipers. I'm also indebted to the ministers, rabbis, and priests all over the country who have taken me into their congregations to lead workshops, especially the generous Reverend John Buchanan of the Fourth Presbyterian Church in Chicago; Bill Weber of the New York Theological Seminary; Bob Reber of Auburn Theological Seminary; and Jeff Weber and Linda Hanick of Trinity Church and VISN network in New York. Friendly help and sponsorship have come from Nancy Lunney and Mike Murphy of the Esalen Institute and other influential learning centers, such as the Omega Institute, Interface in Boston, and the Boston Center for Adult Education, which gave my workshop its start.

DeWitt Henry of Emerson College and Les Standiford of Florida International University have provided me with important opportunities for teaching in their distinguished writing programs, and I count them as friends as well as colleagues.

I would not be in mental condition without the physical disciplines I've learned, beginning with the stationary bicycle and diet program of Boston's Dr. Howard Hartley and nurse Jane Sherwood, which set me on a new path in 1980. Thanks to *GQ* magazine, I went to the health spa Rancho La Puerta in Tecate, Mexico, to write an article about it in 1985 and have returned every year since to give talks and workshops and participate in the morning mountain hikes and bodywork classes that give me physical renewal and a fresh start. For this opportunity I am grateful to Deborah Szekely, the visionary co-founder of Rancho; Phyllis Pilgrim, the fitness director; and Victoria Larrea, program director. I am also grateful for the all-important stretching and meditation practices learned from marvelous yoga teachers who are now good friends, such as Danielle Levi Alvarez, Carol Nelson, Mara Carrico, Jennifer Fox, Paul Gould, Beryl Bender, Thom Birch, and Nancy Evans.

I have stretched and made breakthroughs as a result of the work I have done with Werner Erhard and cannot fail to acknowledge him. Like teachers such as Gurdjief and Trungpa, he is a controversial figure, denigrated and admired with equal fervor. I can only judge the man by my personal experience of his conduct at workshops I have taken or reported on, in which I found him challenging, insightful, and—unlike his image—nurturing and supportive of participants, empowering people to think for themselves.

Whenever I wanted to learn about miracles from other faiths I had only to call on Father Gerry O'Rourke, who introduced me to knowing representatives, including the Muslim Dr. Siddiqi and the Hindu Sister Chandru. In Sister Chandru's sunny living room I was given *prasada*, a holy food that tastes pleasantly of childhood rice pudding, and I felt blessed by the nourishment of both the food and her presence.

Before this book could be undertaken I had to get a contract with enough of an advance to enable me to live while I did the research and writing, a task handled by Lynn Nesbit, the famous miracle agent whose firm, Janklow and Nesbit, represents everyone from the pope to Phil Jackson, coach of the Chicago Bulls. I wasn't worried. The first time Lynn represented me, it was with Art Cooper, editor of *GQ*, who later told me he'd rather negotiate with Saddam Hussein. I haven't worried since. Another miracle.

About the Author

Dan Wakefield is a novelist, journalist, and screenwriter who grew up in Indianapolis and graduated from Columbia College in New York City. His book *Returning: A Spiritual Journey* originated with an article in the *New York Times Magazine* called "Returning to Church" and became a selection of the Quality Paperback Book Club in its Penguin edition. He is a member of King's Chapel in Boston, where he served as cochair of the Adult Religious Education Committee, was a member of the Vestry, and served on the board of the Unitarian-Universalist Christian Fellowship. His book *The Story of Your Life: Writing a Spiritual Autobiography* won a Silver Gryphon Award from *Publishers Weekly* as one of the ten outstanding religious books of 1990. The book evolved from workshops he gives in spiritual autobiography in churches and adult education centers across the country and in Ireland and Mexico. He also gives workshops in "Creating from the Spirit" and will publish a book with that title in January 1996.

Wakefield created the NBC-TV series *James at Fifteen* and wrote and coproduced the CBS movie *The Seduction of Miss Leona,* starring Lynn Redgrave, and a ninety-minute PBS drama, *Mark Twain's "The Innocents Abroad."*

He has won a Rockefeller Foundation grant for creative writing, a National Endowment for the Arts Award for the short story, and a Bernard Devoto Fellowship to the Bread Loaf Writers Conference. He was writer in residence at Emerson College and is distinguished visiting writer at Florida International University. He serves on the national advisory board of the National Writers Union.

Inquiries about his workshops may be addressed to Dan Wakefield Workshops, P.O. Box 1190, Burlington, MA 01803–6190.